D1112115

THEO PADNOS

My Life Had Stood a Loaded Gun

ADOLESCENTS AT THE APOCALYPSE: A TEACHER'S NOTES

MIRAMAX BOOKS

ISBN 0-7868-6909-7

Printed in the United States of America

For information address:
Hyperion
77 West 66th Street
New York, New York 10023-6298

FIRST EDITION

374.9743
PAONOS

10 9 8 7 6 5 4 3 2 1

CONTENTS

The prisoner is a great dreamer.
—Dostoyevsky

Long before they met me, they'd been looking to hook up, to make a connection, to tighten their bonds. They wanted heightened, infallible, permanent partnerships. You embrace me; I embrace you—and on and on it goes, basically forever.

Frenchie had taken a sixteen-year-old runaway on a two-day tour of Vermont. The two of them drove up and down I-91 like tourists, stopping into towns, buying things, and returning to the highway. The trip was her punishment for having been unfaithful to him. Over forty-eight hours, he beat her and sodomized her and forced her to perform oral sex on him. He said he'd enjoy killing her, and that if she told on him, she would certainly die. She believed him and fled only when he collapsed from exhaustion in an apartment in Newport, Vermont.

I didn't know the details of Frenchie's crime when he was my student and anyway, I wasn't judging. I liked Frenchie. I liked his dumb hairdo, a pompadour, and enjoyed hearing about his tourism and his latest undertaking, a campaign to dupe the state psychiatrists. I guessed that the campaign would never work but when a headline appeared in the *Valley News* ("Experts: Suspect is Mildly Retarded"), I had to acknowledge that he was a better actor than I took him for.

Slash was accused of holding a gun in his girlfriend's mouth while he forced her to have sex—"repeatedly raped the victim over a thirty-six-hour period" said the newspapers. He wouldn't talk about it. He did, however, like to instruct my class in how to commit murder (close range, bullet through the temple, wipe away the burn marks; of course, no witnesses). He often talked about the glorious rampage he was planning upon his release. His might would spill over from the jail to encompass the entire town of Woodstock. We would all go with him when he went.

Will Emerson had brought his Saturday Night Special into a convenience store with the intention of robbing the safe. It was something he and his best friend, Rodney, had wanted to do for a long time. They planned to share the loot. Afterward, Will wanted to whisk his girlfriend away to Florida like a retiree. He knew beforehand that the clerk had a shotgun behind the counter. "He could have shot me or I could have shot him or I could have gotten the money. Or, um, some combination of those things could have happened, I guess," he told the class. He was intrigued by the possibilities. Each one held its own special appeal. He didn't count on a fourth scenario, the one that really happened: he got no money, Rodney abandoned him at the scene of the crime, no one was shot, and his mom turned him in.

One of the kids in class for whom I had the strongest feelings, Laird Stanard, had murdered his mother with the family shotgun. They had had an argument. He felt unloved and cold toward both of his parents that evening. When his mom was dead, he shot at his father but missed. He planned to take the family credit cards, the gun, $200 in cash, and the family car. He planned to go to Port Elizabeth, Maine, straight to the home of a girl he was trying to woo. In the event, he did manage to get the cash, the gun, and the car, but as he was leaving the scene of the crime, he crashed into the family mailbox. Then he hit a tree. He'd been driving for less than a year and couldn't steer well. From the house of an acquaintance, six miles away in the village of Brownsville, he called the police. "There's been an accident at my house," he reported, not altogether falsely.

My students' crimes earned them passage into the outlaw world, such as it was, of the Woodstock Regional Correctional Facility in Woodstock, Vermont. It was too dull and too small a place to measure up to its cousins in American myth and movies. It couldn't even measure up to the other lockups in Vermont. There were no gangs, no rituals of initiation, no secret tunnels, hardly any drugs, and no jailhouse hooch. The place was overrun with rural pedophiles and drunk drivers. It was cramped and moldy. The inmates spent their days watching TV and sleeping and shooting the breeze in the cell block common room. Occasionally they'd slip down to the basement "school" to play with the computers and to attend a class or two.

The bonding possibilities—the likelihood of deepening those partnerships they'd dreamed of—were all but eliminated. Laird mooned by the telephone, hoping to get through to his would-be girlfriend in Maine. Frenchie wrote letters to ex-girlfriends in which he pleaded with them to "put the smack down" on his accuser. But the inmates were much too cut off from the world to have any effect on it anymore. When they wanted to make an impression on a credulous, willing person, they had to look to the part-time English teacher—me—who was anxious to be taken into their circle. I didn't mind bonding with them on whatever terms they stipulated. I was all too eager to do it, in fact. I was in their habitat and felt, especially at first, the impassioned gratitude of a well-welcomed tourist.

When that feeling ebbed, I stared wondering, as all the inmates do, about what the future would bring us. We ought to have had little difficulty in taking the augurs. Any reasonable person could have done it. The "suspects" were guilty. They were possibly going to be transferred from the Woodstock jail, a holding pen, to some other, longer-term facility, but that would hardly permit them to look any differently at the future. In jail, the future is the easiest thing in the world to read because nothing ever changes. Tomorrow will be today's exact replica; next year will deviate in only the minutest particulars from this year. Look at the razor wire; look at the inflexible scowl on the guard's face; stare at the piles of black meat on the cafeteria trays: that's how life has always appeared in the Vermont jails and how it always will appear.

Who could deny that? What sane person could see things any other way?

We all could see things exactly as we pleased, it turned out. It was no fun imagining a life of growing old indoors, of staring at derelicts and bored guards all day and having them stare back at you. It was no fun reflecting on an eternity of chewing the cafeteria meat. More to the point, we weren't capable of seeing the future that way. It was too implausible, too dull, and altogether unfit for the adventurers and outcasts and desperadoes with whom we had ourselves confused.

We preferred to imagine that, instead of jail, something fabulous and awe-inspiring was in the offing. We saw great personal transformations in the not-too-distant future. The more ambitious kids like Laird and Will imagined that social upheavals might well follow on the heels of their private transformations.

As the weeks passed by and nothing much happened, some of us started to fret. We experienced the anxiety of the doubter, and the deepened faith of the zealot. We hoped that we could somehow provoke the world into a new, more favorable alignment. A brilliant assertion of ourselves, a deployment of our innermost strength was in order. We didn't doubt that that strength, when it was finally revealed to the world, would make a devastating mark. It would lay waste to every obstacle and catapult us the hell away from dreary, prissy Woodstock, Vermont. Of course it would! For the time being, we were laying our plans. We bided our time and prepared ourselves for what would happen when we would rise like a dirigible, like a phoenix, over the insipid lives we'd been leading.

Some of the clever prisoners in Woodstock sensed that this time of transformation had already come. They sensed that, in ruining their lives, they had already blundered into sympathy with a primitive, unruly power. They were stuck with it now and none too unhappy about their lot. It was where they belonged. It was what they had been wishing for all along without knowing it.

Early on in my time in Woodstock, my friend Slash passed me a poem on a torn up sheet of paper. It was called "Purgatory" and described what I assumed was his experience of jail. It had a lilting rhythm and catchy rhymes. It passed easily into my memory. Now when I think about the emotional climate of my year in jail—the sense of dread and catastrophe and, most of all, the sense of internal wishes fulfilled—I think of the words on that scrap of notebook paper:

> As time stands still,
> I'm sure I'm dead and buried,
> Back on the hill.
> This must be the hereafter.
> When did I stray?
> I must have died violently
> And demons took me away...

♣

Laird had just been arrested for killing his mom. He had a lot on his mind. He wanted me to hear about his relationship with Elizabeth in Maine. She had deserted him at the Christmas dance but afterward they'd made up. He missed his other friends, Emily and Sara and Reid. He was also interested in talking about his favorite movies, his feelings on guns ("too many of them!"), his frustration with school, the loving ambivalence he held for his parents, and the general disapprobation he felt when he contemplated the state of the world. I heard him out. I had many of the same feelings and sympathized. I demurred once or twice but not strenuously. Sometimes, he stopped talking altogether and then the shame and horror that was engulfing his life seemed to flood into his face. He was overwhelmed. He couldn't talk. My instinct was to ward off the horror for him, to make it withdraw so that he could say his piece. This is how I got drawn in.

We talked a lot about movies.

"Someday a real rain is going to come and wash the scum off the streets"—that was one of his favorite movie lines. He'd memorized it in like sixth grade—maybe even earlier. From that movie, *Taxi Driver*, he also liked: "Now I see this clearly: my whole life pointed in one direction. There has never been a choice for me."

When he sat in a dark theater next to a girl and watched *American Beauty* that day had been one of the happiest of his life. On that day he had been bathed in certainty. The dad in that movie is dead in the first scene—he floats serenely above the neighborhood—a leisurely transcendence, the sort of perspective you get as a passenger in an airplane, cruising through the late afternoon sun. There is death there, but there's no punishment or violence, only release.

After he saw the movie, he thought about failure and what it would lead to. He thought about walking out on his life as some of the characters in the movie had walked out on theirs. It had obviously taken courage to do that. It had taken a rare form of self-confidence, something zen-like and deep that was practically a religious feeling; no one else knew that he had it, but he did. He liked himself best when he wasn't afraid, when he was at peace with himself and sensitive to the small, beautiful things in his life. That's what he took from the movie: look for the beautiful things, and know not to be afraid.

The more Laird talked, the more I saw the murder taking shape in his head. It appeared that he'd been planning it in an absent, careless way for a month. As the time grew closer, he talked himself through the stressful periods. Now, in jail, the echoes of this conversation could be heard as he talked. I heard them especially in his lies and his half-confessions and his bragging.

He knew himself to be much smarter than any typical kid who sees a movie and goes out to duplicate some stupid movie stunt. Unlike Hollywood, his plans had nothing to do with faking reality or acting out the directions written out on some sheet of paper. His plans were original to him. They were also flexible, smart, military-style plans that respected stealth above all. They had a director maybe but the actors were invisible. No one would ever know who they were.

What he was was soldier smart when he wanted to be—smarter than the cops, smarter than anybody who might ask him questions; smart enough, in other words, to get away with it.

But supposing he did get caught. He wouldn't get caught because he would leave no evidence and no witnesses, yet he sometimes played out in his mind what would happen if he did get caught. He'd go to jail. That would be real—unlike Hollywood reality.

With his parents dead and the cops blaming him, he would tough it out. He liked to think about jail. In fact, he was haunted by jails. They sometimes filtered into his dreams—these were nightmares, really—in which he was punished and lead off in silence to a filthy cell. When he saw the actual cell in his sleep, he saw himself laying out his body on the mattress, and resting his head on a pile of clothing belonging to the other killers. Their sweatpants and T-shirts were caked in dry blood and stank of blood, as you'd expect. He went to sleep at that moment in the dreams—as soon as his head touched the rolled-up sweatpants—and it was a powerful relief, a tender mercy to be napping on their clothing.

If the course of his life did take him to jail, then he'd be fine with it. He had come to accept, unhappily, that all signs did not point to the Ivy League. But neither did all signs point to "A Job in the Real World." Too dull. They didn't point to Second-Rate College either. He was too smart for that. Sometimes, he felt that the signs in his life pointed to Vermont State Penitentiary.

Down every corridor, in every cell and closet and weight room and bathroom, there would be a different kind of close encounter on offer.

Garden variety killers here, Aryan Nation dudes there, a real-life Freddy Krueger pining away over there in front of his TV. Or maybe there would just be some innocent folks—or some teenagers who'd made some big mistakes in their lives. Somewhere in that labyrinth—he was certain of this—there would be people like him. But mostly the people would be so foreign, so exotic and strange that what they taught him would have no parallel in the outside world. There would be secret, occult knowledge in there, and there was only one way to find out about it because it sure as hell wasn't in the movies. A close encounter with those people would be a real life close encounter of the third kind—he'd be in the presence of aliens. They'd just talk to him and he'd listen.

The experience would pretty much take care of the problem of where he should go in life. It would take care of the problem of his current boring existence and what he should make of his boring self. Within a week or so—within a month (or, how can you know? maybe it would take a year; he had nothing but time so it didn't matter)—he'd be locked into one of those encounters. His whole life would turn into a series of close encounters, each one dangerous, each one an education beyond anything his parents had ever conceived of. Those experiences would change him forever. They would draw their mark on his forehead. It would be an outward and visible sign, legible to those who knew about it, easily pointed out to those who didn't. Wherever he went afterward, people would see what he'd been through or probably they'd just sense it, perhaps just in his physical presence. Perhaps just in the way he carried himself and expressed himself.

Okay. Honestly? He didn't take this seriously. Because he was an insightful person and he couldn't take anything seriously, he couldn't take this seriously. Because he didn't go around longing to be in a jail, he probably never would be. And if somehow he was threatened with jail, if ever it seemed imminent, his credentials—his family, his knowledge of how the system works, his personal charm—all of that would keep him out of real trouble. So every time he thought about going to jail, or dreamt about it, he was comforted in a weird way, like reading a fortune you know won't ever come true. He just knew it was something he would never have to deal with in real life.

Yet he could of course be wrong. If somehow everything failed and he did by accident have to deal with going to jail, he knew the whole thing would be fine for him, even great, and that he'd come out of jail a little while later, or maybe even a long while later, feeling stronger than ever. On the day he emerged, he'd stand there in front of the jail in his patch of sunlight, proud, his muscles jacked, his knowledge of the dark side etched on his heart. As the cars passed along in front of him on Route 4, he would smile at them wistfully, in slow motion, like someone who's been born again.

PART ONE

CHAPTER ONE

Amherst

You must lie upon the daisies and discourse in novel phrases upon your
complicated state of mind,
The meaning doesn't matter,
it's only idle chatter of a transcendental kind.
And everyone will say,
As you walk your mystic way,
"If this young man expresses himself in terms too deep for me,
Why, what a very singularly deep young man
this deep young man must be."

Graduate school fell apart for me on a lovely afternoon in Amherst in the spring of 1997. It happened as we were discussing Flaubert's voyage through Egypt in a seminar on Orientalism. We all loved the professor. Other professors asked to be called professor or mister or doctor. He asked that we call him Robbie and frequently invited us to dinner at his house. He was a stylish, leather-jacketed up and comer, already tenured in his mid-thirties. He spoke beautiful French.

In preparation for the seminar that week, we had to read Flaubert's description of standing atop one of the pyramids at Giza. The twenty-eight-year-old author of a book about rambling on foot through Normandy, Gustave Flaubert was far too sophisticated to swoon over the majesty of ancient monuments. His eye tended to dwell on the squalid details of the Egyptian tourist's life. At the summit of his pyramid, Flaubert noted a pile of bird droppings, the graffiti of a Parisian tourist, and the business card of a hatter in Rouen. It had been deposited there as a joke by Flaubert's companion, Maxime du Camp. For the first hour and a half of class, Robbie lectured us. He was interested in the power of the gaze, the thematics of looking, the discourse of tourism, the relationality of sight and seeing, and the erotics of being seen—and many other things like that. I don't remember what the larger point of the lecture was. I remember directing the power of my gaze out the window at April in Amherst. Students were sailing across a cement plaza on their bicycles; buses were disgorging their passengers and other buses were swallowing up other passengers. In the distance on a swath of lawn a cluster of students lay on their backs, watching the gulls circle in the air. They'd deposited their books and various articles of clothing across a wide stretch of nearby grass like bread crumbs. From our window on the fifth floor, I kept my eye on the scene and kept hoping that a gull would pluck up his courage and steal something from the students. Maybe he could dive bomb for a Walkman or spirit one of the stranded T-shirts away into the sky. Maybe he could attack one of the book bags. I wished for something to happen. I crossed my fingers and stared at the gulls and willed them into action. I willed other things into action: in silence I urged the buses to crash, and the students to come spilling out across the pavement like marbles. Nothing happened.

I remember trying out the thematics of my gaze on my fellow students. There was a crisp goatee on one of them and tiny black glasses on several of them. One guy in his twenties, in homage to someone much older than he, wore a full, pointy black beard. He looked like a very depressed, ruined Lincoln. I checked out the silver traveling espresso mugs my fellow students had brought to class and thought about how I could use a cup of coffee. I thought about the girls in the class. I meditated on the topic for a while. The girls in the class weren't girls but married women, married to other graduate students. All of them were slowly, glacially advancing on their Ph.D.s, as was I. I took a moment to wish that I went to some other university where there were younger girls in the classes, desirable, intellectual ones who spoke to each other only in German and had deep, black eyes. They would come to class in clingy black outfits. They would wear dark mascara and would exchange meaningful glances with me during class. They would adjust the straps of their dresses while they looked at me. I concentrated on that topic for a while. Then I looked out the window again.

Robbie had a lot to say about Flaubert on the top of the pyramid. It was an ironized conquest; the noting of the bird droppings was a gesture that undercut the whole movement of tourist discourse. Flaubert had taken tourist discourse and turned it on its head; he had thematized the scatalogical throughout his travel narrative. Or maybe Robbie said that Flaubert had inquired into the thematics of scatology, or the relationality of scat and themes. I stopped paying close attention pretty early on. I did take some notes, though, even after I lost interest, because I liked Robbie and didn't want to be rude. Most of all, I took notes because I was twenty-eight years old and in graduate school. I was still, in a lame, listless way, trying to take things seriously. This was my life after all and I thought I should somehow try to make it into a success.

During the mid-seminar break, I bought a coffee from the French department coffee table and walked outside into the sunshine to chat with my fellow students. With their quiet, ultrasophisticated, listless talk, the other grad students reliably summoned up my inner thug. I normally have to strain to be thuggish but their company threw back a distasteful reflection of what I was becoming—unhappy. I couldn't behave around them. I was constantly restraining myself from abusing them.

The fellow students were smoking cigarettes beneath a concrete passageway. I approached the pointy-bearded guy and stood next to him for a moment, stroking my chin. "Dude," I said. I tried to think of something shocking to say but nothing in heaven or earth can shock a graduate student in comparative literature. They know everything there is to know and have read the critical discussion surrounding Everything many hundreds of times. "Can you believe that horseshit motherfucking shit going on up there?" I asked. Silence. One of the graduate students dropped her cigarette on the ground and scuffed it out beneath a boot. I tried some more random profanity:

"Motherfucker," I said to no one in particular.

Jonathan, the owner of the pointy beard, smiled. "Robbie's not a motherfucker. He's a structuralist, Theo," he counseled. "You have to know that about him."

"Holy shit," I said. "He's boring the piss out of me. He's boring the piss out of everyone."

Jonathan shrugged. "Actually, I don't think so," he said.

Climbing up the stairs on the way back to class I felt a sharp pain jolt through my spine. It made my knees buckle. I'd been drinking a lot of coffee during the morning and then much more as I was preparing for class in the early afternoon. Maybe that had something to do with it—my lightheadedness. I'd also taken my bike out for a ride in the hill towns off to the west of Northampton. I rode past peacenicky goat farms, Archibald MacLeish's house, and maple sugar shacks, recently idle after the end of spring sap run. Then I rode down into the Pioneer Valley, through Smith College, across the Connecticut River, and past the giant forsythias that reached their branches out into Main Street, just before Emily Dickinson's house. I was probably tired from all of that pedaling. The pain pulsed into my stomach and jerked at my shoulders. I swooned for a second and grabbed the railing.

It wasn't just that morning that I'd been riding my bike. I was spending a lot of time in serious cyclist mode in those days and perhaps because of all that time in the saddle—or perhaps, I don't know, for dietary reasons—I was developing a wicked hemorrhoid problem. It's a common thing among cyclists. You ride for two hours and during that time there's no pain at all but it comes back afterward twice as bad. My problem was serious enough that I had been to the surgeon at the university health services for a consultation. She told me that I could have the offending veins snipped out if I wanted. She also said there was a sort of hemorrhoid tourniquet-garroting-strangulation procedure that I could look into. That might be appropriate, she said, for the gravest cases, such as mine. However, if I did elect that treatment option, I should expect severe pain and I should know that the garrote had to be applied and then left in place for several days. Both procedures would of course mean no bike racing or training for six weeks. Alternatively, I could learn to live with my problem. I thought about it and thought that instead of surgery, I would strive for mental peace and mental harmony with my body. I left the consulting room almost on the verge of tears but also laughing a little bit because I was still coming to terms with how ridiculous and funny it was to have the problem that I had. I pedaled to the drug store for aspirin. Then I pedaled home.

The truth was that the pain, at least for me, was never so anguishing that I didn't also want to laugh and giggle about the absurdity of it—and of course the gross disgustingness of the situation, which I won't go into. Laughing made it hurt worse and the fact that laughter caused pain made me laugh more. After the fateful surgical prognosis, I let a few of my friends in on my secret. They laughed as hard as they could laugh, like I'd never seen anyone laugh before. They made a horrible, monkey-screeching din and fell over themselves clutching their ribs and sobbing. Later, they chased me around with ski poles and hockey sticks. It was all in good fun and I was laughing too, even though it hurt to laugh.

As I climbed back up to the seminar room, I felt a fit of giggles coming on. I started to think of how absurd and comical it was that I was going back into that seminar room to sit down on my bum. I would have to do it gently, without wincing. But then what? Then I would be stuck there listening to Robbie and sipping my coffee and listening to the other students muse about Flaubert. I would look at the girls. I would concentrate mightily and sweat and probably come across as a weirdo pervert.

What with the coffee and the renewed stress of another hour and a half of seminar, I began to worry that I might degenerate somehow—start grinding my teeth inadvertently or drift from consciousness or—I didn't know what to expect. I thought that probably, if I could just lead the conversation away from Flaubert and segue somehow into a brief personal account, an intellectual account of pain, and an intellectual account of bike riding, and do it in French, the students might somehow be grateful to me. Maybe I could make it funny. I'd do it in the most abstract French I could dream up, of course. *"L'agonie du corps et du discours de la vie d'un cycliste"*—something like that. Anyway, unlike the detached theorizing we were doing, my commentary would be personal. It would introduce a human into a classroom that had previously been populated by comp lit androids. Someone would appreciate that. We'd choked Flaubert half to death in the first half of the class. Anything that could bring life back into the room would be appreciated.

When I got back to the classroom, I stood in the doorway. I looked at the beards and the glasses. I lost my nerve. I was turning pale, and sweating badly. Robbie paused politely when he saw me swaying in the door frame. He gave me a discreet, inquiring look and stepped away from the table. Another jolt of pain surged through my spine. I was pretty nervous, probably from the coffee, probably also from the twelve pairs of eyes that were suddenly staring at me. *"Mais, merde,"* I muttered. Nobody blinked. I thought I detected a shudder from the bearded guy. Repulsion? Fear? What? I couldn't put it together—too nervous.

"*Ça va, Théo?*" Robbie asked.

"*Ça va pas,*" I said. "*Ça va pas de tout, mon gars.*" I felt that if I could block out the class and focus on the very real experience of being in private torment, I could execute the maneuver I had in mind. I clutched my abdomen and staggered forward into the class. I clutched at the edge of the seminar table. I was pretty sure Robbie would be okay with my performance. I looked at him as I tripped over a book bag. He was smiling his pleased, ironic smile. I let my papers cascade across the seat of my chair.

Catching the eyes of some of my fellows students, I let go of a powerful moan: "Ohh. Aye. Ohhh," I groaned. "*Je perds la tête un peu, mes amis.*" I doubled over like a soldier wounded in battle and pretended to swab around on the ground for my papers. I kicked them further under the table. I got down on all fours and pretended to chase after them, but really I was scattering them into the corners of the room. After a few seconds I emerged from beneath the table. I stood up, clutching my kidney, and pointed with my foot at my lower back. Then I slumped into a chair. The other students were not amused. The pointy-bearded guy had lost interest right away it seemed. As soon as he saw me acting up, he buried his nose in his book. Two of the women were staring daggers at Robbie, as if my monkeying around was his fault.

Since no one was giving me much of a reaction, I started whimpering and sobbing a little. I was laughing as I was doing it, so that probably took away from the effect. I swayed woozily in my chair. "*J'ai mal,*" I groaned. "*Oh la la la la la la. Qu'est ce que j'ai mal.*" I crossed my eyes and concentrated on turning pale.

Robbie had a sense of humor. He laughed, at least in his eyes. He asked me again if I was okay. That encouraged me. Some of the women pulled out their highlighters and began running them over passages in their Flaubert in even, rigid strokes. That sort of pissed me off. I was in pain, after all. Agnes, the only real French person in class, finally indulged me.

"*Tu as mal, Théo?*"

"*Mal?*" I whimpered. I tried to weep. I was forcing if not tears then at least some angry redness into my eyes.

I stood up and moved a few feet away from the table. I lay down very slowly across the linoleum. Then I rolled myself into a ball and started rocking back and forth. I moaned and sobbed. With my chin and my feet

I tried to indicate where the source of the problem was. I called out to Robbie from the floor.

"Robbie, mon vieux," I said. *"C'est terminé pour moi. Je suis perdue. Je suis assassiné. Justice, juste ciel. O voleur! O voleur! A l'assassin! O muetrier!"*

He was silent for a little while. I heard some feet scuffing on the ground. Finally he asked if I was done. He looked down at me from his chair with a long, mildly pained face.

"It's a secret ailment," I whispered. "I wish I could tell you about it but I can't."

"Can you ail silently?" he asked.

I couldn't. The whole point was the noise, the performance. I tried my best to keep quiet.

After a minute or two of lying on the ground, I lost interest. I didn't feel like ailing at all anymore. The floor was filthy. It was littered with strands of hair and sandy grit and balls of Kleenex. I looked at the feet of my fellow graduate students and contemplated my own feet for a bit. Finally there was nothing more to do. I hoisted myself up and returned to my chair. I had thought to put my coffee cup in place before collapsing and it was still there, lukewarm and acidic. That liquid was not at all good for me, but I drank it down anyway out of idleness and disappointment.

The other students hardly noticed my recovery. I sat listening to Robbie for a while and actually took some notes. Outside, over the greensward, the sun was arcing through the sky. The sunbathing students had moved on. Robbie was on to Flaubert in the brothels and smelly tents of Egypt: his fetishization of the courtesan; his courting fetishistic narrative. Gradually, and without my being aware of it at first, a feeling of genuine accomplishment came over me. It felt as though I'd done something decent, something that I should be proud of. There wasn't a ton of excitement or pleasure in the feeling but it was there, warm and germinating inside my head. I was sort of ashamed too and vaguely worried for myself because I'd kind of lost control for a moment—albeit in a willful way—and I didn't know if episodes like that would be written down somehow on my permanent academic record. *Theo Padnos has a fine future as a theoretician of postcolonial discourse. He is, however, a fucking idiot.* I worried about that for a moment but in my post-performance haze, I was, for the most part, beyond unhappy thoughts.

Perhaps, I thought, Robbie the professor was grateful to me for having made my scene. Perhaps he too secretly preferred a scene to a class. It occurred to me that perhaps he and I could work in synch somehow in the future. Maybe we could perform acts of lit crit sabotage together. We'd target horrible professors and horrible literary theory and we'd work from the very heart of the French department. Or, alternatively, I could get into some of his theorizing somehow, become his protégé, and climb up the academic ladder under his tutelage. All of those notions passed through my head briefly, like a wave of drunkenness, and then they were gone.

Later on, however, when I was out riding my bike again, I started to get really depressed about the episode. I started to feel the old comp lit feeling of being trapped, of self-loathing, of life piddling away.

"The highlight of my day is rolling around on a filthy linoleum floor of a seminar room," I said to myself. That had been the highlight of the day when I was in eighth grade. I was twenty-eight years old. At least when I was twelve I had cool friends. And there had been beautiful girls in French class, girls blossoming and conjugating their verbs and daring me to speak to them. (I didn't dare but at least the challenge was there.) Best of all, back in those days there was some honor in sending up the idea of French class. Now there was just futility.

On bike rides over the succeeding days, all the other grad school problems started bothering me more than ever before. Never mind that a Ph.D. in comparative literature from the second-rate university where I was a student was unlikely to get me a job. Never mind that in order to get the Ph.D. I would have to idle away in Amherst for an undetermined further number of years. Never mind that I would have to write a dissertation and didn't have any interest in doing so. What bothered me most was that I was learning to hate something I used to love, namely reading— really studying—works of literature. I was learning to hold reading and the whole university apparatus around it in contempt: the professors, the way they lectured incomprehensibly at the students—especially the undergraduates—the way the undergrads read the newspaper contemptuously back at them. I hated the dumb student newspaper everyone read and I hated the arrogant buildings that, massed together, passed for a campus. I hated my poor fellow graduate students, though I knew even then that they didn't deserve my enmity.

Of course, once you fall out of love with something, it quickly falls out of love with you, too. I started to see in my own professors' eyes—the professors I liked and trusted—a pitying look, a look that acknowledged the dead-endedness of grad-studenthood, and quickly suppressed the acknowledgment in favor of a weak smile. I passed that wan look along, I'm sure, to people nearby. They, in their turn—undergrads and grads, mostly—flashed it back at me.

What brought the shamefulness of the situation into focus for me was the picture I had in my head of a body—mine—rolling around on the floor in French class. Yes, I was inviting people's contempt. Yes, that was an idiotic way to spend my time. But worse than that, I was drifting backward in life to a truly helpless, preadolescent, literature-hating state. More years in graduate school would have me heading further in that direction. I would be pushing ten and then eight and who could say where it would end? I would go on having no money of course. And I would go on making useless fun of people. But I would be getting older and would be descending every day into the life of a clown—a svelte, bike-riding, intellectual clown, but a clown nonetheless. It was clear to me, after a few days of thinking over the French class incident, that I had to leave school.

Naturally, I did no such thing. Out of cowardice and because I loved riding my bike in the hills above Amherst and because I loved teaching the undergraduate classes, I stayed. Two more years of inching on toward the passivity of a child passed. When I was close to finishing my dissertation, I started sending cover letters to universities across the country and in Europe. "I am particularly interested in your job announcement," I wrote, "because it asks for a specialist in nineteenth-century French poetry." To other universities I wrote that I was particularly interested in their job announcements because they asked for a specialist in literary theory, or Flaubert, or English composition, or American travel narratives. There are only so many job announcements and you're supposed to apply for anything that comes vaguely close to what you might be able to do. At first I checked the mail a lot, and then later, when I saw that nothing was happening, not at all. The department heads call on the phone when they're interested, they don't write. I started writing to tiny little colleges in Vermont, even when they hadn't advertised. I sent one pleading letter to the father of a girlfriend of a former bike racing teammate of mine. He was the dean of a ratty college in Rutland. Could he pass along a good word about me to the English department? I asked. No, it turned out, he couldn't. There was a still tinier college in Rutland and I drove around in the rain one day looking for it but couldn't find the damn thing, cursed it, and cursed my car, which didn't like to run in rain, and finally went home, mission unaccomplished.

My dad had some good advice to offer me about what I should do with my life. I used to go visit him a lot during this time and I listened to his speeches for hours on end as he drank his wine and fell on his coq au vin.

"Jesus H. Christ. My *god*," my dad said. "But what do you do in Amherst? You live in a fucking backwater, Theophilus," he advised. "You sit around and think deep thoughts all day. You're finishing your dissertation? Well, I don't know because I don't see you every day but let me tell you how it seems to me. It seems to me that you paddle this way in your backwater—very nice—and then you turn around and paddle that way. Is that about what you do?" He gave me his beloved incredulous stare. He paused. He allowed a dramatic interval of silence to pass. I could see him envisioning his former life as a lawyer. I was a witness; this was a cross. He was arguing on behalf of Truth. Out in the gallery, auditors were inching forward to the very outermost cusp of the courtroom benches.

"Let me ask you a question, Theophilus. What do you intend to do with your dissertation once you're finished with it? Will you publish it?" Silence. "Do you think a publisher would be interested in your dissertation?" Silence. "According to what I've read, dissertations do *not* get published. But I don't know—maybe you'll find someone. Maybe the University of Tennessee Extension Teacher's Fucking Auxiliary will publish it for you. How much do you think you would get? Ten thousand dollars? One thousand dollars? I don't think so. I think you might have to pay them. But with what? People your age are making *money*, Theophilus. People your age are traveling to Russia. People your age are traveling to China. They're starting *companies*. They're *investing*. Do you have a fucking red cent to invest? People your age are becoming *millionaires* Theophilus, for god's sakes."

At this point, he usually took a deep breath.

"Theophilus, kiddo. You are becoming a bit long in the tooth, I think, for this. I don't mean to insult you. I've always told you to do what you love. Apparently, God knows why, you love this: your academic fantasy. Am I not right?" Silence. "As your loving father, I want you to be happy. And I have been happy without money myself, as you know. I don't have a pot to piss in and look at me. I'm a very, unusually happy man. But as you know there have been some very, very difficult moments." He would stamp his foot at this point. A pained look crossed his brow. He forged onward. "At my age—at any age, for god's sakes, money is important. It's necessary to have money. I have lived, as you know, through some excruciatingly painful moments on the subject of money. My house was taken away. I could not own credit cards. I still can't own a credit card. I have lived through those moments. I'm here to tell you, kiddo. It's not fun. I never cared about making money when I was your age either. I cared about love and beauty and art, as you know. At this advanced age, I am here to tell you: *people* need *money*. Honey, I'm sorry. But you are becoming sicklied o'er with the pale cast of thought, Theophilus. And that may be fine for you. Fine! Far be it from me. But you have no *fucking money*. Listen: you can be a brilliant intellectual and make some goddamn fucking *money*, too. Did you ever think of that?"

Perhaps the best thing I did in graduate school was something I did completely by accident. All told, it probably took me about three hours. One dream followed by one short paper. I was taking a class in Freud and was asked, along with all the other students, to analyze one of my dreams in a formal academic paper. I delayed and wrote nothing until the day before the assignment was due. I couldn't think of a worthwhile dream to write about and was bored with all of those that I could remember. On the night before the assignment was due, I dreamt about myself as a smiling murderer who carried beneath his coat a giant, gleaming knife. In the dream, I was master-killer, the sort of Professor Moriarty type who slits people's throats for the sheer intellectual challenge of it. He outwits his victims, the police, the whole world. I wore a cravat and greatcoat and was much taller than I am in real life. In the beginning, I walked across an empty lawn in Amherst but then, in a magic burst, I was in Vermont at my mom's house, holding a rake. A thick bed of leaves covered the lawn. I was knee-deep in leaves. My father emerged from the house and began wading across the lawn. *You're not supposed to be here,* I thought. That's contrary to the divorce agreement. There are rules.... And then he was lying in a garden cart, clutching his abdomen. I had ripped open his belly. I had run him through with my knife. Blood gurgled out between his fingers—it was a viscous, inky fluid like motor oil that kept pumping and pumping through his hands. *Serves him right,* I thought to myself. The words appeared in front of my eyes: *Serves that motherfucker right.* I dumped his body in a garden cart that I had on hand just for this purpose. He was evidently dead, or dying. His eyes were shutting slowly and he made no noise.

I had to dispose of the corpse before I was found out. Holy shit, I thought. I have nowhere to put the body. *Holy fucking shit, why the hell didn't I think of that in advance?* I started to panic. I decided to store it temporarily in the barn, though I was certain the cops would look there. The cart, however, was too heavy to move. Its soft bike tires burrowed into the leaves on the lawn; I would have needed a tank to pull it. In addition to the corpse, the cart was filled with purple paperback copies of the Russian novel *We* by Eugene Zamiatin. (I happened to be reading it at the time.) The corpse lay on a giant pillow made up of *We*s. That's right, I thought. That's exactly right. We're both of us stuck together in this, aren't we? That's the fate you've given us. That's *We.*

Some of the copies spilled out over the sides of the cart as I shoved it across the lawn. I knew I couldn't possibly clean up so many tumbling, blood spattered copies of *We* before the police arrived. So I abandoned the project. I took a nap on a rotting mattress in the mud room of Mom's house. And then the police were there, looking through the windows for evidence and chatting with my mother. They arrived in the company of my father's family. Everyone was polite but everyone, especially my mother, was disappointed with me. They scowled. "Such a shame," mumbled an older policeman as he ran his fingertips along his jowls. Mom was ashamed that I had been found out. I had done it for her, after all. I had ruined myself for her. She and I had been anticipating happy, work-filled time alone in Vermont. I knew that and she knew it. Now it wasn't going to happen. My future, the plans that I'd set my heart on, that I didn't even know how badly I wanted to come true, were finished. I watched her watching me as I was taken away to jail. She tried to apologize to the relatives on my behalf, but they were glad to see me punished and wouldn't stand still for her apologies. They cast their eyes at the police car.

I asked the police: "How long will I be in jail?"

"Twenty years," they said.

At first I was horrified. I had the sensation of observing a prophecy fulfilled. *So now you've done it,* I thought to myself. *He's really dead, for real. You did it. Your fault. And you knew all along what was going to happen. Jail.*

There was no taking it back. The police had me dead to rights. Twenty years in the slammer, I knew. Case closed. I groaned: *"You fucking, fucking idiot. How could you do this to yourself?"* But as we were driving down Route 4 toward the jail, my mood changed. I knew that all the other people in the Woodstock jail had ruined themselves too, that I would have murderous brothers on every side, and that there would be absolutely nothing for us to do for twenty years. I would be indolent and incapacitated for twenty years. No expectations, no disappointing anyone, and punished for hubris. I relaxed into the idea. It was what I deserved; a just fate.

In the paper I wrote for the professor, I backed away from my crime. I was simply murdering those aspects in me that are like my father, I said. He had passed on a certain strain of DNA. It was expressing itself in real life in a thousand small but disturbing ways. This, represented by the thousand copies of the novel *We*, was what I really wanted to kill. So I was killing a pattern of resemblances more than a person. The professor didn't buy it. "No, you're also killing your dad," he wrote.

I also wrote in my paper that I had a screwy, wracked kind of ambition. I wanted to be cleverer than everyone—thus the Professor Moriarty persona—but I had no confidence in my ability to execute. I usually ended up falling laughably short of my ambitions. "Yes!" said the professor.

I wrote that it probably was an Oedipal dream in that I wanted to displace my father and be alone with my mom. I was confident, at first, that I could pull off my scheme brilliantly but all my ideas evidently lead to the same place—public shame, crippling failure. Perhaps some insidious part of me, I wrote, perhaps the part I had inherited from my shiftless, do-nothing dad, was zealously aspiring to failure. My ambition was to sabotage myself. "Yes!" The professor wrote. "The master–mind killer transformed into a bungler!" he declared, proudly. "You've got it—good work, Theo."

At the end of the paper, the professor penciled in some nice comments about my future in grad school—a sunny forecast. He gave me an A for the paper. Afterward, I congratulated myself on the whole deal. I guess I'm psychologically aware of all that business about hating my dad now, I thought. Thank god. And plus, I like the old man now, that toothless codger. I humor him. I'll find new, better fatherly types kicking around when I need someone to father me.

I liked the Freud professor, for instance.

CHAPTER TWO

Families

I was lulled by the slamming of iron;
A slow drip over the stones,
Toads brooding in wells.
All the leaves stuck out their tongues;
I shook the softening chalk of my bones,
Saying,
Snail, snail, glister me forward,
Bird, soft-sigh me home,
Worm, be with me.
This is my hard time.
    —Theodore Roethke, *The Lost Son*

In the spring of 1999, after teaching my last class of undergraduates, I moved to Vermont and started painting houses. I wasn't thrilled about leaving Amherst and graduate school behind but I had been ambling along in pursuit of my Ph.D. for six years, still hadn't gotten the thing, and had run out of one-semester teaching contracts. The comp lit department gave its graduate students only so many and I had exhausted my supply. In Vermont, I grew a cluster of smelly purple marijuana plants in the corner of a field. Late in the summer, I harvested them with trembling hands, searching the sky for helicopters.

Almost every day during that period, I drove my car along Route 4 in front of the Woodstock jail. I liked to peer through the stand of cedars, through the chain-link fence and the looping ribbons of razor wire, into the jail rec yard. I drove by at the speed of a frightened granny, squinting, craning my neck, and veering dangerously toward the curb and the defunct gas station on the right. Day after day, my peering afforded me, basically, nothing: cedars and a single stretch of chain-link fence. There wasn't so much as a burglar or a drunk in sight. In my mind's eye, the rec yard was a secret garden, short on the flora, but possibly long on the fauna; it was a state of nature anyway, but in order to lay eyes on the thing itself, the *Ding an Sich*, I evidently had to go exploring on foot.

When I walked by on the sidewalk, I was able to certify that there was in fact no secret anything in the rec yard. There was a swath of empty yellow grass. On the western side of the jail, under the shade of a neighboring elm, the ground swelled to a high point: a tiny bluff on top of which sat a lone wooden bench. I checked every day, and every day there was no wildlife perched anywhere nearby, not even a crow. I had thought prisons were overcrowded. I had thought that they pullulated with human flesh. This place was deserted. Even its park was abandoned. The place needed visitors, apparently. I started wondering if the inside of the jail was still inhabited. But I knew from reading the newspaper that it was. When I stopped by the convenience store on the jail's eastern side, I dawdled by my car. With actorly subtlety, I peered up at the bank of cell windows that gave out over the gas pumps: mesh grating, black film over the panes, a dull reflective darkness in the windows where there should have been depth. I couldn't discern so much as a shadow hovering behind the glass. It was like staring through a burkha to a pair of sunglasses. This darkness in the windows, it turned out, was to prevent criminals on the inside from sending signals to their brother criminals, potential aids to an escape, on the outside. As for the secret garden, it turned out that the inmates were permitted into their park for an hour a day at noon. Often they were too lazy or too afraid of the cold or the wet to make the trip. So the bench sat by itself most of the time, looking out over the disused railroad switching yard at Woodstock's east end.

In the fall of 1999, as my own secret garden of marijuana ripened in the field, and the first leaves started to turn on the hillsides, I started to get a little nostalgic for school. I had taken a year off from studying after college, but every other fall in living memory had meant returning to bells and steeples, to pathways and libraries. I felt as though I'd been shown my way off of those premises, and that instead of moving on with dignity, I had refused to leave. Only when the university didn't have an ounce of tolerance left for me or my dissertation had I slunk away into the bushes. Now I wondered if there wasn't some way to slink back through the bushes to a leafy campus somewhere. I decided that I would forgive the academic world its having slighted me if somehow it would agree to take me back. I wrote more letters to more universities: the University of Presque Isle, Iona, River Falls, Stuttgart, L'Université de Montreal.

Though I kept sending out applications, a trickle of malice began dribbling into my cover letters. What I wanted to say—"Dear Chairman Dick, My dissertation explores early American museums in the western states and territories. But you'd never hire me, so rot in hell"—couldn't be said. Instead I wrote orthodox, official academic cover letters, in which every sentence made mocking, lying claims. The paragraphs were like snakes: I laid them down and hoped that someone passing innocently over them would get a bite in the ankle. Thus: *Professor Levine, the theoretician, has submitted my dissertation to the Bakhtin Society of Utah in Folk, Utah, for consideration in its annual Relationality of Discourse competition.*

This is all BS in a place called FU, said the letters, in code.

The readers deserved this joking, lying nonsense, I thought, for having written such nonsensical and stuffy ads. Shorn of their jokes, my letters also said: "Idiots like you probably like reading this sort of academic hocus-pocus, though I don't. Nevertheless, I need a job, so please hire me." Strangely, I got no interviews.

The house painting season was drawing to a close. I started eyeing the jail rec yard more closely whenever I stopped in at the auto parts store, which was the jail's neighbor to the west. As I chatted with Charlie Dubois, the owner, I wondered what I might teach the criminals. I would begin with Franz Kafka: "Before the Law" is a parable about a man who resolves to turn away from the workaday world in favor of an encounter with the all-powerful realm of *Das Gesetz,* the Law. I would stand in front of the felons in their classroom, hold the book out in my left hand like a Bible, shut it sadly, and then recite from memory: "Before the law there stands a doorkeeper. To this doorkeeper there comes a man from the country and begs for admittance to the law." Ah ha! I would say. A man from the country arrives at the great edifice of the Law! "In the original German," I would say, as I modestly exhibited my fluency, "Kafka calls this man a *Landsman,* a word which can mean a rural person, a simple man, or a representative human—or all of these things. What we are dealing with here," I would say, "is a parable about what happens when an average person, a person like you or me, is confronted by the might and the vastness of the Law!"

Our first novel would be Fyodor Dostoyevsky's *Notes from Underground*. I would begin the class with a flourish: "'I am a sick man....I am a most unpleasant man. I think my liver is diseased,'" I would sing.

"In Russia, the *pechen*, the liver, is the target of a national poisoning campaign. Everyone's *pechen* is diseased because everyone marinates it in vodka from childhood. Over time, it fills with a corrosive, acidic nastiness; every once in a while this substance overflows. What we are about to read," I would say, "is an outpouring of something people in Russia—and here perhaps, as well—have felt inside but rarely express in words, something that's gradually, wickedly turning against us. The *pechen!*"

We would smile at first about the Underground Man's rat-like self-knowledge. Over the next days, however, he would introduce us to philosophical speculation, to what lies in store for people who examine themselves. We would be chastened by his bitterness and his black-heartedness and yet fascinated by his resemblance to the company present in the room. The experience would heighten everything you're supposed to feel when you read Dostoyevsky: the room would shimmer with claustrophobia, nastiness, sadness, and the distant, infinitely remote possibility of transcendence.

I also had Samuel Beckett in mind because I knew that jail would be, among other things, excruciatingly boring, and I knew that the absurdity of waiting for lord knows what to happen lord knows when would resonate among inmates. I had Jean-Paul Sartre's *No Exit* in mind because I imagined that reading about a hell in which the definition of hellishness is *other people* would provoke in inmates some chord striking, some appropriate self-awareness. "Yes, Sartre's right, that old bastard!" they would exclaim. "This place is a kind of hell: boring and airless and filled to the bursting point with repugnant people." They would conclude that henceforth in life, they would do everything possible to keep from living in hell.

I thought that I would eventually get around to teaching Albert Camus' *The Stranger* because of its beautiful ending in a cell in Algiers. Having committed the senseless murder of an Arab on a strand of beach, the hero of the book wakes on the night before his execution to find the starlight drifting through the bars in his cell; it falls against his face and offers dim, inscrutable comfort. A plainspoken, entirely secular redemption ensues that's so quiet and natural it could be mistaken for a gentle breeze passing over the pages of the book. There's no religion involved, no twelve steps, no pledges to anything or anyone anywhere in sight. I wouldn't be pushing a thing by having the inmates read this: I would be opening up a window and permitting the slightest current of air to snake through the room.

I also contemplated a more up-to-date, get-them-where-they-live syllabus. I might teach Raymond Carver's short stories, one after the next after the next. Carver's drunks, his liars, the way they kept wondering what was wrong with a little champagne in the morning to wash down the pills: these characters would become a shadowy presence in class. And as we spent more time with them, Carver's people would begin murmuring to us from the bookshelves. They would warn us away from coming apart, as they have come apart. They would show us that there's always another level of decadence beneath the one we currently occupy and that full scale disintegration—of the liver and everything else—is a realistic possibility. One of my favorite Carver stories is called, simply, "Careful." We could begin there.

I had something else in mind as well: there's a certain kind of Vermont dude I've always admired. I've had to admire him from a distance because I'm not part of the car racing scene, haven't worked in a Jiffy Lube or a Howard Johnson's or on a highway painting crew. I've had to admire him from a distance because I'm a little intimidated by him. He's often called Mike or Mark; often he has a French last name. For twenty-five of his thirty years, he's lived by the sweat of his brow. His dad worked harder than he did and fought in Vietnam. His dad's dad before him dragged giant oaks from the forest for half a century, erected stone walls on the crests of mountains, and paused only to invade Normandy. The scion of all that physicality is an intensely physical being himself. He thrashes his snowmobile through the woods in the winter and humps his dirt bike over the hills in the summer. His hands have turned a dark gray shade of engine oil. He stalks bears in the fall, has a collection of guns, and believes, like Robert DeNiro's character in *The Deerhunter,* that one bullet is all you should ever need.

When this guy is throwing his beer cans at me as I'm riding my bike on the side of the road, I hate him. When he's yelling "Faggot!" and "Nice ass, motherfucker!" out of his window I flash him the bird and feel murderous rage toward him. But I've always thought that if somehow he could be stilled, if I could hang out with the guy in quiet conversation, he and I would get along well. Some of his toughness might rub off on me; some of his fuck-my-future and fuck-the-world indifference might do me some good. And maybe I could do him some good as well—an Allen Ginsberg poem here, a Theodore Roethke poem there. We could conceivably clear away a little swatch of common ground. We would sit down at its center and swap what we had to swap: his stories, my poetry anthologies. His anger, my admiration. I'd give him some cigarettes if the rules permitted it.

As the fall turned colder, an awareness, perhaps related to this fantasy, was pressing in on me. I needed some damn friends. I was pretty lonely and getting sick of bike riding. I wanted a specific kind of friend though, the volatile kind who runs aground in jail. I imagined myself his advocate. I saw myself filling up on his righteous anger and taking it abroad to walk around in the free world. Maybe I would prosecute his grievances around the county as a favor to him. Maybe I would let them drop when I left the jail and turn his anger toward my private causes. Anyway, my mom and dad, those disapproving, unappeasable, not-yet-senescent authority figures in my life would soon guess that I was changing. Perhaps other people who were getting in my way would guess the same thing. The whole world would see a new stoicism and wisdom in me; it would be the wisdom of someone who has knocked around a bit, who has broken bread with society's monsters, its nightmares. I would drop a few names whenever I met people I didn't like—this famous wife-stabber, my friend; that famous torturer, my confidant. I would intimate that other similar friends were being released soon. My footfalls would then resound a little louder in the halls at the university (I was still in slow pursuit of the degree though I didn't live in Amherst anymore and didn't visit the university often). Whenever I got some money together—three or four hundred dollars—I imagined that I might buy one of the inmate's idle high-rise trucks.

I guessed that there wasn't much point in thinking too much about the monsters and famous wife-stabbers. They would surely be locked away, I incorrectly assumed, in other, more serious jails. Wife-stabbers probably wouldn't want to hang out with me anyway, and probably wouldn't appreciate my loving appreciation of Camus and Dostoyevsky and so forth. So I often let my thoughts settle on the average Vermont jailbird, the professional collector of DWIs, the lonely, slightly twisted dad with a stepdaughter, the heroin addict, the Oxycontin thief. These are the people who fill up the crime columns in the *Valley News* and the *Rutland Herald*. What could I do for these people? I wondered.

To the undergraduates in Amherst, I used to love to teach a James Baldwin story called "Sonny's Blues." It's a short, bittersweet saga that follows the path of a troubled family, living among other troubled families in postwar Harlem. Sonny, the jazz pianist son, is a heroin addict. The story's narrator, Sonny's brother, has recently lost his infant daughter to polio and leads a colorless life in his colorless city. There are other sorrows in the family past: an uncle was run down on a highway by a carful of joyriding good ol' boys. The father never entirely got over it and died in a sort of unhappy bewilderment. Then, in the recent narrative past, the mother passed on as well.

The undergraduates often said they didn't like the story on account of its length. I remember a conversation during class one day in Comp Lit 131, International Short Story, with a young woman who was put out by the twenty-seven pages she'd had to read through in preparation for the class. "Baldwin whatever could have cut a lot out and he would still have gotten his point across," she announced at the beginning of class. Out of the corner of her eye, she looked at her friend, a young woman who wasn't quite as pretty but held reliably fiercer opinions.

"Right!" I said to the first girl. "It is too long. Let's pretend you're the editor. James Baldwin comes to you in your office. You tell him his story needs a trim. Which part goes first?"

She thumbed through her text for a moment and pointed to a description of a Sunday afternoon in the life of the narrator's family, a Sunday afternoon as they used to unfold back when Sonny and his brother were little children. "This part here," she said, glancing at me and running her pencil over a block of text. She eyed her friend.

The passage she pointed to describes how Sonny's mother used to sit on a sofa on those Sunday afternoons, while the father sat on an easy chair nearby. "In the living room," writes Baldwin, "there would be church folks and relatives." The kids would lie on the floor. As the narrator summons the memory, it swims into the present tense:

> There they sit, in chairs all around the living room, and the night is
> creeping up outside, but nobody knows it yet. You can see the
> darkness growing against the window panes and you hear the street
> noises every now and again, or maybe the jangling beat of a
> tambourine from one of the churches close by, but it's real quiet in
> the room.

If I had had adequate presence of mind, I would have given that student an
intelligent response: "It's a story about encroaching darkness," I would
have said. "It's about how you can keep it at bay. It's about *whether* you can
keep it at bay. Only the luckiest of kids, you know, have families like this
one that do some of the work for you. And even then. Even then you grow
up and the family goes away. Suppose later on, when you turn into an
adult, you get into trouble somehow. It could be drugs, but it could also be
an awful marriage or an illness or some stretch of shit luck. Who can say
what it will be? I can't because, look at me, I haven't really grown up all that
much myself. But suppose something bad does happen, and your family
can't be there for you. What do you turn to? What do you have left?" Some
smart kid in the back would have said, "The blues?" and I would have had
the whole class flip immediately to a passage illustrating how the blues
soothes the poison out of people, how it's a lament, passed down through
the generations, that must be met and explored and made new by each
player before it can be surpassed.

As it was, I didn't have the presence of mind to make the speech.
Instead I talked about the importance of family in the story and the
importance for the students of reading through the whole text whether
they were bored or not.

Since that class, however, I've read and reread the passage through a
half dozen times and have taught it to other classes several times as well.
I'm the perfect reader for that scene since it gives such an apt description
of what it was like for me to be a happy kid, hanging out with Mom and
Dad, lolling on the rug, never guessing that the silence around us was
actually the calm before the storm. For me, the scene is as real as a home
movie. I like it for that reason alone, but in my mind it's been more than

that as well since I've often found in it a hint of career advice. Like the narrator in "Sonny's Blues" I was the son who tried to knit the unraveling family together. When I was twelve and my dad came unwound, as he occasionally did, and he threw the TV out the window or needlessly murdered the chickens or mowed down the neighborhood maples with his chainsaw. Mom could be found sobbing in the kitchen. Sophia, my sister, would be upstairs in her room, poring over C. S. Lewis's *The Chronicles of Narnia*. In such moments of family disintegration, I knew just what to do. I wended my way through the downed trees or the chicken carcasses or whatever it was, and sidled up to the old man. He'd be pouring sweat and swearing like a sailor. I would scour my brain for jokes. I'm sure what came out was the humor of an average twelve-year-old and none of it particularly funny, but eventually he would allow himself to be distracted. He would abandon his chainsaw and return to the kitchen for lunch. There he and my red-eyed mom, under the supervising eye of their kid, would effect a temporary reconciliation. Often, remarkable though it may seem, this patching together would hold out. Dad's mania would subside and we could go for weeks, maybe months, without another episode. During those tranquil interludes, Dad would sometimes mention to my teachers or to family friends that little Theo had quite a mature, warmhearted nature and that he had done a lot lately to help the family through a *passage difficile*. "He's our family counselor," Dad would say, "I have him on retainer." Since I was only twelve, I didn't know what the expression meant but I did know that I liked the sound of the word. I knew "retainer" to be connected to the idea of possession, of continuing to hold, of keeping a structure together. That was my life's goal at twelve: a continuous holding together. I went about it like a missionary. Nothing could stand in my way. I lied and stole and made myself into a clown at school, surely making matters worse, in order to distract my parents from each other. Of course, over time my scheme failed. Probably even in the short term, my tactics didn't amount to much. My parents were probably touched by the notion of me as the lynchpin, the binding agent for the family and graciously allowed me my belief. Anyway, when Mom and Dad finally did split up for good, I wasn't at all sad. Dad moved away; papers were filed, pets were kidnapped, shrinks and lawyers were enlisted. Even at the time, I thought it was all a big cliché. There was hardly a tear to be shed. I was about sixteen by then and already out of the house, already indifferent to the falling maples and the crying mom.

Well, not totally indifferent. I had escaped from the hurly-burly of a marriage war and was grateful for that, but by that point, my nature was fixed. After those half-dozen years in an unhappy family, I knew what I liked. I knew where I could make myself feel at home, how I could put myself to use and find appreciative audiences for jokes and spiels. I sought out families in distress. I honed in on them like a crow. When I couldn't find an entire family, I made friends with the remnants of families, the stragglers and the bewildered survivors. Even now, when I stumble into the midst of an unhappy family, I think: this is my milieu, my type of hang out, my moveable feast.

So it's happened that at times when I haven't had a clue as to where to go in life—this is where I was in the fall of 1999—I've looked for places where the family and its discontents were likely to be the subject of conversation. It's a sort of homing instinct. Well, maybe I'm not going to make a big impact elsewhere, I think to myself, but here, in this mess, I can make myself heard.

In the scene in "Sonny's Blues" that mattered so much to me as a teacher of undergrads, the family has just returned from church; it has arrayed itself across its living room. Lunch is now finished. There's not much left to do in the day. The family, by this time, is doomed to taste the bitterness of life and sort of knows it. Mom and Dad are doing what they can to keep the trouble at bay, and are talking quietly to each other. There's not much that they can do and what they do do doesn't really help. One of the kids is lying on the couch, half asleep and somehow all the more alert for that. His mom is gently stroking his forehead. The narrator remembers what the boy on the couch is thinking:

> something deep and watchful in the child knows that this is bound
> to end. Is already ending. In a moment, someone will get up and
> turn on the light. Then the old folks will remember the children and
> they won't talk any more that day. And when the light fills the room,
> the child is filled with darkness. He knows that every time this
> happens, he's moved just a little closer to that darkness outside. The
> darkness outside is what the old folks have been talking about. It's
> what they've come from. It's what they endure. The child knows that

they won't talk anymore because if he knows too much about what's happened to them, he'll know too much too soon about what's going to happen to him.

When I was thinking about teaching this story to prisoners, I had no idea there were going to be children in the jail. I had no idea that part of the job was going to involve my trying to shield the actual kid-prisoners from what was coming their way. As it turned out, there were kids, and of course they were in deep trouble, but before I walked through the cafeteria for the first time, I wasn't thinking *kids* at all. I was thinking that I'd try to sequester the local screw-up adults in one of the classrooms. Hopefully it would have a view of the stately Norwegian spruce forest on Mt. Tom to the north of the Woodstock jail. Maybe it would look out over the Billings Farm Museum whose furthest corn rows stretch to within a stone's throw of the razor wire. In a classroom occupied by a band of society's failures and one earnest teacher, it would become obvious after a bit that there were no reassuring wise old folks to be had. We adults would basically be the kids. I would turn to them when the time was right and say: "Looks like we're going to have to deal with this situation—there's no better word for it but darkness—on our own. The trials, the publicity, what you did, your memories—all of that. That's what we're dealing with."

I also intended to fire up these adults. My speeches would include an inspiring, humbling call to literature. I would declare: "Look, obviously we don't have the answers. And—correct me if I'm wrong—but I doubt the lawyers and shrinks and judges do either. But we do have this syllabus." I'd hold out a sheaf of Xeroxes and the inmates would stare at my hand as if I were dealing cards in a casino.

Well, why the hell not, they'd figure.

By the end of "Sonny's Blues," Sonny has made a tentative truce with his heroin problem. He rejoins his old bandmates at a club and invites his brother to hear him play. He plays a Charlie Parker tune called "Am I Blue." My immediate idea was that I would find, out of the ninety-five inmates in the Woodstock jail, one or two—perhaps three, perhaps a half dozen—who could read the passage that describes how Sonny plays, or any lyrical passage for that matter, and *do* something with it. Take it into themselves, as Sonny absorbs "Am I Blue." It wouldn't happen right away,

I knew. The inmates might be awkward at first or resentful or suspicious but my job, I thought, would be to push them along. Probably, in an environment like that, people would be more than willing to be pushed—and to give in. They wouldn't have much else to do. If I worked hard, and sorted through the throng of general-population inmates until I came to the right people, I thought I stood a decent chance of witnessing a performance something like Sonny's at the end of "Sonny's Blues." In the last scene, Sonny is at his piano up on stage and, not having played for a while, he struggles at first. "Exactly like someone in torment," says his brother, the narrator. Then:

> Then he began to make it his. It was very beautiful because it wasn't hurried and it was no longer a lament. I seemed to hear with what burning he had made it his, with what burning we had yet to make it ours, how we could cease lamenting. Freedom lurked around us and I understood at last, that he could help us to be free if we would listen, that he would never be free until we did. Yet, there was no battle in his face now. I heard what he had gone through and would continue to go through until he had come to rest in earth. He had made it his, that long line of which we knew only Mama and Daddy. And he was giving it back, as everything must be given back, so that it can live forever.

As long as they didn't murder me while I was trying to get something like this to happen, I would be okay waiting around while the inmates gathered themselves together. And as we waited, I meant to extend to them every conceivable liberty I could extend—favors, treats, permissions, whatever vain gestures were available to me—in order to demonstrate my good faith. I hoped these gestures would go beyond that, though. I wanted to create a small pocket of healthy, even unruly, human exchange—liberty, in other words—within the jail. I knew that the place would have its unfriendly, inhuman side, and I figured it probably could use a local, in-house opposition.

CHAPTER THREE

Duane B.

It's not easy to get yourself hired by a fantasy. I called it a few times at various offices around the state, was directed hither and yon, left messages for this one and that one, and heard nothing. I buzzed at the Woodstock jail front door one afternoon. A voice spoke to me from a metal box bolted to the bricks. It told me that the person I wanted to speak to wasn't available.

I made another, last-ditch effort to get myself an academic job, this time by driving up to Montreal to an academic conference. The result was that my car broke down. When I returned, there was message on the machine telling me that my application to work for the Department of Corrections had been reviewed, that I should come in for an interview, and that if all went well, I could start on Monday of the following week.

I got a haircut. I passed the interview. On Monday of the following week, I clothed myself in my stiffest, most police-like clothes. I washed my car. On a spectacular November afternoon, with snow on the mountain peaks and leaves the color of ripe peaches fluttering under the wheelwells of the car, I drove myself along the Queechee River, through Woodstock, and pulled in under the elm on the west side of the jail.

The guards gave me crisp nods when I opened the front door. I gave them fervent, angry nods in return. I walked through the cafeteria. There I saw four or five picnic-bench-size lunch tables, a lone mopper swabbing his deck, a bank of high windows to the east, permitting a view of sky and rooftops. Looking through them was like looking at a censored landscape painting. There was a strip of scenery at the top—the crowns of trees, a line of sky—and rows of whitewashed panes beneath. You kept trying to lower your gaze to the level of the traffic on the street. You kept boring your eyes into the whitewash as if it might somehow give way. The place reeked of disinfectant. I heard a guard's squawking radio in the distance behind a door and could make out the sound of passing trucks outside. Otherwise, the cafeteria was perfectly silent, perfectly empty, and immaculate. It had the glistening, unreal quality of a movie set.

At the back end of the chow hall, I pushed open a heavy gray door and stepped into a cement stairwell. There was no natural light. I was in the bowels of the institution now and I had seen one inmate so far, the mopper. I listened for the sound of people, heard shouts to my left, coming from behind a heavy steel door. It had a square foot of window cut into it at eye level. The back of someone's neck was pressed up against the pane on the other side. It was a stout, well-shaven weight-lifting neck.

I didn't know where to go. Left? Right? Up? I gazed at the wall phone. Was I supposed to call someone? Above me, yellow light, as if from the inside of a microwave, flooded from a recessed fixture; it discolored my books and made my hands look like parchment. More shouts from behind the door. The stairwell reeked too: sour sweat and cafeteria disinfectant. I descended two flights of stairs and came to another heavy prison door: it clicked open in front of me. I stepped through it, feeling like the hapless pilgrim in "Before the Law," nervous and earnest and ready to meet my fate.

I beheld Duane Bedell poring over the *Valley News*; to his left was Jim Candon, who had hired me a few days before, his *Rutland Herald* unfurled in his lap.

It was hard to tell what the room I was standing in was used for. There were no rows of desks, no blackboards, no throng of students. There were no lockers or student belongings or evidence of ongoing school projects. A wooden plaque hung over Candon's desk. The plaque said "Community High School of Vermont" in green block letters and then in smaller type, between quotation marks: "Living, Learning, Working." Directly in front of me were three long lunch tables lined up end to end. A scattering of mismatched chairs were pushed in neatly at two-foot intervals so that a dozen inmates or so could sit comfortably in a semicircle. The cinderblock walls were covered in sticky, shiny white paint. There was a poster of a hang glider on one wall, a white dry erase board against another, a waist-high shelf of encyclopedias to the left of the entrance, and a massive Xerox machine behind Candon's desk. There was a bank of aged, idle computers behind the lunch tables. A coffee urn stood on a small table next to the computers.

There wasn't much to remind you of who you were or what you were doing there; it was a bit like a conference room in a hotel in this sense. The theme of the décor was versatile indirection. I was reminded that I was inside the bowels of a jail by the wire mesh on the windows, the squawk of Jim Candon's radio, and the video camera mounted on a bracket high in a corner of the room. I had passed by at least three such cameras and one bank of video monitors on the way in. Now, at the entrance to the schoolroom, I felt myself sufficiently monitored. I almost always had this sensation in the main schoolroom, in the cafeteria, and in the hallways. I felt, accurately enough, that every gesture and every word was being scrutinized by professionals. There was nothing for it but to relax and enjoy the attention. That's what the inmates did, anyway.

When I opened the door on that Monday afternoon, I stepped into a scene of quiet fraternity. Two duffers were reading the newspaper in silence. I could practically smell them heeding one another and sighing together and aging together. In fact it turned out that they had known each other for only a few months, but in that time they had apparently fallen into a halcyon domestic routine. It helped that Duane was a perfect prisoner, the sort of inmate who volunteers for unpleasant jobs, signs up for every jail-sponsored activity on offer, never displays aggression, and never complains. He was in his late thirties, had taken to high school only lately apparently, and Jim had begun to reward him for his interest. He was permitted more frequent access to the schoolrooms for instance, and was always welcome, even when he hadn't signed up for classes in advance.

Duane and Jim were resting their hands on the plastic laminate surface of one of the tables. A twitch in the arm of either party would have brought their skin together. I wondered if maybe they had pushed up against one another for comfort, for a sense of human solidarity beneath the cinder blocks and the cameras and the shelves of encyclopedias. I said nothing.

It was, at any rate, a heart softening scene. I wasn't invited to join in so I stared at Jim and Duane. I saw them exchanging collegial glances. After a moment, Jim introduced me to Duane. Like old couples everywhere, they required only the barest noises and a gesture or two to carry on an intelligible conversation. Jim nodded and mumbled; Duane nodded and mumbled; I followed suit. We were introduced.

I checked out Duane's duds. Like all Vermont inmates, he wore clothing from home. He had on a black woolen sweater checked with bright purple and yellow squares. His hair, once curly, perhaps, and now wiry, rose from his forehead in bristles. When he mumbled to Jim, I heard him gently eliding his consonants as he spoke, and adding soft *as* to the ends of words, as the old-timers in untouristy, un-Woodstockish parts of Vermont do. "Nisa meetya," he nodded.

I mumbled something in response. I said that nobody, it seemed, had signed up for either one of my afternoon classes. "Doanmadda," Duane shrugged, barely touching his *ds*. "Doanmadda, rye?"

"Right," I said.

A feeling crept up on me. It came along slowly and then was suddenly filling my head and sending excited tingles along my spine. I decided that I liked Duane. I decided that I loved him or could love him—as a student, I mean. I decided that a small classroom full of Duanes could make my life meaningful and satisfactory, at least for the time being. I decided that I had to get to know him and I knew the only way for that to happen would be in private, away from the cameras and the radios and Jim's fraternal supervision.

Duane did not return my affection. He was the first inmate I ever hung out with, my first criminal student, my first encounter with someone who had disgraced himself before the world. He held my glance for a moment and shrugged. He seemed shy but not furtive. I couldn't take my eyes off him. I inventoried his physical self: slight, slender shoulders, chalky skin, apologetic eyes. I was riveted by his sweater—was it possibly homemade? What a beautiful artifact it was, I thought, with its checks and its colors, a true Vermont handcraft, I decided, and not at all like the hokey pullovers sold at tourist expos. I gazed at his work boots and his Ames jeans. They were immaculate, old things, carefully husbanded.

He seemed to me an especially mild criminal—he wasn't much like the hearty Vermont dude I had been imagining, the fellow named Mike or Mark with engine-colored hands, but he was there in front of me and I was wholly satisfied. I wanted him to stand up from the table. I wanted to walk around to his side of it, and to wrap my arms around him. I wouldn't say it, but I would think it: "*Mon semblable, mon frere.* We are all trapped, more or less, are we not?" Perhaps Duane would think the embrace a little weird, but it would be a meaningful thing to do, like Jimmy Carter embracing Leonid Brezhnev: a greeting across a void.

From his side of the lunch tables, he asked me what I intended to teach. I told him. He said he'd sign up for one of the classes in the future. I thought about how I could pull off the embrace without looking like a freak or a moron. Impossible, I concluded. I restrained myself.

I had no classes to teach on that day and no syllabi to hand out. I was there to sit in on a current events class, to meet people, and to get a feel for the place. Jim suggested that Duane and I go into the library—a smaller, darker room connected to the main schoolroom by a wooden door—and visit with each other for a while. I could tell Duane, if I wanted to, about the classes I meant to teach. Jim suggested that Duane could give me some suggestions about what the guys in his block upstairs might be interested in.

We ambled into the library. A beam of sunlight illuminated a spot of red tiles on the floor. Otherwise, the place was a duskier, smaller copy of the first room, with book shelves on the walls rather than posters of hang gliders and kittens.

I'm finally here. I'm alone with a prisoner! I thought: *What kind of criminal is he? I'm about to find out....*For a moment, my thoughts drifted absently back, 10,000 miles away, to the real world. I could still see, in my mind's eye, the dome of the sky stretched out over the roofs and foothills of Woodstock. I could see the last yellowing leaves still fluttering on the beech trees and the tiny cone summits of the Green Mountains off on the horizon. They were sparkling with new snow.

Duane reached into his shirt pocket for a pen. "So you're a teacher," he mumbled. I certainly didn't want to admit to being a teacher. I would have put out my eyes before admitting that I had come to offer him instruction. I wanted instruction from him. We sat down on opposite sides of the library table and stared at each other for a second. It was up to me to start the conversation. In a voice that was embarrassingly timid, almost moist with regret, I asked him if he thought he might be in jail for a while.

"Yup," he said. He smiled sadly. I smiled sadly in return.

"Man," I said. "That's..." I didn't know how to go on. I apologized. I swore a bit.

"Yup," he agreed. He hadn't been to trial yet. His lawyer was telling him to expect ten years. It could be longer; it could be life. He was taking it day by day. The problem was it was the second time he was charged with the same offense: domestic violence. The first time, when he was innocent, he accepted a plea, which meant that he had a conviction on his record. Now the judge was getting ready to throw the book at him.

I didn't know what to say. I had a hard time wrapping my head around the idea: ten years of your life for two fights with your spouse? It seemed a medieval punishment. He must have done something pretty bad, I assumed.

He said that he wasn't a violent person. In fact he had been trying to leave his house and climb into his truck when it—this conflagration with his girlfriend—happened. He was exhausted from work. He and his girlfriend fell into an argument. A tussle ensued. She called the cops right away, even though he asked her not to, even though, so it seemed to Duane, she was in no danger. She knew she had him over a barrel since he was still on probation for the first offense. At that point, he had nowhere to go. He got in his truck and started driving. He ended up at his deer camp in the mountains. He hid out there for a week. An old friend of his from childhood, now a cop, came to arrest him.

When he wasn't fighting with his girlfriend, he lived with her and her three kids in West Addison, Vermont, at the southern end of the Champlain Valley. He managed a two-hundred-acre farm on the shores of Lake Champlain; he was the sole full-time worker. He took care of the cows and the corn and the equipment. He was up every morning at four, every day of the year. Between April and September, he generally worked about fifteen hours a day. He was of course on call all the time. He had every other Christmas off, but even when he was off, he was on, since he was the one who knew how to do things correctly.

I didn't know how to sympathize. Everything I could think of to say sounded in my ears like a mockery of sympathy. "Man," I finally said. "Wow." I wanted to laugh at the absurdity of my idiotic words and a smile cracked my lips. I shut it down immediately. "Man," I said again. "Ten years?"

"Yup. Ten yeahs." Duane agreed.

In moments of especially intense incompetence, I sometimes remember the story of a country doctor who's wakened in the middle of the night to attend to an ailing patient. Panic overtakes him as he's flying to the bedside and when he arrives, he realizes he knows nothing about medicine. He examines a glistening wound in the patient's side and lets go a low whistle. A hole like an open-faced mine writhes with worms. The doctor's too dizzy to know what he's seen. A chorus of schoolchildren and wandering peasants gather in the darkness outside. They sing:

> Let him heal us
> If he doesn't, kill him dead.
> Only a doctor, only a doctor.

Dwelling on this doctor's paralysis of course only makes mine worse. I assumed Duane might not be telling me the whole truth. I assumed he probably tangled perhaps a bit more viciously with his girlfriend than he was letting on. Maybe he'd made a bad mistake. And that mistake, compounded with his earlier charges, meant that he was currently treading in some dangerously hot water. But ten years? What on earth could I do for him?

"You didn't even hit her?" I wondered moronically.

"I'll be doing five years at least," he said. "I'm not looking forward to it," he said.

I imagined him restored to his tractor in Addison. I saw him rolling over the bluffs with it, a tiny figure in a massive blue panorama—he would be holding on to the tractor with one hand, and swaying like a cowboy in a Frederic Remington painting. From behind his head and through the undercarriage of the tractor, the lake would be shooting little sparkles of blue sunlight.

"Duane," I said, "can you cut them a deal somehow? Don't you have work to do back on that farm? The cows... Who else is going to get up at four in the fucking morning?"

His face, already long, was falling. He fastened his eyes on his hands, which were clasped together, in the posture of an honest man, on the table in front of him. A difficult silence ensued. "A deal?" he murmured at last. "Nope. I'm fucked."

About six months later, I found out that he did cut a deal. Leafing through the *Addison County Independent* one day—a paper devoted mostly to news of corn harvests and announcements of agricultural fairs—I noticed a headline: "Child Molester Sentenced to Six to 20 Years in Prison." Duane had been charged with lewd and lascivious conduct, domestic assault, and sexual assault on a child, said the paper. The article continued: "Det. Trooper Ruth Whitney conducted an investigation which revealed that Bedell had been molesting the children of the woman with whom he was residing over a period of years. Bedell admitted in court on Thursday that he had fondled two young children and engaged in sexual intercourse with the eleven-year-old girl."

I was unnerved by the news, but not drastically unnerved. I wasn't sure if I should believe it. I couldn't see Duane doing that. But I knew by then, after six months in jail, that when it comes to inmates, you should expect the worst. I knew by then that the inmates, even the nice ones, especially the nice ones, rarely tell the truth. They lie out of shame or habit or self-delusion or malice. They especially liked lying to me since I was no investigator and I sincerely wanted to believe the best about them. Or the worst. Whatever they wanted to tell me, I was happy to listen. By the time I read about Duane and his girlfriend's children I knew that finding truth in the jail is like finding truth in a weird, experimental novel; it's certainly there, it's all over the place, in fact, but you have to puzzle it together ingeniously, like an artist and a scholar, and when you do, you're never entirely sure what you've got. Some version of truth perhaps but *the* truth? Unlikely. I, for my part, preferred to think that Duane was lying in court and telling the truth to me.

In those first few weeks, I had two favorite students: Duane Bedell and a school bus driver, Joe Emmons, who was from a village in the mountains just south of Barre. The two of them were my *only* students on most days, so it was a good thing I liked them. Fortunately, I did, very much. I escorted them into the library, after their current events class, turned on the light, and closed the door. Neither of those inmates were well liked by their fellows. Perhaps we were let alone for this reason: the new teacher and the two loser kiss-asses who wanted to be his buddy. The scenario was fine with me.

Out of Jim's hearing, Duane complained that the regular classes in jail school—U.S. Constitution, Science, Logical Thinking, "and all that *shit*" —didn't give him the academic challenge he had had in mind when he signed up for the adult ed program. An unhappy look clouded his face as he talked; he gestured toward Jim's desk: "That kindergarten shit in there," he grimaced and stopped, out of words. "What the fuck is it supposed to do...?" He said he was hoping to actually learn something during this time in his life.

Did he have anything particular in mind? I asked.

"Sure," he said. "Shakespeare or poetry or just...shit." He was sick and tired of being treated like "a shit kindergartener," he said.

I'm good at adult ed, I thought. That's my thing. Sort of. It wasn't at all my thing until that moment, but I was anxious to make a difference and anxious to claim an expertise for myself. In that cavern of idle, functionless people, I badly wanted a function for myself.

I had met Joe when I was loitering one day in Jim's current events class. Jim had scheduled my Literature of War course during that time slot—one to two in the afternoon—but since no one had signed up, I signed myself up for his current events class. Sitting next to Joe one day, with my *Valley News* unfolded in my lap, I noticed a hairy finger nosing its way across the text. It settled on an ad for an iMac. It tapped up and down. "That's how my wife meets her boyfriends," Joe muttered into my ear. He looked at the ad for a moment longer and gave me a sad look. "So I smashed its guts out and threw it in the Dumpster." He moved his finger down the page. "Then she got one of these." He pointed to a laptop model. "When I get out I'm gonna put that one in the Dumpster too."

"In that case, Joe," I said, "she might just get another one."

He gave me a hangdog look. His mouth fell. "I know it," he replied sadly and shrugged his shoulders.

A few days later, in the same current events class, the discussion settled somehow, after skipping through several news items, on the topic of women's dress. The one thing we were prohibited from talking about, local crime, was the only thing everyone wanted to talk about. Since we couldn't go there, we followed Joe toward his topic of choice. In Joe's view, women in the world today dressed themselves in outrageous, blatant attempts to provoke. It was "bad morals," he insisted and gestured angrily at the windows beyond which those morals were stalking the streets. He scanned the room for a local example, found nothing, and then slapped the newsprint with his hand. "Look at fucking Barbie," he declared.

"Look at the things they dress her up in. And that's just for little kids. The bigger kids...the bigger kids...the women...The women!" He turned his widened eyes toward me. His mouth hung astonished in the air.

Joe had been in court in the morning and was wearing his best shirt, a candy cane–striped oxford, tucked in at the waist. He'd been on a suicide watch, so he was beltless. His hair, which is normally frizzy and blond, was combed into a moist clump. It lay defeated across his forehead. He was rapidly gaining weight in jail and already had a sack of flesh pouring out onto his lap. Joe was in his late twenties then but looked several years younger.

His fellow inmates had been listening calmly to him, but they'd had enough. One hot-tempered guy whose name I didn't know interrupted him at last.

"What's wrong with you, Joe?" he asked. "You don't like tits, Joe?"

"What kind of tits, fat ass, do you like?" someone else asked. "Only tits like yours?"

"No," he said examining his shirt front, "not like mine." He looked down into his lap and reddened. He lost himself for a moment in reflection. "I like..." The word wouldn't come to him. He tapped his foot on the floor and made his belly bounce along to the rhythm. He muttered: "When they're...When they're like..." He paused. He was out of words. His eyes found mine across the table. I searched my brain for the word he wanted. *Melons? Water balloons? Submarines?* He reached his arms in front of his chest and curled his elbows upward as if he were carrying a load of firewood. "I like 'em like *this!*" he exclaimed. "Just like fuckin' *this!*" He turned his shoulders to demonstrate for the windows and the video camera.

The problem, in his view, was that nowadays women who had big freaking melons like that went out in tiny bras, in see-through shirts. "It's like they don't nobody have morals anymore. It's like they don't even care. Nobody cares anymore. Nobody gives a fuck." His hands gripped at the table edge in front of him. But by this time, the other inmates were losing interest in him. Was this all he had to say? Apparently so. He tried to go on, but he could see that his listeners were turning away. He was a hopeless case, they'd decided. He couldn't be rescued. They were giving up. Gradually, Joe let his shoulders relax. Somebody else carried the conversation off to a different aspect of the same subject: the women employees of the Woodstock jail. But Joe kept looking at me and smiling apologetically, as if he'd just delivered himself of an opinion that mattered tremendously to him. He knew it was a dumb opinion, but still it held deep personal significance and he wanted it out there, known to everyone. Barbie had bad morals; she reflected the state of the world. He shook his head and smiled slowly at me, his mouth quivering, as if he was almost on the verge of tears. He seemed so saddened by it all, by society's waywardness, its long decline. And he took it personally, as if America had in mind to rebuke him of all people; it wanted to spit in his eye, the eye of an honest man. That was too much; that was just plain outrageous.

The current events conversation moved on to the topic of how female lawyers dress—very well, according to the consensus of the class. There were some lucky bastard husbands running around out there, the class thought, that were getting some fine lawyer trim every night. The hot-tempered prisoner—a batterer I learned later—announced that he had a woman lawyer. He had offered his services to her. It would be the old jail-house swap: she would get him off and then he would get her off, over and over again. Everyone laughed.

Joe had nothing to say about the jailhouse swap. The eight other inmates in the class took some time to evaluate a few of the other local attorneys. Joe kept staring at me. I looked away and then a few minutes later, he found my eyes again. "You should meet my wife," he offered.

A few days later, as Duane and I were waiting for Joe to show up in class, I fell into deep conversation with Duane about the book I'd recom-mended he read in his cell. He had asked me earlier in the week to suggest a long, good novel—something he could sink himself into, something that would make the jail go away. I walked to the library bookshelf, scanned the spines, passed over the jail's encyclopedic collection of Robert Ludlum and its reserves of James Michener. Many of the books had their covers torn off. Many of the spines—the script in which the titles were spelled out—suggested early seventies to me; I didn't recognize the names of the authors. I alighted at last on Leo Tolstoy's *Anna Karenina*. It was a book about unhappy families. There were spectacular scenes of farming in it. Duane might find himself at home in those pages if he gave them a shot. Duane had duly taken the book up to his cell. He had puzzled through the first few pages. Now, as we waited for Joe to show up, he was wondering why the hell I had given him such a book: so many long names; so many balls and cousins and old-fashioned debates.

I reached across the table and took the paperback from his hand. Joe wandered in. "This, in this passage," I said, giving him a sage glance, "this paragraph I think will help you understand what you're meant to see in the story." I had in mind a paragraph that seemed to me to crystallize the genius of the book. It cut past the ostensible subjects of the book—adultery, marital disillusion—to the meaty heart of the matter. I flipped to the passage I had in mind and read it out loud:

> He felt that he was standing face to face with something illogical and irrational and did not know what was to be done. Alexey Alexandrovich was standing face to face with life, with the possibility of his wife's loving someone other than himself, and this seemed to him very irrational and incomprehensible because it was life itself. All his life Alexey Alexandrovitch had lived and worked in official spheres, having to do with the reflection of life. And every time he had stumbled against life itself, he had shrunk away from it. Now he experienced a feeling akin to a man who, while calmly crossing a bridge over a precipice, should suddenly discover that the bridge is broken, and that there is a chasm below. That chasm was life itself, the bridge that artificial life in which he, Alexey Alexandrovitch, had lived. For the first time, the question presented itself of his wife's loving someone else and he was horrified by it.

As I read, I could see Duane out of the corner of my eye, shifting his weight in his chair; he plucked at his sweater for lint. He closed his eyes. His head lolled gently on his shoulders. But Joe was fascinated. He slowly circled the table. Instead of sitting in his chair across from me as he normally did, he stood behind me, and then he was brushing the back of my head with his belly. Then he put a hand on my shoulder and one on the arm of my chair. I flipped the book over on its face.

"I wanna read that fuckin' book," Joe declared, almost bellowing. "My wife," he explained. "Is that about adultery?"

An idea came to me: I would use the passage as a platform announcing the ambitions of my class. I said that one of the reasons I came to jail was because I had worked and lived my life in official spheres. I paused and looked out at Duane Bedell and Joe Emmons, my only two students. I imagined them as tutees and myself as a young don. Perhaps my idea of official, I said, wasn't Alexey Alexandrovitch's idea of official—what I meant was I had lived a relatively narrow, officially approved life with officially approvable people. I had lived in a safe, even timid way and I wanted to put myself up there on that bridge, no, I wanted to put everyone—everyone who came to class—up there on the bridge. Then I wanted to walk down into that chasm, which Tolstoy was calling life. The books we would read would illuminate our way: they would help us see more and the things we would see we would see in great detail. The books would involve us in other chasms and the crossing of other bridges. "And you guys," I said, "your stories, your reflections, your experience, will make something great. Out of nothing." The life experience that six or eight prisoners could offer combined with the books on my syllabus would amount, I said, to the richest educational experience in the country, richer than anything the richest university—Harvard, Yale—had to offer. For we would be offering ourselves a true education about life, not about books. Books would simply be the means to an end. After all, I began, we were interested in something very mysterious and elusive, namely life itself, and therefore we would have to permit all available data into the conversation. I started off on a new tangent, but Joe interrupted.

"Is that book there about being obsessed with your wife?" he asked. "Because I'm fuckin' so obsessed with my wife right now."

"Right!" I said. "I'm glad that that's . . . well, it's good that that's something we can talk about openly. . . . And I think my point is that many of us have come to the edge of something here. I mean, we've all been put in a place—"

"I'd like to read that fuckin' book," Joe offered again. "Not the whole thing, though. Just the part about the wife."

He asked Duane if he could borrow the book for the evening. Duane turned the book over to Joe directly.

After that conversation I didn't see Joe for a week. It turned out that he'd been put in the jail jail, a single-man cell also known as "the hole." He'd had a "disagreement" with a guard; he'd called a guard a name and was sent to the hole until he calmed down. He'd forgotten to take his book. And then it was lost—maybe it was somewhere up in the cell block—he didn't know exactly where it had gotten to. I never heard or saw anything of the book again.

When he came back a week later, Joe was his old affable self. The time alone had made him talkative and even more chummy than usual. He offered to tell me the story of his arrest. I demurred at first—I suspected that he was going to lie, and I had school business to take care of, but he persisted, starting to tell the story anyway, and I eventually shut myself up. By that time I had netted two more regulars in class, for a total of four students.

Joe had planned his crime carefully. He parked his car blocks away from his wife's house, so the cops wouldn't know that he was in the neighborhood. They knew him well. Before he even drove over to his wife's house, he got good and drunk: half a bottle of Smirnoff's, many shots of schnapps, and four bottles of Jägermeister. He said that he knew he was going to be afraid; he didn't want to have any inhibitions when it came time to carry out his crime. After parking his car, he walked twenty minutes to his wife's apartment building. He wore his best clothing: an Izod shirt and pleated pants from Sears and Roebuck. He climbed through her second-story window thanks to a fire ladder and a landing just outside her living room window. There he removed his shoes so as not to leave footprints. He had a pair of socks in his pocket for his hands in case he had to touch anything.

He popped the window with a screwdriver. He stepped inside, "like a cat burglar," he said. The place was a terrible mess—food on the couch, dishes in the sink, newspaper and trash on the floors. He brought out the vacuum cleaner. It took him a half an hour to vacuum the way she likes it. He had to put the socks on his hands and fumbled with everything—the cord, the attachments, the scraps of paper and lint on the ground. "That's not easy to do with socks on your hands," he reminded us. It took him another half an hour to wash all the dishes. He popped a video into the VCR. It was a Christmasy thing—something with Bill Murray in it.

"Where was your wife?" I asked.

She was hiding at her father's house. She knew he was coming over, so she left.

One of the new students, Stephen Brooks on the official student roster (Slash to his friends), was running his hand through his moptop as Joe talked.

His eyes were deepset pools of blue; they were shooting out two blue lasers of hatred. He massaged his scalp. Joe shut up. Joe pushed himself away from the table and smiled. Softly, with his palms turning upward, he asked: "What?"

"I think you're borderline retarded, Joe," Slash spat. "I honestly think you're fucking borderline." He spat again. "Yuh. Right?" There was silence. I was glad Slash wasn't looking at me that way. I would have been tempted to call for help if he had. "You're criminally insane, Emmons," Slash continued. "Did you know that, ya fuck?"

I interrupted. "Why did you want to go over there at all, Joe?" I asked.

"I just wanted to show her. I can be jus' big cuddly Joe, but I can also do what I want. I wanted to show her I can do what I want. And I did."

He got caught, he said, because he brought her a bouquet of flowers. On the way out, before putting his shoes back on, he wrote out a note and left it under the bouquet. "I love you very much—Joe," it said. "That's how the cops knew, I guess," he concluded. They picked him up later on that evening. He was still drunk. He didn't know what to say to them. He was embarrassed because it wasn't the first time he'd violated a restraining order. He felt he might as well go out in style as long as he was being arrested. He started yelling. "I'm going to kill her," he screamed. "I'm going to kill myself." He grinned ashamedly and a flush of red filled his temples as he told us that part.

"But you weren't thinking of actually killing her, right?" I asked.

"Not killing her, no," he said. "Maybe...maybe I was thinking—"

"Ya fuckin' gorilla," Slash said.

"Well, I'm glad to hear that you weren't," I interrupted.

"Ya fuckin' fat gorilla," Slash taunted. "Planet of the fucking apes. That's where I live now."

Joe shot me a glance. "Maybe I was going to do something else to her," he suggested.

"On the syllabus today," I announced, "you all have read a story by the writer Joyce Carol Oates. Right? And everyone has their Xeroxes?"

I felt, by that point, a panicky urge to take over the dialogue. Yet my syllabus, filled as it was with works that played into the personalities of my students, seemed not at all the right thing. It seemed to put me in the position of leading the students onward, deeper into the subject. I needed something to take them away from all that. I plowed forward.

For twenty minutes, I lectured about "Where Are You Going, Where Have You Been?" I said it was a story about coming of age in America, and about the forces that threaten women and kids. I lectured about the toxic commercial culture that America thrusts into the faces of people who aren't equipped to respond to it. "The story sees things this way, at least," I apologized. The subject, it turned out, held no interest for the students. Most of them allowed their attention to wander while I read from my notes. I described the origins of the story—the murder and rape of a Texas teenager—and the central metaphor of the story: a flimsy screen door attached to a flimsy house. This is all the protection the girl—Connie, in the story—is offered by home and hearth. No sooner do the parents step away than the girl herself is summoning that alien, family-destroying presence to come pouring into the house. Eventually something truly evil, in the form of Arnold Friend, a smooth talker and a rapist, shows up. The girl—body of a woman, mind of a child—doesn't stand a chance. Joe seemed vaguely interested in this scenario, but not at all for the right reasons, and I didn't think it was a good idea to kindle his interest.

CHAPTER FOUR

Settling In

Once Slash started coming to class, other inmates began coming as well. Despite his aggression, or perhaps because of it, wayward inmates tended to follow him from room to room. He was thirty-nine, pint-sized (five foot two), a pro-snowboarder (so he said), and a carpenter from West Dover, Vermont. He wore his hair in a blond surfer moptop; he wore immaculate jeans, button-up short-sleeve surfer shirts, and, on most days, a pencil stuffed behind his ear. He looked like a clerk in a ski shop. He also looked as though he spent a lot of time pumping the jail's Nautilus machines. Perhaps he was just formed that way by nature: stumpy with a broad, rolling chest that nearly burst from his clothing. He never talked about his own crime. He said that he'd been in jail for about four years off and on, and that he'd been on probation since 1996. Whenever he was asked what he'd done, he gave his questioner a blinding stare and shouted: "Obstruction of justice. You?" I found out later that an unhappy, violent relationship had ended in a series of clashes with his girlfriend. The newspaper articles said that he'd put a gun in her mouth, held a knife to her, and had assaulted her during the course of one very long day and night. For these crimes, he'd been arrested one morning as he slept, charged with aggravated sexual assault, kidnapping, and possession of a weapon. He was arraigned and then released. He immediately returned to his girlfriend's house. He might have or might not have assaulted her again. He might have demanded that she withdraw the allegations. He did violate a restraining order. Once the police had sorted everything out, they decided to drop the charges stemming from the initial incident. The witness didn't want to go forward. Slash was eventually charged instead with obstructing the police investigation. He pled guilty and got probation and a five-year suspended sentence. When he violated his probation, he was sent off to the Woodstock jail to begin serving his term.

Slash was the most literate and canniest prisoner I had met. I liked him right away. He wanted to talk to me about the Michel Foucault history *Discipline and Punish;* his favorite books were G. Hirliman and W. G. Stone's *The Hate Factory* (about a prison riot) and Alexandre Dumas' *The Count of Monte Cristo.* He was proud of his family, particularly his grandfather, a colonel, and scorned the other prisoners for their white-trashy ways. I liked Slash's verbal trickery. I liked the way he translated prison terms into his own language of contempt: public defenders (PDs) were public pretenders; when they succeeded in showing you the way to the lockup, they were penitentiary directors. The Department of Corrections was the Department of Corruptions; the hole was "the little cage"; the Woodstock jail was "the big cage" or "the fucking petting zoo" or "day care." The guards were his "butlers." He bragged, "I say to them: take me to my lunch. Take me to my doctor. Take me to exercise. Now!"

I also liked him for his firm hand, which was a hundred times firmer than mine when it came to dealing with the other inmates. When they annoyed him, he would stare with azure eyes; sometimes he would slap the table with his hand. They would shut up. In the first week that I knew him, I watched while he vowed in front of a roomful of current events students to exact revenge against his parole officer. I could see his words sinking into the hearts of every person in the room. He walked the class through the murder that was forming in his mind. He described her office, how he would approach it, what he would say to her in her final seconds on earth, where he would put the gun, how many bullets he would pump into her, and who else he would kill while he was at it. "I will go to the dark side if I have to," he promised.

There was silence in the room. "Right?" he asked. The twelve newspaper readers nodded as if he'd just read them a psalm. He would do everything he said he'd do and more, he went on, if she convinced the parole board to deny him his probation. He said he'd make Carl Drega, a psycho gun freak who'd shot up the town of Colebrook, New Hampshire, look like a toddler. He said he'd make Dylan Klebold and Eric Harris from Littleton, Colorado, look like kindergartners.

The next day, in the library, after thinking about how to respond to Slash, I countered with my own speech. It was no tour de force but it did the trick. The gist of it was that the dark side was an interesting place, well worth exploring, but that Slash needn't go nuts in order to go there. He could explore the place through study, through his imagination; I said that he'd be likely to go much farther if he did it that way. Moreover, he could come back whenever he wanted to. Something in the speech caught his attention. I could see his eyes taking in my points. After class, he clasped my upper arm in a two-handed embrace. "Nice fucking class today, Theo," he assured me. "Keep that shit up, bro, okay?" he said.

"I'll try," I said. After that, we were bonded. He quieted unruly inmates when I asked him to and sometimes, though not always, quieted himself.

When I knew that I had Slash on my side, I knew that I was succeeding in the task that most daunted me: getting the inmates to trust me. After my Nietzschean speech about the dark side—it occurred in mid-December of '99, after I'd been working inside for about a month—I knew that if I could corral my students into the library and close the door, I could conduct a relatively civil, intelligent conversation with them. That, however, was a big if. It didn't help that everything about the jail, with the exception of my growing group of students, scared the hell out of me.

I was afraid, first of all, of the guards. I thought that they could see through me, or, failing that, smell through me to a distilled pot-growing essence, trapped in my clothes. I had gotten an aggressive haircut and wore conservative tortoiseshell glasses, but weighing against that evidence was my disheveled car, my disheveled raincoat and backpack, and the bleeding-heart mission itself that I had signed up for. I assumed that these gave me away to the guards. I assumed that the guards had me ID'd from the moment I set foot in the jail as a head-in-the-clouds-do-gooder. (I was right about that and only underestimated the annoyance guards tend to feel for people of this nature.) I guessed that the guards were waiting for me to commit my first and only error. Then I'd be out on my ear, having gotten to know only four inmates, having accomplished nothing.

When I wasn't afraid of the guards, I was anxious in the presence of the other teachers. I had displayed my résumé to Jim and others above him in the jail administration. On it I wrote, optimistically, Ph.D. Comparative Literature, *expected*, June 2000. "It's just a matter of finishing up some formalities," I lied, in my interview. The result was that I arrived having proclaimed myself to be a do-gooder *and* a fancy-pants. It was a wicked combination of high-mindedness and pointy-headedness, a double whammy. It was bound to go over poorly with overworked, burned-out teachers and of course it did. But then I didn't like these two aspects of my personality either, and I'm sure I invited the other teachers to hold my qualifications in contempt. Naturally, that made matters worse.

On many afternoons during those weeks, I slipped through the schoolroom door into a stony silence. Jim would be reading the newspaper at his desk. Dottie, the special ed teacher, would be gazing into her computer screen. The inmates would be perched on their bunks upstairs, waiting for the radio call from Jim that would permit them into the stairwell. I would slip through the steel door, cradling an armload of *Norton Anthologies*. Jim would look up: "Hiya," he would blurt, in our instant of eye contact. It was a low, effortful blurting, more like a sheep baaing in the distance than a human voice. I rarely made eye contact with Dottie at all, certainly not at predictable moments like this. I had the distinct impression that the two of them rolled their eyes when I wasn't looking at them. Maybe I was being paranoid. I had the impression that they were hoping, anyway, for me to dispatch myself somehow from my mission: perhaps I would get myself fired or would quit or would find some other, better job. I suspected that they were hoping they weren't going to have to wait me out.

When I was done being anxious about Jim's and Dottie's attitudes, I turned my anxieties toward the general inmate population. It turns out that many inmates don't feel even a twinge of friendliness toward the local ex-college kid who wants to teach English at the county jail. Some of them don't like to be looked at by outsiders; some of them hate well-meaning outsiders most of all. They like the cops better than they like any other kind of noncriminal, because with the cops you always know where you stand. A cop will usually be honest about his contempt. Often, an outsider won't know how to do even that. Certain inmates in those first months looked into my eyes as if they could barely keep themselves from spitting. Some of them were too filled with contempt to look at all.

I didn't make things easy on myself. I proselytized on behalf of "Literature" and the liberal arts way too much. I went after anyone who looked, even from a distance, as though he might be capable of holding a book in his hands. One inmate sitting by himself in the library calmly informed me that I was an uppity motherfucker and that uppity motherfuckers like me sometimes found their short stories shoved up their assholes, maybe with the aid of barbed fucking shank, so that it would get stuck up there good and tight. His black eyes flashed with pleasure as he talked.

Almost every day, during this first month, I considered how long the jail had existed without my presence. According to the official town history, the first jail in Woodstock was carved into the side of a bedrock wall in the spring of 1797. Woodstock has had a jail ever since because it has always been the county seat, though the criminal court was moved to White River Junction in the seventies. Anyway, some form of penal institution had been operating safely and efficiently in town for about 203 years. It seemed likely that the penal institution could probably carry on, also without me, for another 203 years. The people who ran the jail had enormous skill and practice in waiting. I began to reflect that they probably had a general sense of how long it takes someone to get discouraged, how long the person's reserves of courage will last, and how long he can carry on running on empty. They tote up the figures, check their watches, and start the wait. The more blindingly obvious it is to everyone that the wait is on, the better.

Yet I had big plans for the jail. When I looked at the situation from some remove—from the end of a weekend away for instance, or from the living room at home—I wasn't at all bothered by the sour face the jail presented to outsiders. It wanted to be left alone. Fair enough. I didn't see why its desire to be left in peace should interfere with my desire to start my own university. The place had the raw makings of a campus—an outdoor park, a rec room, a suite of classrooms, and blocks of living quarters. There was a cafeteria with lousy coffee. There were twenty unarmed guards in case of civil unrest.

My first order of business was to recruit a student body. It turned out that the student body, such as it was, recruited me. Some of them, it's true, weren't actively recruiting. They just cherished the privacy of the library and didn't mind that I conducted a class while they were lounging around in there. But others, like Slash, actively sought me out.

When he sat by my side in the current events class, he sometimes lowered his newspaper to peer in amazement at the condition of his fellow inmates. He'd nudge me under the table and point out a mountain of inmate flesh quietly slipping staples into his mouth. "Why's he doing that?" I would ask.

"Tattoo gun," he'd whisper. The inmates would burn carbon paper to ashes in their cells, he explained, mix it with toothpaste and water, and daub their staples in the resultant muck. The fat man was an artist; he was paid to prick the other inmates with staples.

Sometimes Slash would point at a prisoner whose eyeballs were bobbling erratically beneath their lids. He would gaze and then turn his head to catch my eyes and then slowly begin shaking his head back and forth. I'd lower my newspaper too. "How would you like to live here with these fucking apes?" he would ask. We would look out over the collection of inmates like generals on a reviewing stand—and Slash would whisper to me about what a hellhole the place really was. This one had molested his grandchildren, he would tell me; that one over there had used a crow bar to threaten a woman as he raped her in front of her kids. He narrowed his eyes in cold fury sometimes and stared at the people he couldn't bear. If one of them laughed too loud in current events class, he would crash his newspaper down on the table and kick at its leg. The offending prisoner would look up to see Slash staring wildly. He would straighten himself in his chair. His face would turn blank.

I was also adopted initially by Mike Tobin. The newspaper described him as a "drifter" from the White River Junction "area"; he was offended by the word *drifter,* though, and suggested instead "man about town" or just simply "man." "I live in different apartments," he said. "In the summer I live in a tent." He told me that he wanted to come to class to talk about some poems he'd written.

"Where are they?" I asked.

"In my head," he said. When I asked him to recite a few lines for us he blushed. "Nah. Okay," he mumbled. "Jus' . . . forget it."

Just before Christmas, an article about his sentencing appeared in the newspaper. He folded the local and regional section up in quarters so that the column with his name in it was positioned in the upper left, just beneath the fold. He passed the newspaper to me underneath the table. "Man Sentenced to Five Years in Sex Assault Case," it said. I scanned the article and turned to look at him.

"I admitted it, at least," he said. It was his second offense. There had been kids involved—his own. What he actually pleaded to, he said, were two inappropriate touches and one lewd and lascivious conduct.

Later on in the library he told me about his coming clean: "I didn't have to come to jail. I chose to come here and I'm glad about it." I wondered how that could be. Had he knocked on the door? How did that work? If he turned himself in, he would've had to encourage his children to come forward as well to testify against him. "Yup," he said. "That's what I done."

When he was talking to me about his crimes, he let his bangs fall forward into his eyes. He wore a stringy curtain of dark brown hair over his forehead. If he was embarrassed he would drop a lock or two or the whole mess over his eyes and then he'd pull his turtleneck up over his mouth. The other inmates hated him because he was HIV positive and because he was a snapper—a child molester. When he was present they talked about the fucking sick-ass motherfuckers who littered the jail, the human refuse who should be exterminated with the rodents and the flies. Tobin could sit through a lot of this, but when Slash would point to him in current events and announce: "This man knows all about butt fucking. He's got AIDS, boys—watch the fuck out," Tobin would let his bangs drop into his eyes. He'd pull his turtleneck up over his chin and stare at us from behind his curtain of hair. Then after a little while, if Slash kept talking—about the "sniveling bitches" who live in the jail, "the rat fuckers" and the "human weeds"—Tobin would sweep his books from the table. He'd move off into the library and sit down by himself. By the time I got there a few minutes later, he'd be in a really good mood, smiling and cheerful and looking forward to class.

The inmates in Woodstock were waiting for sentences to be handed down, or for trials to begin, or for plea bargains to be worked out. Then they moved on. To keep a class of a half-dozen people intact over the course of three weeks was a major accomplishment, for everyone was on the move except the staff. Many inmates were parole or probation violators, sent back to jail by their POs for having disregarded court orders. Others had been transferred to Woodstock from elsewhere in expectation of imminent release. Those who had been returned to jail by their POs sometimes had to wait around only for a day or a week; other times the violations were grave and meant, among other things, that the violators were likely to be stuck in Woodstock indefinitely while the police tried to figure out what exactly they'd done. To have the same configuration of students every day in class for a week was like having a straight flush five times in a row. It never happened.

Still, a group did coalesce around my two o'clock fiction class in the library. In addition to Slash, Joe, Tobin, and Duane, a young robber named Will Emerson began signing up for class every day. Occasionally, we were visited by Woodstock's alpha male, a twenty-nine-year-old career criminal from Putney, Vermont, named Brian Argeros. He called himself Rhino, perhaps in honor of his heft, perhaps because he was constantly threatening to bugger the other inmates with his "horn." Rhino had smashed into a neighbor of his in Putney with his truck. The neighbor was strolling down the highway at the time. Rhino fled the scene. The man was not killed but suffered broken bones and a concussion. Why had Rhino done it? "I was drunk," he said, "and plus I didn't like the guy."

In December 1999, I began trying out a formal syllabus on these students. I began with Kafka. Standing next to Rhino but looking over his head toward Duane and Tobin, I held my Kafka volume in my left hand, just as I had envisioned, and read through the first lines in silence. I then closed it in ceremonious, priest-like solemnity. "Before the Law there stands a doorkeeper," I intoned as Tobin emptied his nostrils into a Kleenex. Slash glared at him.

"Shut the *fuck* up," he roared. Reflexively, I shut up. Everyone laughed. I continued with the story. The man from the country, I explained, has given up everything in order to beg for admittance to the law.

"Why doesn't the man just go the fuck home?" Slash wanted to know.

It's his life's ambition to know the secrets of the law, I explained.

"What is he, a fucking lawyer? I mean a liar?" he asked.

I explained: "No—he believes, perhaps reasonably, that a great truth is to be had in the codices and commentaries and in the book of the law themselves."

Duane was thinking things over: "That dude is fucked up," he announced. "Why should we care about some lunatic?"

I was nearly stumped. I couldn't keep my eyes off Rhino; he was digging a pencil into the skin on his forearm. The carbon tip was probing after a vein a like a hypodermic needle. "You see," I explained to no one in particular, "the man gives away everything he owns—all his material possessions—in an attempt to bribe the doorkeeper. He wants that badly to be admitted into the very first of many doors that guard the law. He knows that something, something glorious is inside. And of course he's right! See?

See, he begins to perceive this *inextinguishable radiance*, remember, streaming from beneath the outer door."

Duane clasped his hands together neatly on the table. Rhino pushed
his pencil deeper into his arm. Slash opened a magazine. I talked for ten
minutes more. When I was finished, I asked Duane if he had in any way
understood anything of what I was trying to get at. He narrowed his eyes
as if he were condensing all the information I'd given him into a single
point in his mind.

"Yup," he said calmly. "I certainly did."

I was thrilled and relieved. "You see," I told the class, "the law in this
parable is housed in a mansion of secrets. It's a vast, sprawling, forbidden
empire, this mansion, and of course it contains, well, there's an intensity
to it, a power—even a sinister beauty. A person would give years of his life
to know these immensely powerful secrets, the secrets of a special elite
tribe of scholars."

"Yup," Duane said.

I turned to the other students. "Well, what are you guys thinking?" I
asked. "I mean I hope it's clear that the law here is a metaphorical thing—
it's not just strictly a set of legal codes. It's a massive codification of life
itself, of the mysteries of human existence. It's all written down. It can be
studied and pored over like a book. In fact, it is being studied...you
know?"

"Yup," Duane agreed, nodding his head rhythmically as I talked.

For a moment it seemed almost as though he and I had arrived at a
concord. Or maybe he'd arrived at his concord with Kafka. But as I looked
at the other students I had to wonder at Duane's attention. I inched forward on my chair and peered into his lap. The papers that I had assumed
were his Xeroxed copies of Kafka were in fact legal documents. He was
scanning through them as I talked, making eye contact as needed, and giving up an occasional "Yup." He was too polite to tell me that he was preoccupied with other things, or maybe he was partially interested in what I
was saying and his affirmations were a blend of his response to the legal
papers and to me. When he saw that I had discovered what he was up to,
he reddened, put away his papers, and sank into a funk.

The following day, I was anxious to get on with Dostoyevsky. The
Underground Man, I thought, might appear to them as a comical, wickedly

perceptive alter-ego for imprisoned people, fulminating out the truth of their lives. Every prisoner lives at the mercy of psychiatrists and lawyers and phalanxes of guards. It's the job of these people to settle the inmates into an orderly society. But the inmates are, almost by definition, hostile to settlement. They refuse to permit themselves to be accommodated, even when it's patently in their best interests, even when they have no other choice. I had thought that this dilemma might be context enough for *Notes from Underground*, but, sadly, no, it wasn't.

Perhaps I should have provided more background for Dostoyevsky himself. I tried to explain about his mistrust of Western humanism, his contempt for logic and reason as powerful forces in human affairs. "Dostoyevsky said: No. No to Aristotle. No to Europe. Man is no rational animal!" I exclaimed to Slash and Tobin and a handful of drunks, recently tossed into the slammer, who happened to be dropping by class that day. I could have been talking to a row of cabbages. I decided to hurry past the background sketch and plunge directly into the text. I ought perhaps to have plunged directly into a description of Dostoyevsky's experience as a prisoner in Siberia. I should have described what Dostoyevsky made of his fellow captives; how they had impressed him as innocent brutes, as childish and murderous and utterly beyond the scope of any thing or person imagined thus far by Western philosophy. I should have done this, but such a good idea didn't come to me in time, and by the time I did think of it, it was impossible to get a hold of *Memoirs from the House of the Dead*, which describes Dostoyevsky's experience in Siberia. I combed the shelves in the basement library for the book, found *Crime and Punishment* and Aleksandr Solzhenitsyn's *The Gulag Archipelago*, but no *Memoirs from the House of the Dead*.

Nevertheless, Duane and Slash did make it through some thirty or forty pages. They came to class armed with perfectly reasonable questions: What's this Crystal Palace he keeps mumbling about? What the hell is an *homme de la nature et de la verité?* Is this Underground Man really physically underground or what?

Paragraphs of answers tumbled out of my mouth but I could see, even as I talked, that the students had extracted their questions from the book, as required, and then closed it altogether. The obstacles were too daunting, the ranting of the Underground Man too formless and too foreign.

Among other things, there's no plot to that book, nothing to which a beginning reader can bind his attention. Because neither Tobin nor any of the drunks had apparently tried to read at all, it was easy for all of us to write off *Notes from Underground* as a mistake—mine.

I took back the paperback Penguins I'd collected from used bookstores and stuffed them down into the bottom of my backpack. I didn't want Jim and Dottie to see me carting them ignominiously out of the jail, especially since only days before, I'd made a solemn display of carting them in. But there was no use in concealing anything in that tiny institution. Dottie and Jim knew everything anyway. They probably knew before I knew. I might have simply asked for their advice at that point, but I was too proud, too swept away with my scheme of Dostoyevsky in jail to actually consult anyone. I meant for my University Within Walls to achieve a smashing success. Then, after announcing what had happened—how I had brought illumination and self-knowledge to the dark souls of the inmates—I would maybe, maybe, solicit some opinions for future syllabus items.

After the failure of Dostoyevsky, I decided to bring the material in the course more directly into the orbit of the inmates' lives. It was shortly before Christmas, 1999. I took a week to read Ken Kesey's *One Flew Over the Cuckoo's Nest* with the students. It was a week in which a dozen strangers trooped through the classroom at various points, took copies of the book, and never returned. Slash and Tobin and Joe said they loved it; I'm not sure if Duane ever got around to reading it. In fact I'm not sure that anyone got around to reading it. Our discussions were strangely preoccupied with the movie version of the story: Jack Nicholson was the protagonist; it came out in the seventies, they insisted. It won all kinds of Oscars.

"No," I corrected, "it came out in 1962. It was written by Ken Kesey."

"The movie came out in '75," Slash declared. "You haven't seen the fuckin' movie, buddy?" Rhino shook his head. "You should show us the fuckin' movie and shut your fuckin' mouth," he counseled.

I thought I might have some success with "Where I'm Calling From," a Raymond Carver story about a group of men in a drying-out bin.

Slash threw his copy of the story down on the table on the day we were to discuss it in class. "Theo, buddy. That is the most boringest shit I've ever read," he announced. He circled the table, furious, enraged and not just with Carver but with me. He'd given it a fair shot. He'd read with an open mind. He was starting to wonder about me and my college bull-shit. I turned to look at Joe.

"Yeah," Joe said, "Sorry." I decided that I needed a new student body. At least, I needed a retinue of younger, book-reading people—prisoners closer to college age than middle age.

I had to look toward the younger kids, toward those for whom high school was not a distant haze. Will Emerson, who was from Springfield, was the source of the chaos that occasionally overcame Jim and the other students in current events class. Will was about twenty-one; he'd dyed his hair with a dark purple and had ripped his clothing into a carefully hus-banded skein of shreds. It might have made an alluring impression on girls in his set on the outside, but in jail, his clothing and his wraith-like frame made him look like a beggar child, like Oliver Twist. When he wasn't talk-ing, he'd squat on the seat of chair and disappear into himself. His eyes would drift up under his lids; he'd curl his arms around his knees. He could sit like that for fifteen minutes, like a frog—no movement at all, not so much as the bat of an eye. When he wasn't doing that, however, he was yammering away. He often had a hard time shutting himself up. During his first week in jail, we discussed how he'd been arrested for robbing a con-venience store. He talked affably, garrulously about that. It was going to be his third felony conviction, which would mean ten to fifteen years in jail, possibly longer. He was going to have to start lifting weights, he said, with more than a little bit of uncertainty in his voice, in order to protect himself.

Will seemed to love the current events class. In every article, he found evidence of the evil nexus that linked IBM, China, and the mighty, blood-thirsty executives at the Chase Manhattan Bank. Half of what he said, it turned out, was lifted from *There Comes a Pale Horse*, William Cooper's ur-text for conspiracy theorists. The other half, a sunnier, happier half of his dialogue, was made up from the cheerful stuff of Vermont's many Rainbow Gatherings and Phish concerts and Ben and Jerry's Festivals. "Live free and die stoned," he counseled; "Never met a joint I couldn't smoke," he bragged. Despite the right-wing cant of his *Comes a Pale Horse* nonsense, Will was for civil unions, for anarchy, for free health care, for organic everything, and for the use of hemp as a soy-like universal foodstuff.

After a few days of listening to him harangue Jim with his theories, it was obvious to me that Will was arguing because he liked arguing. A lot of what he said would probably have baffled William Cooper himself. It seemed clear to me that he valued the truth of his claims much less than he did the pleasure of making them. Those tense, argufying moments were what he did to engage the people around him. In this way, he deepened his ties. And yet he wasn't making friends. The other inmates despised him for dragging out the same nonsensical, arcane claims day after day—the Rockefellers controlled the UN, China was an archvillain, a planetwide nuclear holocaust was advancing on us every day. Probably it would be started by China. But maybe Clinton or Gore or George Bush would also want to launch a weapon or two, just for the hell of it. Every inmate and all the teachers, after a few days of this, wanted Will just to shut the hell up and yet he wouldn't.

I decided that I, alone, could bring Will under control. I decided that I needed more people like him in class: amateur theorists who were anxious for data to back up their theories and not averse to reading. I could supply them with data if data was what they wanted.

I knew that in the early mornings, when I wasn't at the jail, a troop of high school age inmates were brought into the school for mandatory classes. On any given day, there were fifteen to twenty of them. I saw them afterward in the cafeteria and then later at ease in front of the TVs in the cell blocks. Occasionally, in the afternoons, they condescended to come down to the schoolrooms, but since they weren't required to enroll in any afternoon classes, they rarely signed up for mine. Instead, they played with the IBM 386s; sometimes they sequestered themselves inside the guitar practice cell, a closet next door to the library, and banged on the jail's broken guitars. Among these kids were characters who fascinated me. For instance, there was Steve, whose blond dreadlocks hung like wet ropes around his shoulders. Judging strictly by his preppie clothes, his bright blue eyes, and his languid, "dude!"-filled speech, he seemed to me like an averagely ambitious English major on an average American campus. But he'd never been past eighth grade; he graduated from there straight into drug dealing. He had a beautiful deep voice and sang songs in the practice room that amazed me for being in tune and for containing verse after verse of intact lyrics. He knew how to play a greatest hits selection of college-kid anthems: "Wish You Were Here" by Pink Floyd, "Knockin' on Heaven's Door" by Bob Dylan, "Wild Horses" by the Stones, and Van Morrison's

"Brown-Eyed Girl." But on some afternoons he sang from an older, folkier play list that, at least to my mind, seemed more appropriate for the jail: "Goodnight Irene" as sung by Huddie Ledbetter, Johnny Cash's "I Walk the Line," "Hurricane" by Dylan, the Woody Guthrie ballad "I Ain't Got No Home." The lyrics in that song proudly announce the failure of a life: "I ain't got no home, I'm just a-wandrin' roun'. I'm just a wandering worker. I go from town to town. The police make it hard whereever I may go and I ain't got no home in this world anymore."

Matt sat in on a few of those jam sessions. Occasionally, he appeared at the current events table. Whereas most of the teenagers dressed in Ralph Lauren and Tommy H. and came to school reeking of cologne, Matt wore a tired wife-beater T-shirt and rarely shaved. He didn't belong to the crowd of jail hippies either; he sat by himself when he came to class, dropped his face into hands, and massaged his temples as Jim talked. He'd skipped out of his furlough program, had hightailed it to Florida, and had been brought back by the U.S. Marshals. Now he was looking at a five-year escape charge, in addition to all the other charges, which were drug offenses he didn't want to describe. He was nineteen, but he moved with the listlessness and resignation of the middle-aged prisoners. Still, he gave me a disarmingly sweet smile when I pushed a copy of my syllabus at him and the next day he did indeed sign up for my class. He sat through the whole thing, having no idea, apparently, what I was talking about, and just before I was done made a request: "We should read some fucking Edgar Allan Poe in here," he suggested, "that dude was a fucking quack snapper drug addict, bro. But he wrote some good stories, bro."

"Okay," I said. "I'll see what I can dig up."

Among the teenage crowd, I also kept my eye on a group of seventeen-year-olds who'd been arrested in a single round-up of miscreants in Bellows Falls. They'd been part of a burglary ring run by a twenty-two-year-old woman named Christina Boyce. She'd needed $8,000 to make a down payment on a house and had sent a small legion of teenagers out into the world to thieve on her behalf. She'd been arrested eventually as well and was charged with various sex crimes stemming from her connection with the boys, some of whom had been underage at the time of their involvement. The woman had three children of her own already. She'd wanted a quiet house, a cheap place in the flood plains on the banks of the Connecticut, in which she could live with her friends and her children. The plan recalled in my mind the basic plot structure of many of the articles on kids and crime in the *Valley News*. I was just beginning to pay close attention to them, just beginning to get a sense of their elements. The mixture looked something like this: a bit of criminal mischief, some dreamy middle-class yearning, some poorly executed scheme, shock and horror in the community. Each kid blended the elements in his unique way, and each kid was stunned in turn by the result: jail.

The scheme also reminded me of Lennie and George in John Steinbeck's *Of Mice and Men*, and I started to think that I should teach that book. I went around to used book stores and picked up as many copies as I could. The teenagers in jail were younger by a decade or so than Lennie and George, but the way they banded together and their improvised, ill-conceived travels made me think they might find something disturbing and personal in *Of Mice and Men*. Of course, Lennie and George had worked hard, and these kids were migrant slackers, not migrant laborers. Instead of raising money from the sweat of their brows, they had raised it through robberies and drug deals and car thievery. But there was a moving evocation in that book of labor; maybe that would help. In the end, the students—those who'd read the book—focused to the exclusion of everything else on the sex crime at the heart of the book. What had Lennie done? Why wasn't it spelled out? Hadn't the writer missed something if he didn't let Lennie have his way? I answered the questions and moved on.

The most successful class I had during those first six weeks took place on a sunny December afternoon when a fortunate combination of teenagers and middle-agers took up a Stephen King story called "The Raft." Mike and Brandon from Bellows Falls were there: both seventeen, both facing a half dozen charges each, both excited and frightened to be in jail for the first time with the big boys. Steve, the folksinger with the ropey hair, was present. So also were Joe and Slash and Will. Rhino glided in halfway through; he could come and go as he liked. He commanded respect, even among the teachers, because he'd spent the most amount of time in jail of any of the regular students.

"The Raft" belongs to the early King oeuvre. Like a lot of his writing from that period it's sincerely in love with goop and viscous things gener- ally. Its hero-villain is a malevolent jellyfish-like creature ("it floated on the water, round and regular, like the top of a large steel drum") that swal- lows up four strapping college kids. They've made the mistake of going out late in the afternoon—late on a late fall afternoon, during their last year of college, which also happens to be, for at least one of them, the last year of teenagerdom. Worse still, they're going back to a swimming hole that's been chained off to prevent such late-season adventures. The kids have to hop a fence to get inside.

It's a place that's laden with memories for the story's characters. Of Rachel, the diffident, child-like victim-to-be, King writes: "[She] said that summers seemed to last forever when she was a girl, but now that she was an adult ('a doddering, senile nineteen,' Deke joked and she kicked his ankle) they got shorter every year. 'It seemed like I spent my life out at Cascade Lake,' she said." Now, it seems, she will lose her life out at Cascade Lake.

She will, as often happens to Stephen King characters of this era, lose it in pursuit of the pleasures of adolescence. In fact, everyone in the story makes the tragic mistake of plunging backward through time: they vault a fence, plunge into the water, swim, and then perch themselves on the white raft in the center of the black lake. There they glory in the simple, ecstatic pleasures of youth. "One of them," writes King helpfully, "looked like Sandy Duncan, the actress who had played in the revival of *Peter Pan* on Broadway." The blob approaches.

I like the story not so much for its heart-pounding, *sexy! spine-tingling!* terror, although there is a bit of that on hand, but because of its mean twist on the coming-of-age story. Here the kids already have come of age. They're adults by any legal definition and yet they're still in love with being children. And why not? They're still innocent in all the important ways and more physically radiant and fresh than ever before. Yet now they're also freer and full of sexual desire and alcohol. In other words, they're teenagers. But their time has come. And they've gone scurrying off into the pleasant oblivion of childhood. You can't do that, says the story. In time, the adult world will devour you whole. And you kids, hints the author, you frustrated Peter Pans, will have deserved it.

In class, perhaps because the story came to them emblazoned with a brand name, every last prisoner came to the library prepared for discussion.

The sun was setting through the basement windows of the library when we finally got through our customary round of insults and small talk. It was an effect that meshed well with the atmosphere of the story; I said nothing but watched the slanting rays falling through the window grates. It can be kind of homey in a jail when the inmates are gathered around a seminar table and the sunlight is playing on the spines of the books and illuminating the clothing of the inmates. Anyway, it felt so then. I talked quietly with the students—not, for once, at them—about themes in Stephen King in general: the moral purity of childhood, the alcohol and violence and corruption of the adult world. It got quieter and darker in the room as we talked. No one wanted to turn on the light, a good sign.

Will knew his Stephen King. To him, the whiteness of the raft was a symbol of the untainted, untaintable sphere of childhood. "Everyone has a place like that, at least in their memory," he suggested. Brandon and Matt seemed to agree. So did Steve.

"Right on," he said. "Right fucking on, dude."

Will made sure to point out that the blob can't get at the actual raft. The raft itself is a sort of sacred sphere, immune to the dangers lurking on its periphery. "If the blob is what's coming at the kids, if it's adulthood or whatever," he paused, apparently having lost his train of thought, "it can only get the kids when they put their feet in the water," he resumed, "or when their hair touches it. When they leave their sphere, know what I mean? And when they were actual kids, they swam in the water all the time. The whole lake was part of the sphere. The whole world was. So the blob respects childhood. It just doesn't respect people who keep on trying to go back there when they're sort of too old for it. Know what I mean?"

I understood him perfectly and said so.

Some of the younger kids, I think, were impressed by the predicament of the last two surviving teenagers. The blob has devoured their friends. On every side is sickening, encroaching menace. The only thing for it is to plunge in and make for the shore, but that would mean gory dismemberment and death. Alternatively, they could huddle on the raft.

Steve said, "Dude! You just got to stay out of the fucking water! Just wait there to get rescued, man."

"Right!" I said. "There's still some safety there, there's still a tiny bit of light falling across the lake. Just sort of hunker down right?"

Mike from Bellows Falls wasn't sure that was the solution. "There's no way out," he concluded.

"What are you saying?" I asked. "Can you please say that again?"

Steve hit the table with the Xeroxed pages. "There's no fucking, fucking way out, dude, is what he said."

"Okay," I replied. "I'm not sure I agree with you. There is a way out of this mess. Perhaps there's no way off the raft in a literal sense. But we're talking about a coming-of-age story here," I reminded the students. "We're talking about a way out through growing up. It's a figurative, that is, a metaphorical, image-based way to depict leaving childhood. That's what this story is about, in my view."

"There's no fucking way out," Steve said again, as if it was the first time the thought had occurred to him. A pause ensued.

"Doesn't he fuck the girl on the raft?" Slash asked. "That's what I would do."

From here, I remember the class eventually dissolving itself into a discussion of what you should do if you're on an airplane and you find out that it will crash in five minutes. We also talked about what you should do if you have cancer and you learn you're going to die in two weeks. The teenagers gave predictable teenage answers. They would get drunk and high and rob as many banks as possible and go to Las Vegas. Tobin, who was older, in his late thirties, and inclined to philosophize, especially about death, kept himself poised and silent. He listened politely and seemed to appreciate each teenage suggestion for its resourcefulness and its vigor. I think it probably occurred to him, as it occurred to me, that many of the kids were going to be in jail for a long time and might already have forfeited their last best shot at youthful abandon. They didn't seem to know that they had, however, or if they did, they weren't letting on.

Yet in some of the faces, especially after the sun went down and we were all sitting there with not much left to do or talk about, I think I detected a dawning awareness of what was coming. It wasn't the dramatic death-sex crescendo as presented in the story; it was instead the adult world of prison, an adult world that would slowly draw the life out of these hyped-up kids. Maybe my sense of their intuition was overdetermined. It came from their unusual quietness, their stillness, and the way they focused their eyes on the Xerox paper in front of them. You could hear the pipes thumping overhead. In the booking room, you could hear the cops strolling around, scuffing their shoes on the floor, moving chairs and cameras and clothing in preparation for the next intake.

After a while of sitting in the quiet, Will said, "I fucking love fucking Stephen King, yo."

CHAPTER FIVE

Woodstock

Our beautiful streams, our pleasant valleys, our mountains with the
wooded summits, surrounding us as the mountains stood round
about Jerusalem—these constitute the pride and glory of
Woodstock; and as we look at them, we may well say, "Our lines
have fallen to us in pleasant places, and we have a goodly heritage.
—Henry Swan Dana, *History of Woodstock, Vermont,* 1889

It looked like the set for an Andy Hardy movie.
—William Least Heat Moon (referring to Woodstock, Vermont),
Blue Highways, 1982

Because of my positive experience with Stephen King, I planned a new,
twenty-day syllabus. Half of it would survey gothic American writers of the
nineteenth century. I would give Matt his crack at Poe. The succeeding ten
days would show how America is still deeply absorbed in its gothic heritage. We would read stories about doomed families by Flannery O'Connor and doomed children by Joyce Carol Oates. Of course, we'd pick up with
Stephen King again.

On the day we were to begin this syllabus, Monday, December 20,
1999, I brought a small mountain of books into the jail and deposited them
on the current events table.

"Hiya," said Jim. His eyes hardly moved. He was absorbed in the
newspaper as usual. I had some Xeroxing to do and went away to a corner
of the room in order to get done my busywork before the arrival of the
inmates. It's never a good idea to leave anything—books, coat, gloves—
unattended on the table when inmates are in the room. I returned from the

Xerox machine in time—no inmates yet—and sank into my chair with a copy of the *Valley News*. On the front page, above the fold, I read the headline "Apparent Homicide Probed" and then, with increasing interest, the text beneath:

> A 51-year-old woman was the victim of an apparent homicide in West Windsor over the weekend, Vermont State Police said.
>
> Police spent the entire day at Bill and Paula Stanard's home yesterday, but released few details. Later in the evening, they removed a body from 1768 Blood Hill Road.
>
> The homicide, believed to be a shooting, was reported at about 2 AM yesterday. In a brief news release, state police said only where the incident took place and that the victim was a 51-year-old female. In interviews, investigators said they would not disclose the cause of death, whether they had a suspect, or if anyone had been arrested.
>
> "It's a suspicious death at this point," Detective Sgt. Jim Cruise of the state police barracks in Rutland said at the scene.
>
> Additional information is expected to be released at noon today.
>
> "There's not going to be any comment from the family tonight," a friend of the Stanards said in a telephone interview.

In 1999, there were seventeen homicides in Vermont, a figure slightly above the average number of killings per year in the state.

Vermont is not so tiny or remote or insulated by quaintness that a murder story cannot be easily absorbed with the morning paper. Earlier in the year, I had read about a man who had bludgeoned his houseguest to death as the guest slumbered on a rollaway cot. I had read about the naked body of a woman that had been deposited by the side of the highway several miles to the north of the Massachusetts border. That, I had thought, was how killers disposed of their victims in LA. Perhaps the method was catching on. Something about the case did flummox the police, it seemed, for the killer was never caught. In early December, the balding head of fifty-year-old Carl Sears beamed from the front pages of every newspaper in the state; it flashed from TV screens at the beginning of every local news broadcast. He had attacked his estranged wife, Patricia, as she walked through a strip mall parking lot on her way to work. She was a cashier at the Hannaford's supermarket in South Burlington. The day before she died, she had taken out a relief from abuse order against her husband. In her affidavit, she wrote, "I have a great fear that given the chance Carl will kill me." The following morning Sears stabbed his wife nineteen times in the head, neck, and torso. The news reports had her co-workers cradling her in their arms. She tried to pronounce the name of her attacker but the sound was obscured by vomited blood; the co-workers thought they distinguished the word "Sears." She died on the spot.

There were other hideous deaths in Vermont in 1999; shaken babies, drug killings, and four other spousal abuse cases. When the victims and murderers touched down in the newspapers, they lingered there for a news cycle or two, usually no more, and then they were gone. It took something remarkable, something beyond the scope of the normal angry-man-shoots/stabs/bludgeons story, to keep the case in the headlines. It took sex or multiple victims or the aura of deep bank accounts. As unspeakable as Sears's crime was, it was also too numbingly typical, too dreary, and too downmarket to merit coverage day in and day out. The shakers of babies and bludgeoners of houseguests were similarly easy to overlook.

I could tell right away, however, that in the Stanard case at least one of the requisite hooks was present: money. I knew enough about the neighborhood around Blood Hill to know that the area was populated by a special kind of Vermonter. The skier, the horse person, the early retiree and his family, flush with money from the big city—these were denizens of Blood Hill Road. They lived up there in splendid, sylvan isolation. They had horse paddocks and barns and stands of towering maples for company.

It was easy for me to conjure a picture of Blood Hill itself. About ten miles south of Woodstock, the landscape rises to a high point beneath Mount Ascutney. From there, the hills roll gently down on top of one another to the Connecticut River. The whole network of farms and trails between Woodstock and Mount Ascutney has been carefully barbered and groomed to resemble Shropshire or Sussex, with lanterns imported from Polo Country. Blood Hill is a little summit in the middle of that sort-of shire.

I often ride a trail on my bike that winds through corkscrew turns and tops out in a field; an outcropping there gives a sweeping view of the countryside. The stone walls at the field's edge have been restored to their early-nineteenth-century sturdiness. They plunge neatly into a woody gulch at the bottom of the hill. They are level and clear of undergrowth; they do not crumble or totter. Not a block of granite is out of place. The woods that are visible from this outcropping have been prudently arranged as well; a birch copse to the left would do nicely as set decoration for a Chekhov play. About a mile to the south of this copse, slightly lower down and topped with a radio tower, is Blood Hill.

I know that Blood Hill; that's a beautiful place, I thought to myself as I read the article. I flipped to page A6 where the story was continued:

The home belongs to Paula Stanard, a former town lister and school activist, and her husband, Bill Stanard, a boat enthusiast who works at Logic Associates in Wilder. Their teenage son, Laird, attends Gould Academy in Bethel, Maine, and is home for the holidays.

Rick Fallon, who lives down the road from the Stanards, said he did not hear anything Saturday night, but received a call from his daughter at 1:30 AM yesterday. "She was quite upset," Fallon recalled. "She said that they had heard there was a shooting. She was afraid that there was someone still up on the hill."

Fallon drove to Brownsville General Store and picked up his daughter, who had been at a party. He took his daughter to a friend's house away from the immediate area and drove home.

Police said the area was safe, according to Fallon.

News of the apparent homicide spread quickly through Windsor and West Windsor yesterday. By late afternoon, two television news crews were at the scene.

I stared at the type and tried to arrange the elements of the story into a narrative that made sense to me. On Saturday night, somewhere in West Windsor, there had been a party. Probably it had been attended by teenagers; probably Fallon's daughter and her friends had been there. They seemed to know something. They might have sounded the alarm. The police were telling people to remain calm, but a local mom had been murdered in the night inside her house and the killer was still out there. He was kicking around in the woods somewhere. Maybe he was having lunch at the general store. Basically, no one knew where the hell he (or she?) was. Mr. and Mrs. Fallon had decided to send their daughter to sleep elsewhere.

I read the paragraphs over several times and wondered about the domestic arrangement of the stricken family. Something there caught my eye. Apparently, the mom did not work, though she'd been active, formerly, in the community, especially in the schools. Her husband worked and the son was away at his prep school. Perhaps somehow, I thought, in their isolation, up on that hillside with only each other around for company, things had gone badly wrong.

But there were teenagers involved. That complicated my husband-kills-wife theory a bit. The shooting was reported to the police at "about 2 AM"; the Fallon daughter called her parents from the party at 1:30 AM. There was thus a half hour of lag time between the phone calls. Why did the teenagers know what was going on before the police did? Why hadn't they called earlier?

I assumed that the police would probably begin their investigation there, with the teenagers at the party.

I flipped through a few other articles in the newspaper (the millennium was coming; terrorists were trying to sneak down from Canada, presumably to blow things up on New Year's Eve). As the minutes ticked by, my thoughts kept lapsing back toward Blood Hill. I imagined what nervousness and dread would be taking hold in the households up there that evening. Whoever owned a gun would probably have plucked it from the closet; whoever had a connection with the police would probably be dialing his friends at the sheriff's office to find out what was really going on.

I folded the *Valley News* into sections in my lap and looked across the table at Jim. "You ready?" he asked.

I nodded. He pressed the button on his walkie-talkie and summoned the inmates from their cell blocks. Fourteen inmates, their faces drawn from excessive sleep, excessive TV watching, and excessive arguing with each other over the weekend, filed into the room. One fled straight to the law library without a word; another two took their places in front of the computers. The rest settled in to ruminate on the news.

Jim gave the inmates the normal ten minutes of newspaper leafing time. Then he hiked his ankle up over his knee and lowered his newspaper to the table.

"What piqued your interest in the news today, gentlemen?" he wondered.

"There's an article here that says the millennium's coming," Joe suggested. "Then there's one here that says you're fucked when you get to jail, basically," he murmured.

Jim invited him to summarize the contents of the latter article. Prisoners' rights advocates were objecting to the Vermont Department of Corrections policy of shipping inmates to a Virginia state prison. It was hard on the families of the inmates because visits were impractical and phone calls expensive. The inmates themselves, according to the article, missed looking out the window at the Green Mountains.

We spent the first forty minutes of class grousing about the Vermont DOC. Slash fulminated. In his view, the Department of Corrections had a single overriding mission in life in comparison to which everything else it did had no meaning. "The DOC is one giant mother-effing cash robbery operation," he announced. He laid out the sordid details of the scam: the state threw people in jail, most of the time on niggling, picayune charges, then billed the federal government for its trouble. The officials lined their pockets with federal money. Then they scammed money from the hapless inmates while the inmates were in custody. The speech was directed at me and Jim. He wanted us to know that we worked for a criminal organization.

"They want their fucking pound of flesh," Slash repeated not once but three time times. Jim urged him to pass on to the next topic of discussion.

Steve the folksinger had a story: a friend of his, best friend since grade school, came to jail on a fucking pot possession charge. Cops stole all the pot: ten fucking pounds. That's not what they reported but that's what they took. Guy stayed for one year. He had $500 in his commissary account when he left. The DOC gave him back fifty-nine fucking cents. Steve glared at Jim. "And you say it's not about money?"

Jim drew in his breath and held it. Steve's face was contorted with indignation. "You're gonna tell me it's not about fucking money, this place?"

"He's gonna tell you it has nothing to do with fucking money," Slash announced, almost laughing with ire. "That's our fucking Jimbo," he said.

Eventually, Jim managed to steer the class back to the newspaper. I had the front page of the *Valley News* unfolded on the table in front of me. In a pretty photograph laid out beneath the masthead, the sun was setting behind Mathew Crumbine, eleven, and Sal Saccarelli, thirteen, as they rollerbladed at Hanover High School. Pretty but dull.

I couldn't get my mind off the dead mom. The article didn't say how she'd been killed. I thought about the husband and the "additional information" that was supposed to be released today. And what about the kid who'd come back to town on Christmas break from Gould Academy? He must have gotten home just in time for his mom to be murdered. I tried to conjure up what I remembered of Gould Academy. The students called themselves Ghoulies; within walking distance of the dorms was a first-class ski resort, Sunday River. There was a golf course next door to the campus.

The inmates in current events were eventually persuaded to consider an article describing mounting Y2K anxiety. Border security had been tightened after explosives were found in a car in Washington State. Someone had wanted to blow up the Space Needle in Seattle. Now, in Beecher's Falls, Vermont, a woman from Montreal had been stopped trying to smuggle a Pakistani man across the border. She was supposed to have ties to a certain Algerian Islamic League. But neither Pakistan nor Algeria nor the shady network of connections, traced through her cell phone to the four corners of the earth, could arouse much debate among the inmates. Jim read paragraphs from the article, paused, listened to the silence, and picked out another, more enticing paragraph to no effect.

I didn't want to call attention to myself but it seemed like Jim was going to let the entire current events class go by the boards without mentioning the killing in West Windsor. I knew that there was an etiquette to be followed. One doesn't drop a gory local crime into the inmates' laps and ask them to have at it. Technically, it was within the rules of current events discussion to bring up crimes not connected to an inmate lodged with us in Woodstock. But somehow it seemed that an unsolved murder of a local mom wasn't the right subject for our group. Jim had scrupulously avoided it.

I can't let this just pass altogether, I thought. I stared out over the inmates' heads. One of their kind—well, some kind of criminal, anyway—was haunting the mountain villages south of Woodstock. Perhaps the captives in here would be willing to speculate, I mused. Perhaps they knew someone who'd heard something. Perhaps, I thought, one of the teenagers might have a word to say about the sort of parties that occurred late on Saturday nights in the condos by Mount Ascutney.

There were five minutes left in the current events class. I rattled my paper. I gestured in casual curiosity toward the headline. "Did anyone read about this thing?"

There were long looks on the faces of the inmates. Jim slowly turned his eyes toward me and slowly turned away. An interval of uncomfortable silence ensued.

"I fucking read that," boomed a tall, silken-haired inmate after a few seconds. He reached for a copy of the newspaper; he scanned the text. Freddie Stockwell's hair was his private arts project. It fell in a graceful, black cascade down to the small of his back. As he read, he swished it to and fro like a horse. Freddie was the one who'd offered, a week earlier, to shove a short story up my bum. His eyes twinkled handsomely. He looked up from the paper. He gave me a long, incredulous stare. With both hands, he scrunched his hair into a ponytail: "Who'd ever go and live on Blood Hill Road?" he wondered, nearly shouting. *"Blood* Fucking Hill?" He spoke as if he were projecting his voice to a theater full of restless patrons. "That's not where I'd go putting my house if I was in the fucking riller state market," he roared.

Slash rolled his eyes. Under his breath he muttered: "All right, Freddie. Go smoke another doobie, ya fucking prick."

Fortunately, Slash was talking to me and not to Freddie. If Freddie heard, he chose not to make a fuss.

After class, when the inmates had left the room, I turned to Dottie, the special ed teacher, and pointed again at the article. "Did you read about this?" I asked. She was married to the chief guard. She struck me as the sort of person who knew things. She knew the criminals who were out on parole, for instance, having spent many special ed hours drawing up plans for their education.

Dottie turned her eyes down toward her hands on her desk: "I did read that. I have no idea," she said softly. She looked up again and shrugged her shoulders: "Maybe the kids," she suggested. "Maybe the kids," she mumbled again. Behind her desk, stuck to the cement wall, a hand-lettered sign in capital letters read: "RESIDENTS ARE OWED NOTHING. YOU MUST WORK FOR YOUR PRIVLIGES."

Over the course of the following week, I learned from follow-up articles in the *Valley News* that a vehicle had collided with a mailbox and a tree at the scene of the crime on Blood Hill. This same car, an Explorer, had been found about six miles away and had been impounded. I learned something about the history of the Stanard family as well. It had been interested in farming: "The couple had renovated their house over the years, and took to raising sheep," said the *Rutland Herald*. I learned also that the family had lived on a slightly fancier version of the pretend farm my parents had bought when I was a little kid. The *Herald* reporter wrote: "Police and the mobile forensic unit spent all of Tuesday searching the Stanard estate, which consists of the renovated farmhouse, a new post-and-beam barn, a three bay garage, and several acres of land where the family raised sheep, horses, and other animals."

I learned that Paula Stanard was well liked by her neighbor, Mrs. Fallon. The *Valley News* quoted her remembering Paula as "a hard-working woman who took pride in her farm... she was educated, intelligent, and well-mannered." The article continued:

> Asked about the homicide, Fallon said she remained in disbelief.
> "We're from New Jersey and this is exactly why we left," she said.
> "It was difficult to watch the evening news."

On Wednesday, the police were interviewing the automobile thieves from nearby Springfield. They were said to be tracking down the people who'd been at the party the night of the crime. I began to suspect, as I think the reporters suspected, that the mystery would resolve itself into a story of class anxiety: a mountain retreat guarded by sheep had been invaded by dangerous youth. Since no suspect had yet been produced, the *Rutland Herald* reported that West Windsor was beginning to seem a frightened small town. Something unnamed was menacing a village. The last paragraph of "Murder Suspect, Details Elusive" on December 22, 1999, read: "While police say they have no reason to believe that the public is in any danger, the fact that they have yet to declare a suspect or make an arrest has created a disconcerting atmosphere in the area."

CHAPTER SIX

Laird

Laird was arrested on Thursday, December 23, 1999. Friday was Christmas Eve. On Friday morning I stopped in the Bridgewater Mill to pick up the newspaper and to chat with Akankha Perkins, who owns the bookstore there. The newsstand was decked out in front-page color pictures of Laird: wavy red hair, a black fleece vest, his face turned away from the camera. "Son Held in Mother's Murder," said the headline. I scanned the text: "...17-year-old Laird H. Stanard...20-gauge shotgun...explain how he could murder his mother and then fire at and come within inches of killing his father.... The judge ordered Stanard held without bail at the Woodstock Regional Correctional Facility."

As I put the *Valley News* on the counter I put my finger under the headline: "Oh my god," I said. "Can you believe this?"

Akankha fiddled for her glasses—they were bifocals that she kept on a loop of string tied around her neck. "Is that the woman from West Windsor? My god!" she exclaimed. "I've been so *worried* about that." She stared at me for a moment and shook her head in wonder, as if it had been her son. "I can't read it," she whispered and pushed the newspaper toward me. I grabbed a *Rutland Herald* too and made for the exit quickly, feeling like I was doing something furtive and wrong.

The jail was closed for Christmas that Friday; at least it was closed to the teachers. I went home to study the newspapers. Now the content of the articles doubled back to details that suggested a family, lost in its wealth, had also lost their kid—in what, it was difficult to say. And being lost, he'd tried to drag his parents into the void with him.

The papers, relying on an affidavit filed with the Windsor County Court, said that Laird had stolen his mother's credit card and "racked up" more than $5,000 in charges. He had refused to return to his "exclusive" boarding school; he had "recently told his parents he was bisexual" and believed that they had had a hard time accepting the news. Yet the father, William Stanard, told police that he had had no problem with Laird's coming out and had said so openly to Laird. If the motive was repressed sexuality gone haywire, it had gone haywire despite the father, apparently, and not because of him.

But Laird had clearly been unsettled in other ways. He'd been in trouble at Gould for skipping classes. A suicide attempt—possibly more of a suicidal "gesture"—had been made earlier in the fall. And there was this: a young woman classmate of his, contacted by the police during their investigation, had told police that three weeks earlier, Laird had said that he might get a gun and kill both his parents.

That would suggest premeditation.

The police had pieced together a narrative of the night in question. From what I could tell by reading the papers, it went as follows: Saturday night, December 19. Laird is at home. He waits until his parents go to sleep. Sometime around midnight, he sneaks away in the family car. He shows up at Destiny's nightclub on Route 5 in Ascutney, Vermont, fifteen minutes later. At around 12:30 AM, he leaves, giving two acquaintances he met there a ride to a party at the Mountain Edge Condos. He leaves this party by himself shortly after 1:00 AM. At 1:24 AM on Blood Hill, Bill Stanard wakes to hear his wife "reading the riot act" (his words) to Laird. The *Valley News* reporter, reading from the police affidavit, described what happened next:

> Stanard said he did not hear any other voices, but a moment later heard a "pop" coming from downstairs.
>
> Hearing nothing but the beeping of the phone off its hook, and perhaps the sliding of a glass door, Stanard told police he walked downstairs. He was walking through a doorway "when a gun went off in his face," the affidavit said. He remembered the muzzle being about eye level and a little to his right at a very close distance.

The police affidavit, which I checked out at the court, said that shortly thereafter Laird returned to the Mountain Edge Condos. In a panic, he recounted a story of a car-jacking: A man had been lying in the road.

Laird had stopped to help. Then suddenly the man had taken hold of Laird and pressed a gun into his face; he spirited Laird away to Blood Hill. The man wore a trench coat and had a scruffy beard. After that there had been, said Laird, an accident. He didn't know what had happened. "Call the police," he whimpered to his fellow partygoers. "I think my mom's been shot."

Things changed for me as a teacher when Laird showed up in the Woodstock jail. He turned out to be so much like me or like a nightmare version of myself—a bumbler, a blusterer, an ungainly kid refusing to grow up—that I was thrown into a panic. Though I knew it was no business of mine, I badly wanted to save the kid. Instead of attending to my teaching, I obsessed about Laird. I stared at him every time I could catch a glimpse of him. He's not here, I said to myself, ogling. Maybe he didn't do it, I daydreamed, examining his clothing for specks of blood. Yet of course he did do it (his father was an eyewitness). I knew in my bones that the police had him nailed.

In those first few days, I saw everything from his point of view. I couldn't get it into my head that he had committed a horrible crime, was possibly still dangerous, and now must live out the life of a convicted murderer. I wanted an exception made in his case. I wanted him to be offered a one-time-only get-out-of-jail-free card. Wasn't he just a child? Wasn't it obvious he was too young and too confused to accept responsibility for such a crime? Hadn't I been witless in a similar way when I was seventeen? Probably, yes. I had been impulsive and spoiled. I couldn't tolerate people who got in my way. Yet I didn't have parents who kept guns and ammo around the house. That circumstance—not really Laird's fault—seemed a crucial difference.

At Christmastime of 1999, Laird's crime hadn't yet acquired the solidity of irreversible history. It still seemed as though dozens of different narratives might emerge from the data the police were collecting. Perhaps Laird had meant to commit suicide, had struggled with his mom over the gun, and the gun had gone off accidentally. A story like that would at least lessen Laird's guilt. But then how to explain the second shot aimed at his dad? Perhaps some other kind of accident had occurred; surely Laird and his lawyer could come up with something.

Every day, I worried that he was going to tell the truth—he blew his mom's head to bits and meant to do the same to his dad—to his new inmate friends. When I caught his eye, I fixed him with what must have seemed an anguished glare. It said: "For god's sakes, Laird, say nothing to anyone!" On his first day in with the general population in Woodstock, I saw him waiting in line in a hallway. He was chatting amiably with a fellow criminal. I resolved to approach him, to introduce myself, to put my hand on his shoulder, and to whisper some advice into his ear. I walked up to within arm's length of him, looked him in the eyes, opened my mouth, and froze. Words did not come to my lips. I murmured "Excuse me" after an awkward interval and pushed my way through the line.

This kind of preoccupation wasn't appropriate for a teacher. I didn't care. In addition to obsessing about Laird himself, I obsessed for a while about the family in West Windsor that had so lately been blown to pieces; ghastly images kept crowding into my field of vision. I thought a lot about his mom; she died as she was scolding him. Now during dull, daydreamy moments in the current events class, I tried to summon up an image of her. The obituary picture had her standing in front of a horse, but in my mind she wagged her finger. She was still furious with Laird, and still keeping an eagle eye on his teachers. Hadn't she been a school activist? Anyway, she hadn't given up on him, despite his crime; she was just angrier now and ruthless.

Her ghost made me sensitive to the other ghosts that trooped regularly through the jail. These were women, mostly, and sometimes children. They were hapless, unlucky, desperate people who'd had the shit luck to become entangled with my students. Now they were back, at least in my mind's eye, mingling with their tormentors.

One of the kids in the current events class, Mike Potter, twenty-four, had, the previous summer, leapt on a sixty-six-year-old woman as she was walking down a dirt road near Woodstock. He slashed her throat and battered her with a rock. He dragged her down an embankment, fondled her, and then left her for dead in a ditch. The woman staggered to the road and hailed a passing car. She was covered, said the driver, from head to toe in blood. At night when I climbed into my car, I imagined this woman and Laird's mom together, watching me from just outside the car window. They shivered and chatted together. By the time I got home, I was engaged in a full-scale dialogue with them. They were curious about their assailants.

They were curious about jail, and wondered what happens to crazy, violent kids after they've been arrested. "I'm pretty sure they're thinking about you a lot now," I apologized groundlessly. "I'm pretty sure they'd like to take it back." But I had no reason to impute remorse to even a single person I'd met in jail. I had to read it into the expression in their eyes, and the more I looked for it, the more I suspected that it wasn't there.

During those first few days of Laird's imprisonment, I lost all interest in teaching. I didn't want to bring the liberalizing influence of the humanities to anyone. I wanted to know about the prisoners; to hell with books. But I had no license to go prying into their affairs and knew in fact that such prying could get me fired. Not wanting to teach and not willing to pry, I simply shut up. My teaching personality sort of deflated, especially in Laird's presence. I watched it lie down in a heap on the floor. I made periodic attempts to puff the thing up again, but the process was like pulling at a mound of tousled sheet. I tugged and primped and it rearranged itself in some other useless attitude. I must have made being in class look like awfully hard work because I remember the students urging me, from the very first week in the new year, not to bother myself so much. "Just relax, bro," Rhino counseled. "You'll get paid no matter what, right?" I nodded and did relax, as advised.

I didn't totally relax, at least not into somnolence as the inmates do. I just ignored my sloughing personality in its heap. It turned out to be an easier and more pleasant way to be among the inmates, though I wasn't necessarily teaching during long stretches of class. Instead, I was searching through my lecture notes, or searching for them, and when I finally found them, I didn't always feel the impulse to read from them. I was more interested in scribbling on them and drawing on them and recording the ambient conversation underway around me. I scribbled in as deliberate and stern a way as I could manage so that people wouldn't mistake me for a slacker or an absentee teacher. They were supposed to assume that I was applying the finishing touches to my lecture. In fact, I was applying the beginning touches to a book about teaching in jail.

I probably made a lamentable sight, doodling away instead of teaching. But it wasn't any more lamentable than what the other inmates did to pass the time. They poked at their hair with their pencils and scratched their bodies with the erasers. I did that too, some. They scribbled over the surfaces of the jail tables, and drew funny pictures into the margins of their newspapers. I might have done that, too. I don't think I stood out.

When the inmates said interesting stuff, I wrote that down. When they said boring stuff, I wrote that down. When Slash turned to me at one point, spitting with rage and spat out at me, "Don't you be fucking writing this down, Theo," I flinched. I covered my notebook with my hand and laughed out loud. "I'm not!" I cried and scribbled our exchange into a corner of the page.

Later on at home, I would sit in front of my computer, absolutely drained from the afternoon at the jail, and as I tried out a new (for me) combination of caffeine and pot, I poured my notes into the computer. I napped, woke up, and wrote some more. In the beginning, in January, I wrote just to myself. I composed little essaylets that summed up my week's experience and filed them in the computer. Almost right away, I got tired of writing to myself and wrote instead to a friend I had seen once or twice during the past several years. Amy Meehan had been a student of mine back in Amherst and was now graduated and fully matriculated into her own life. She had boyfriends and lived in Boston and was trying to move herself forward through entry-level jobs and rotating housemates. I knew all that but didn't know much else. Though it was a bit presumptuous, I began e-mailing her entries from my jail diary.

"Interesting," she wrote back. "Am bored at work. Keep them coming."

This kind of writing didn't feel much different from writing a diary. The only difference was that I was killing time for two people rather than just for one. I had to take a little more care with spelling and fill in some extra context as I wrote. That was all.

I wasn't sure what kind of listener I had been for Amy but for me she was a perfect one: uncritical, interested, tolerant.

Laird was taken into police custody on the night of the crime. It was in the small hours of Sunday morning, actually, December 20, 1999. I learned later that the police questioned him at the Bethel, Vermont, police barracks. They tested his clothing for blowback (blood and tissue splatters), kept him overnight and then let him go. From his lawyer's office on Sunday morning, he called a friend in Windsor, Vermont. She came to pick him up. He called another friend, this one in Massachusetts, from her house. She drove north, picked him up, and drove him to her parents place in

Massachusetts. Laird explained to her parents that there'd been a death in his family. "My mom was hurt in an accident," he lied. He stayed in Massachusetts until Thursday, December 23. He called his lawyer on that day. His lawyer told him to check himself in to the Brattleboro Retreat, a psychiatric hospital in Brattleboro, Vermont. He was driven there in the morning by his prep school friend and was arrested in the afternoon by the state police. A week later, after spending a few days in a holding cell in Rutland, he was transferred to Woodstock and released into the general population of inmates there.

Right after Christmas, I used to see Laird almost every day in the hallway outside his cell block. Inmates were permitted into a foyer there at certain hours in order to make phone calls. Teenager that he was, Laird couldn't stay away from the phone. "Hi, Sarah?" I heard him saying as I passed, "I'm all right. Not too bad. I'm doing fine," he would say. "And you?" I wondered if his prep school girlfriends were reading the same newspapers I was.

I started a clipping file. I tossed in every bit of printed matter that connected to the deeds of the people in jail. I found myself reading Laird's clipping over and over. At first I thought that if I read carefully enough, I might be able to discover the true cause of his crime. I thought perhaps the reporters knew but couldn't say and so had to communicate in journalism code.

So I combed the text like a literary critic, with my eyes peeled for omissions, or double meanings, or anything the reporter might have revealed inadvertently. As it turned out, the reporters didn't know as much as I assumed. They could give a sort of ambience to the crime: Destiny's night club, the party at the Mountain Edge Condos, the fleeting carjacker, and the angry mom waiting up for her son—but they couldn't tell me about the flesh and blood people who made up the ambience. They couldn't, of course, tell me why a nice-looking middle-class kid with a promising future had tried to kill his parents, steal their car, and drive away into the night. I was anxious to find a different order of reading material.

At home, I made amendments to my syllabus in order to take Laird's arrival into account. At first, I proceeded by flipping open anthologies and scattering books across the floor of an upstairs bedroom. I found that I was less interested in creating a useful class program and instead taken with an urge to ransack the bookshelves in search of a diagnosis. I wanted to find a book with an index of themes. I wanted an atlas of mental states. I knew that there was nothing in my library that was going to address the matter of homicidal adolescents specifically, but the Emily Dickinson portion of the Am Lit anthology seemed like it might sketch in the outlines of the landscape I was looking for. I found myself stuck in poem number 754:

> My Life had stood—a Loaded Gun
> In Corners—till a Day
> The Owner passed—identified—
> And carried Me away—

The photograph in the newspaper—a chubby teenager with a small hunch in his back, unsmiling—made it easy for me to see Laird as a loaded gun. His bent shoulders and his persisting baby fat made me think he might well have been picked on in school. He might have taken up residence in the corners of rooms. He was too short—about five foot six—to strike anyone as a fighter. Evidently, however, he was the owner of a powerful aggressive streak. Or maybe not. Maybe he simply felt that the time had come for him to take action, and he had gone to the gun closet under some twisted moral compulsion. He certainly didn't look enraged as Slash and Freddie Stockwell did; his slumped shoulders and tired gait made him seem more passive than angry.

This poem also held my attention for the way it so casually discarded everything that came before a certain fateful *day.* The speaker in the poem had lived out a lifetime as a loaded gun; now all of those years were dispatched with a single sentence: *The owner passed—identified—and carried me away.*

I could see Laird concocting his carjacking story and relying, as he did it, on the emotional truth that those lines happen to evoke. *Yes, my life* had *stood a loaded gun and I haunted the corners of rooms. But someone picked me up and carried me away.*

The next stanza described what would come next for someone whose life was split in two by a day:

> And now We roam in Sovereign Woods—
> And now We hunt the Doe—

And every time I speak for Him—
The Mountains straight reply—

There would be two people, doing things together in a forest. Companionship at last. And the workaday world, that restrictive past in which nothing could be expressed, would dissolve itself into a gloriously free present tense. *And now...And now...And every time...Every time I speak for Him—the Mountains straight reply.* In this new dispensation, you made a statement of identity, an expression of your truest self, and you were heard. The echoes would come rolling back to you across the fields.

I couldn't put this poem on the syllabus. It was a dilettante's take on things, and too literary to make any sense to Laird. To force him to read it would have been to twist his head around to my point of view. There was clearly no point in that. Still, Emily Dickinson was all I was interested in reading for the time being. Her afterlife was a place that Will and Steve and Slash—especially Slash—had sometimes mumbled about in conversation, particularly when they were talking about life after jail: they talked about retiring to a simple wilderness in the company of their lovers. They would take their guns and live life like latter-day Daniel Boones.

Another anthologized Emily Dickinson poem has her being swept from the surface of the earth by a gentleman courtier, Death:

We passed the School, where Children strove
At Recess—in the Ring—
We passed the Fields of Grazing Grain—
We passed the Setting Sun—

On Laird's very first day in jail school, he wandered through the warren of basement rooms like someone treading on a bed of the softest, loamiest earth in the world: he levitated over the floor tiles more than he trod on them. He smiled vaguely when he arrived at the threshold of the music practice cell. He smiled vaguely at his tour guides. He drifted on. Here is the law library. Here are the computers. And look, there is the school supply closet. "People steal things from it all the time," Laird's tour guide promised. As I watched Laird taking his tour, I could see him searching at every step for eye contact from his new friend and guide, Frenchie, a sex criminal. Frenchie was a gallant host, Laird's gentleman courtier:

We slowly drove—He knew no haste
And I had put away
My labor and my leisure too,
For His Civility—

But there was no carriage in our moist, moldy jail basement, nor was there
anything like a "field of grazing grain." There was the musty music practice cell, a windowless cubicle equipped with two metal folding chairs
standing in a puddle. There were the two libraries, a bathroom, and six
IBM 386s.

Still, on that day, Laird seemed delighted. His hands were stuffed
deep into his pockets. His head swiveled. He could tell who the teachers
were—Jim and Dottie were sitting behind two broad teacher's desks—
but, like saucy teenagers everywhere, he ignored them. He breezed past
their desks without making eye contact, without saying a word. He was
on a tour and wanted to see what there was to see.

As I watched Laird over the course of the ensuing week, however, his
enthusiasm for tourism seemed to dampen. He couldn't maintain his
bright-eyed, super-polite smile; he couldn't keep himself from staring in
disgust as the inmates made rude remarks about Dottie, spat on the floor,
and groped themselves when Dottie's back was turned. What kind of
place was this? he seemed to wonder. And who are these animals? As the
time dragged on—three days in jail, then four, then five—he made ever
more ungainly attempts to shore up his identity. The first five minutes of
currents events class became a sort of portfolio exhibition for Laird: he
wanted us all to know, apropos of nothing, that his father had written a
book. He made sure we knew that he, Laird, was on the ski patrol at
Gould, that he taught skiing over at Mt. Ascutney during his vacations,
that he had seven email accounts, and that his dad had "like set up the
entire e-mail system for Windsor County." "He was like the first systems
administrator for this jail!" Laird proclaimed. The inmates, behaving well
beneath the cameras, looked at him with long, uncomprehending faces.
Jim and I made congratulatory noises: "Interesting," said Jim. "I didn't
know that about the Windsor County thing," I muttered.

Laird didn't seem to mind so much being overlooked in the jail. He
didn't want, however, to be overlooked in the media. He wanted the story
to get out. He assumed that it had. He assumed that the networks were

paying attention. In the current events class, a few days after the murder, he wanted to know about a certain segment on the evening news: "Did any of you guys see the CBS Evening News last night?" he piped. Silence. "There was a picture of a banged-up Ford Explorer," he explained. "I was just wondering if that was my car. I was just wondering if they were doing a story on me or something." Later, in that class, I overheard him confiding a secret to Bedell: the story of his murder, said Laird, had gone out on the AP wire. Some girl in Texas had gone and committed a copycat crime, he said. She'd shotgunned her parents as they slept in bed on Christmas morning. Afterward, she said she'd done it because she'd gotten the idea from some kid up in Vermont. She said she'd heard about him on the news. Had Duane heard about that story? No, he hadn't. Laird assured him: "Don't get me wrong. I feel horrible about that. If some girl in Texas...," he paused, his eyes growing wider. "O my god! That would be horrible," he concluded, but I didn't detect all that much sincerity in his voice. After school, I logged on to Lexis-Nexis in search of such an event. Nothing turned up. I asked Laird about the story a few days later: "It's true! It's true!" he insisted, his face flushing as if I had accused him of some further crime. "It really happened!" But it hadn't really happened as far as I could tell and for several days afterward a picture settled in my mind: Laird in the TV room upstairs, clutching the newspaper, scanning the channels. Was no one taking notice anymore of his "situation"? Had it amounted to only a half dozen local stories in the local news? Yes, apparently, it had. In the current events class, Laird persisted: reporters were dying to interview him, he announced. Some shows were, like, offering him money. But his lawyer was forbidding all contact with the press so he couldn't say a thing. I didn't believe him though and the other prisoners ignored him.

JAIL DIARY, JANUARY 9, 2000

I'm going to have to modify my syllabus a bit in order to enlarge my understanding of what's happening to *me* in there. I doubt I can help Laird in his own struggle to make sense of jail, at least not yet. But I'm curious about my own responses. I would like to know why the experience is enveloping my waking thoughts, and reappearing in my dreams as if it's the only kind of film my unconscious is willing to play.

Prison *is* disorienting. There's a *Through the Looking Glass* quality

to the place that comes on like a drug at moments like this. I'm not
used to the way media creations step from the headlines and alight
there, prepared for literature, in my classroom. I'm also not prepared
for the odd blending of true-crime horror and Woodstock, Vermont,
dullness. The kid seems to have planned the killing long in advance;
he stole the gun, and loaded it, and stalked his dad with it. It takes a
certain kind of demented adolescent to do all that. And yet he's also a
normal high school kid, doodling on his notebooks, raising his hand
to answer questions, conscientiously doing his homework.

He's maintaining his innocence. That much I've heard from other
people in his cell block.

Now, when I look at my students, I tend to look at them through a
prism of suspicion. They know how to conceal their guilt, evidently,
but I won't be fooled. The newspaper reports and the eye-rolling of
the other teachers as certain students arrive in my class are beginning
to make me think of my class as a mock-up of a class. No one is what
they really are. They're certainly not here to study. Everyone dissem-
bles. They wear false faces; they're hiding false hearts.

I can imagine that the street kids, and the middle-aged child
molesters who won't make eye contact—even the wife-beaters—are
used to this way of life. They've been furtive creatures for years,
furtively going about their guilty lives. But Laird is no professional
liar. He's just a kid, just a seventeen-year-old in deep trouble. I
strongly suspect that he wants to tell the truth about himself. I doubt
he has the stomach for deceiving all inquirers, on every occasion,
with regard to all things. But who can he talk to? I asked him that
question today. "No one," he said. I nodded toward one of the jail
chaplains who happened to be using the phone on Jim's desk. "Can
you talk to him?" I asked.

He shook his head. "No fucking way," he said.

"Don't talk to any of the other inmates," I warned.

He nodded: "I know." He had a bottled-up, teary look in his eyes.

"What about your dad?" I asked.

"I haven't heard from him," he whispered. "I don't even know
where he is."

I imagine that Laird is used to being able to contact his parents when he needs them. But now one of them is dead and the other is probably in shock somewhere. Laird's on his own now. Now the hours are ticking by. He seems like a kid lost in a mall trying hard to remember the parental instructions, trying hard to stay calm. What was he told to do in situations like this? He racks his brain. There's no answer for that question inside, however: it's one dilemma for which his parents never prepared him.

The only way he can explain himself is by uttering a vexingly circular formula: "If you saw what I saw," he says with his eyes widening, "you'd understand."

CHAPTER SEVEN

Murderers

Every day in jail, I seemed to hear an inmate say something startling. In current events class, Laird piped up: "I wanna learn how to clone a dog! My mom just got a brand new Corgi puppy. I want to clone the thing so it'll be just as cute when I get out!" I stood by the Xerox machine and listened to Joe Emmons: "We can't even pick on the kid or we'll get in trouble with the guards. But we told him we're gonna rape him if he gets in the shower. He hasn't taken a shower yet!" The next day Laird told the current events class, apropos of nothing again: "I used to love violent movies! I can't even watch them anymore! If I saw *Terminator II* right now, I think I'd be like sick or something." Out in the town of Woodstock, people were talking about Laird. A lawyer friend of mine with the good looks and winning ease of a future politician said: "That kid should be lined up against the wall and shot. End of story." A Dartmouth professor friend said, "Theo, do you have Stanard in your class?" I nodded. "My *god,* man. What is he *like?*"Akankha Perkins, the owner of Sun of the Heart Books in Bridgewater said: "Poor child! Poor, poor boy." Laird said: "My dad went to Princeton but I don't want to go there. I just want to play lacrosse and I can do that anywhere." And: "I miss Elizabeth so much. I'd really like to get her to come see me. You know?"

Journeyman prep school kid that he was, Laird was anxious to find friends and fellow travelers and sympathizers. His thoughts seemed to dwell especially on his new peer group, murderers, who could be found here and there in the Woodstock jail and much more frequently in the pages of the newspapers. In the news, he focused on younger killers or wealthy killers or splashy killers. A college kid in Nashua, New Hampshire, named Liam Youens had operated a Web site on which he detailed his plans to murder a young woman with whom he had been infatuated in high school. He also daydreamed on his site about a Columbine-like massacre in the lunchroom of the high school in Nashua. In the fall of 1999, he finally found Amy Boyer after months of scouring the Internet for her home address. He ambushed her in a parking lot in October, shot her to death, and promptly killed himself. During the following winter, newspapers published excerpts from his Web site ("Update: I planned to go to NHS [Nashua High School] for the mass murder but I found that I started screaming and crying. Should I wait until Christmas Eve to kill her [Boyer] instead of [attacking] NHS?").

Laird, I discovered, was fascinated and sympathetic. He shook his head slowly as he read the news. I watched his face slackening with sorrow and fellow feeling as he absorbed the sordid details of the crime. He claimed to have known about the web site all along. I doubted him but said nothing. He was angry that the cops were so far behind the times that they couldn't track the Liam Youens of the world. After all, Laird had been able to follow events, he said, from the privacy of his dorm room.

There were other killers in the news that attracted Laird's attention; at about this time, Michael Skakel, the Kennedy cousin, appeared in the press, and Laird was an expert in the case. Just after Christmas in 1999, a gunfight broke out in a trailer in Tunbridge, a tiny hamlet thirty miles to the north of Woodstock. The wounded and the dead were on the front pages of the local paper. Six men were involved, it turned out, along with their many firearms: a semiautomatic rifle, a .45 caliber handgun, a .40 caliber handgun, and shotguns. One Peter Snape, a small-time criminal who had been haunting the local jails in recent years, including ours, had been killed. The man who was suspected of firing the fatal shot, twenty-year-old Robert Jacques (pronounced Jakes), was not charged right away. Like Laird, he was permitted to wander around the countryside for a few days as the police gathered evidence.

During this interval, Laird wouldn't let the matter drop. The other inmates, even those who'd known Snape well, quickly forgot about the case. Not Laird. "What's happening with Jacques?" Laird would ask every day at the beginning of current events class. No one would answer. A few minutes would pass by, he'd shift uncomfortably in his chair and pipe up again: "Anybody heard anything about that Tunbridge deal?" When Jacques finally slunk into the current events class himself, Laird overflowed with gestures of brotherly hospitality. He pushed his chair up close to Jacques's chair, passed him newspapers, and smiled at him benevolently, as if they were members of the same secret society. Jacques was mystified or alarmed. Anyway, he didn't get what was driving Laird and he finally pushed Laird away with his elbow.

Laird had better luck with Duane Placey. In the fall of 1996, Placey had burst in on his estranged wife and her new boyfriend as they slept in his former home. Placey was thirty-two at the time, a carpenter, a farmer, and a dad. He stabbed the boyfriend twenty-three times, stabbed the wife, apparently by accident, and also stabbed himself. As the boyfriend lay dying by the side of the bed, Placey dragged his wife, the town tax collector, into the bathroom, washed her wounds, and raped her. Sometime afterward, with his wife and daughters looking on, he set the bedroom in which the boyfriend, fifty-eight-year-old Bertis Wheeler, was dying, on fire. He fled the house with his family. Wheeler managed to stagger from the flames but he died before he could get to a hospital.

In jail, Placey was immaculately well behaved. It had been three years since his rampage. He'd become the chief breakfast cook, a trusted advisor to new inmates, and a sort of factotum to the guards. Everyone respected him. He was especially welcoming to Laird and Laird was proud to have such an esteemed presence for a friend. In current events class, Laird mumbled to Placey about the evidence the police had gathered so far, about various defense strategies, and Placey obligingly mumbled back. No one disturbed their colloquies. Laird enjoyed the solemnity he and Placey's discussions were accorded, and drew them out. It was a common sight during Laird's first months in jail to see him pouring words (excuses? lies? prayers?) into Placey's ear. Placey, being a calm, even-keeled inmate, nodded politely throughout.

Not long after Laird was arrested, another Vermont mom was murdered at the hands of a teenager. In this instance, the foster son of a teacher in West Burke, Vermont, opened fire on her as she graded papers at her breakfast table. The woman's stepdaughter, fourteen-year-old Tashia Beers, was, it turned out, the foster son's accomplice. The two of them locked the father in the basement, stole the family car, and fled south on I-91. They were on the lam for no more than two hours; the car was spotted, a fleet of state troopers descended, and Scott Favreau and Tashia Beers were in custody by 11:00 AM. Laird greeted the news with a combination of regret and esprit de corps and excitement. He immediately concluded that the girl had been involved in an abusive relationship with her stepmom; he also concluded that the crime had been a copycat crime, spurred on by his own deed. Laird said that he wished he could have counseled her, wished he could have dissuaded her somehow from her evil deed, but also wished that the stepmom had had the common sense to guess what was coming. "I wish I could have just done *something*," he said in a voice that seemed to me a weird mixture of relish and sincerity. "I feel sort of partly responsible, you know?"

I didn't have useful responses to these remarks, and was often too startled to do anything but stare. Not knowing how to respond or what to do, I scribbled the words I was hearing onto a notepad. At the end of the day, I typed them into my computer at home.

The more I wrote in my jail diary, the more I wanted to keep writing. Unlike the other kinds of writing I had done in the past—dissertation chapters, conference papers, polemics against dissertations and conference papers—the jail diary pretended to a knowledge of, basically, nothing. It was the simplest, most transparent kind of writing imaginable: stuff happened or was said and I wrote it down. It was hardly writing at all; it was dictation. It involved not an instant's worth of thinking. When I had several interesting remarks lined up in a row, I read them through and sent them off to Amy. "Wow!" she wrote back. "Keep them coming. When is Slash getting out?" She was interested, apparently, and so was I, so I kept writing.

In the end, I did modify my Gothic America syllabus slightly. I decided that I would focus as much as possible on kids in flight, on children with an itch for travel, on kids who were capable of floating over "fields of grazing grain." I had a vague itinerary already in mind for the central character of my syllabus. He—or possibly she—would have spent some time as a kid cooped up at home, watching the parents. The character's departure would be thrilling; his voyages would invite the kids in my class into the great American beyond—out West, off to the country, down the river. I resolved to check in with the most mythical of American traveling kids, Huck Finn, to see how he was faring. And I knew I'd get to Whitman by and by, though he would have to serve as a counterexample to the prevailing gothic theme of the class.

The part of the syllabus dealing with home, I thought, might present some problems. A difficulty I had had before in broaching the subject of families was that the inmates were so nostalgic and proud and even pious about their relatives that reasonable discussion about them was impossible. The honor in jail accorded to that famous troubled triangle—a mom, a dad, and a kid—was like a force field. It jolted you with the message "This is sacred to me" before you even got close. But this was a clue. At least, in their piety, they agreed on something. They murmured about their wives and their children from morning to night and made a show of despising anyone who'd harmed a wife or a child. If a Martian visitor had happened by, he would have assumed from the public conversation that wives and children were such adored, such ferociously honored creatures that they lived lives of uninterrupted luxury and indulgence.

I decided I should somehow seek to take advantage of this sentiment. There was no telling how much damage they'd done within their own domestic spheres, but I wasn't concerned with their criminal histories or their hypocrisy. If the wife batterers and delinquents and drunks wanted to come off as Promise Keepers, that was fine with me. I just hoped that the word *family* on the syllabus would inspire them to do the reading.

I didn't know for sure after the Christmas break if Laird would be in class, but as it turned out, Frenchie had given him a syllabus and had recruited him without my having to lift a finger. In any case, my lecture was written out and I was prepared, on Laird's first day in class, to discuss the item on the syllabus—it happened to be Poe's "The Cask of Amontillado," with emphasis on what the story could tell us about the lives of families. I had included the story on the syllabus as a concession to Matt, the drug dealer who'd tried to escape to Florida. I hadn't thought of it as a touchstone for a discussion about family life, but when I went looking for passages in the text that would rhyme with the new theme of the class, I found just what I was looking for.

This is what I wished the students to understand about "The Cask of Amontillado": the story is narrated by the scion of a noble Italian clan. It is the height of carnival season in an Italy of long ago, the end of the eighteenth century or thereabouts. A seasonal madness is erupting in the cafés and through the streets. Montresor, our narrator, happens on his lifelong enemy, Fortunato, and promptly resolves to kill him. It will be an ingenious, drawn-out affair, in which the victim steps into his grave, thinking, as he's doing so, that he's soon to be rewarded with a fabulous cask of Amontillado. The crime scene is the perfect place for a murder: an utterly private, even sacred locale, namely the catacombs upon which the Montresor family palazzo is built.

Some explaining of context and terms (*catacomb*, for instance) was going to be necessary but I wanted the students to figure out on their own that there was profound symbolism in this voyage to the family vaults. I wanted them to notice the damp of the place, the way it was strewn with familial treasures, but also, being a catacomb, with desiccated corpses. I wanted them to see that, literally, in this story, when people ventured beneath the surface of family life, they stumbled on the sprawling empire of the past. It was a darkened realm in which, nevertheless, much was still alive. Instruments of torture were on hand, as were piles of bones and cask upon cask of wine: in other words, the family treasures were down there, waiting to be examined.

Eventually, the students were supposed to work around to an evaluation of the truth of Poe's metaphor: Was it really so that family life was such a foul thing? Was it really the case that in making explorations into the family vaults you were taking your life in your hands? And was Poe recommending the voyage or not? (I meant to argue my opinion: Yes, he is. He recommends going but going utterly in control, lest you end up sealed away in a crypt, like Fortunato.)

In the end, of course, Fortunato gets shackled to the wall and then masoned away for all eternity in a dark, innermost dungeon. I wondered if the students would see the symbolism I saw in this demise: Families can be like prisons. Living among all the family secrets can be a slow death. There was another way to read the story: Fortunato is really an intruder into someone else's family past. He's not at all welcome there, or he's welcome only so that he can be administered punishment for his temerity. Perhaps the inmates would have a word or too for me about my nosy curiosity. Why was Theo in the jail? they might wonder. What business did he have in urging people into conversation about family life?

All of these seemed to me like suitable questions for class discussion. There was a fitting image embedded in the middle of the story with which I meant to begin our conversation. The Montresor family coat of arms depicts, says Montresor, "A huge human foot d'or, in a field, azure; the foot crushes a serpent rampant whose fangs are imbedded in the heel." I liked the venomous circularity in the image—a suitable metaphor for the dangers of treading through family history—and I decided that I would begin there.

Wednesday, January 5, 2000, was the middle of my seventh week in jail; it was Laird's tenth day in Woodstock (he'd been sent, for two days after his arrest, to the Rutland jail), and the first day of several in which my class degenerated into a prolonged, sinister joke.

JAIL DIARY, WEDNESDAY, JANUARY 5, 2000
Laird is good at eye contact; he stares earnestly into my eyes, awaiting instruction; a teacher's pet. If I were a teacher at boarding school, I would spot him from a mile off as the goofy kid, always ready with a smart remark and a charming smile, who never does his homework. He has a flap of red-hennaed hair that keeps falling down in front of his eyes. I recognize the fleece vest in which he was arraigned from the front page of the paper. It's embroidered with the name of his ski team and the league in which he competed. I recognize the shape of his body—his rounded shoulders, his stoop—from the same photograph. There are a dozen more inmates in my class today than on normal days: they lean against the pipes, they lounge on bookcases in the far corner of the room, they're crowded in chairs around the seminar table. They're waiting for Laird to turn up. Apparently, everyone knows he's coming, though I don't. More inmates file in. When he appears in the doorway, Slash flashes him his mile-wide toothy grin:

"Killer! You the *man*, killer!" Slash exclaims.

"This is Laird, everyone," says Frenchie. Laird smiles.

"Ka boom," yells someone from the back of the room. "Yo yo yo yo, ka *boom!*"

There is chuckling and table rapping. I stare at it and am ignored.

"There he is, the *man*," says somebody else.

People who aren't in Laird's cell block upstairs haven't had a chance to lay eyes on him yet. This is their first shot. People, like me and Slash, who haven't yet had a chance to talk to Laird for an extended period or in a semiprivate place—away from the cameras, away from Jim and Dottie—can have at it.

"Shut the door, shut the door," someone yells. The door is shut. Sometimes, the inmates like to come in here to do their thing away from the electronic eye. Our door is also advantageous in that it can be locked from the inside, though Jim and the guards have keys. An inmate I don't know gets up to turn the button in the doorknob. He returns, creeping and smiling stupidly to himself. We're safe now, anyway, from Dottie wandering in.

"This is English class, right?" Laird asks.

"Yes," I say. I turn to the inmate next to me on my right: "Will you shove over for a second?" I ask. He scootches his chair to the right. I unlock the door, walk into the current events room, pick up an extra chair, and return with it in my hand. Laird takes his seat next to me. He turns his face up to look in my eyes.

"This is English class, right?" he asks again.

A lot of the inmates who've never given me much respect seem to be here today. They call me Waldo instead of Theo. They laugh at me when I ask them questions about the homework. I need people to come to my class, but not these people.

"We want to be in your class, Waldo," says one of them in a deadpan.

"We got some real bad guys in here today," says somebody else as he smiles at Laird.

"You fucking kidding? We got the man in here today, the man of the hour," says a toothy prisoner named Leon. Leon's mustache is growing into his mouth. His whiskers are wet at their ends and his mouth is a graveyard of wilting, discolored teeth.

"Some of these guys are going away for a long, long time," says another person. The prisoners like that idea and roll their heads backward on their shoulders.

"Some of them have been away for a long time," says someone else.

Rhino smiles and then announces that it could be worse. He turns to Laird: "You could be going to jail in New Hampshire." Rhino did eight years in Concord, New Hampshire, he says. "Now that's a bad jail," he brags. He was there when the prisoners raped the female

guard. He was smoking pot in his cell. A lady came running naked
down the tier. He was stoned. He thought he was seeing things; he
thought he'd happened on some fine weed. "I was like, 'Now that's
some good shit!'" he yells.

Some of the best sex Rhino ever had in his life was with
somebody's jockey boy down in Concord. He'd go into the unit's
kitchen, put a pack of cigarettes onto the counter, and drop trou.
There'd be packs of cigarettes from previous customers strewn across
the floor. Rhino stands up to thrust his hips into the table a few
times, showing us how it's done. "Oh man," he laughs, looking at
Laird. "Oh dude," he guffaws in mock pity, with the water coming to
his eyes, "you are good and fucked now."

"Literally, he means," Slash helpfully explains.

Rhino and Slash can easily take over my class. They've done it before. I
have a strategy to prevent this. Slash likes me. He hates the others, but he's
decided that he likes me. I ask him if he can get Rhino and the others to
shut up so I can go about my class.

"Yes," he says and raises his arms again. "Quiet! Will everyone shut the
hell up? My lord. And let Theo talk." As the prisoners look at him, he
smiles at me. It takes a little while for the conversations to trail off. People
in our prison pay attention to Slash but they don't want to be seen being
obedient. As we're waiting, Laird notices that Slash and I are trying to
silence the thugs. We're making order. Laird understands. He wants an
orderly class. He beams his prepped-for-class smile at me and then at Slash.

"Okay, Theo. Go ahead," Laird says. "What's on the syllabus? Start
your class. Go ahead." I'm hesitating because some of the others have now
begun to argue among themselves. I want them to quiet down or leave.
"Theo, never mind them. Go...," says Laird.

"For everyone who didn't get a copy of the Xeroxes, here are some
extras," I say, and pour a stack of Xeroxes out across the empty table. The
inmates pass their eyes over my papers but do not reach for them.

Laird's bright eyes and the urgency with which he wants to get our
class underway have thrown me off the scent of his crime. I expected him
to be sullen and angry. His cheerfulness is disconcerting. There must be a
second self, darker, murderous, dripping with blood. But he is a sunny

child, appropriately nervous for the first day of school. He knows that first impressions count, so he makes direct eye contact and smiles.

Slash tells me to hurry up and start my class. I should ignore Rhino and his friends. "They're not here for your class," he says.

"I know that," I say and nod.

Slash gives it one more try. He comes to his feet and pounds his fist on the table. "Everyone shut the *fuck* up!" he yells, loud enough to be overheard next door.

Then, abruptly, everyone really is quiet. The long limbs draped over chairs, the tattoos, the baseball caps, the beards, and tank tops, a wandering elderly man who normally drops in to gaze into the bookshelves: they all are now still. They are not looking at me. They look at Slash. Slash knows exactly what to do. He raises his arms again and takes in a deep breath. He looks straight at Laird and exhales loudly until he's almost out of air—an enormous fake sigh. In a slow whine, a parody of parental disappointment, he asks, "About your fucking mother, dude. What the fuck were you *thinking*, dude?"

Nobody laughs. Nobody stirs. The room, for two seconds, is suspended in silence.

Laird has been bracing himself for this moment and now it's here. He stares hard at Slash: "I didn't do it. I didn't do it. I swear to god." His face is flushed. He looks at me.

"Slash," I say. "Come on, bro." It's not much of a defense but it's all I can manage.

"Come on what?" he demands, turning to me. "I'll tell you what I did. I tell everyone. Obstruction of justice. I did it. I'm guilty. There you are." He turns back to Laird: "So you didn't do it?"

Laird is shaking his head. "No. No. I didn't. I can't talk about it. That's all I can say."

"That's right," Slash replies. "Of course you can't. And we're all innocent here. By the *waayyy*, this entire jail is full of innocent people." He looks around for eye contact from the others. They smile. I can see that Slash has asked the same question and gotten the same response from other new arrivals. He knows what to do. You ask about the cover story. You pick that apart, like any two-bit detective. I know what to do, too. I should interrupt. But I'm dazed and don't know what to say. I can't think of how to swap Poe for Laird. Is such a thing possible? Desirable? I'm not sure. And I want to hear what Laird has to say.

"So you were just minding your own business, and everything was going your way, and then the police arrested you for first-degree murder?" Slash asks. "That's how it happened? Isn't that the way it was? Because that's just what happened to Placey, too." Duane Placey, down at the end of the table, has been listening carefully, impassively, like a judge. He gives Slash a brief courteous nod, as if to acknowledge how inevitable guilt is in a place like this, how it goes without saying that he stabbed his wife's boyfriend to death and torched the house in which he was dying.

Laird is stuck. He doesn't have an answer to Slash's question. Laird clearly identifies as an innocent person, especially in this company of career criminals and hotheads, but he seems to be having trouble remembering if he really is still innocent. He says that he knows something important, that the cops have been interviewing more suspects than just him. He starts in on his defense clutching the edge of the table with both hands; he lets out short stacatto bursts of words and then pauses, his jaw hanging incredulously in the air. "I swear to fucking god! I didn't do it!" Pause. "That night is a fucking nightmare for me, okay?" Pause. "I'm still having nightmares about it, okay?" The inmates lean on the table and crane their necks—their heads are supported on their forearms; their biceps are laid out on the table like giant sausages. Laird is saying that he's just as distraught as anyone over the death of his mother. Much worse, in fact but...But he can't talk about that night. He's got a lot to say and everyone will probably hear about it when he goes to court. He's going to take the stand in his own defense. He pauses, staring. Everyone's listening carefully now, so he continues: He doesn't have any idea what happened that night. But it wasn't him. He knows that. And he knows the police have already started lying about things. So have the lawyers. And the guards. Some guard in Rutland called him a fucking butcher! They're jumping to conclusions. It's a rush to judgment!

It seems like he has many more bits of testimony stored up and ready to deliver, but he stops after a few minutes of this, apparently out of words.

He looks over at me. I'm sitting directly to his left. I ought to be able to help somehow, but so far, I can't think of anything that will work. I have my notebook out in front of me and I'm doodling on it in fake casualness, making believe that I'm just waiting for the banter to subside.

Joey Bergeron, a teenage car thief from Springfield, turns to me. "Can I tell you something, honestly?" he asks.

"Uh-huh," I say. Bergeron has curly blond hair and a wide smile. I'm glad that he's interrupting.

"At first they thought it was me. The cops... They were asking me"— he lets his eyes find Laird across the table—"about that." Bergeron is remarkably polite, it seems. His deferential smile says that he respects Laird and respects me. But Laird doesn't notice. His eyes are narrow, and he's not interested in returning anyone's smile.

"See?" says Laird. "They're taking in more people than just me. You can see that. I swear. I swear to *god.*" He's stuttering. His lawyer says he'll be out soon. His lawyer says the state has no case.

I don't believe him and I don't think anyone else does.

Slash interrupts: "So... Joe. Can I ask you something, Joe?" He's speaking in preposterous, polite, teatime softness: a lampoon of tenderness. "Lemme see... I'm thinking... Please"—he's stroking his chin—"um, how do I put this? Um... Did you do it?"

Bergeron smiles for just a second, like someone with a bright idea. "Nope," he announces. Bergeron is sipping from a plastic peanut butter container that has been converted into a travel mug for instant prison coffee. He keeps smiling into his coffee as if he knows there's a joke coming up.

Slash stands up and cranes his neck around the room. He's peering behind the pipes and into the darkness by the toilet closet. "Did anyone else here do it?" he asks, and cocks his ear for the response. Much grinning and silence.

"Can I say something?" says Bergeron after a moment. "What I've got to say is that someone's going away for a very, very long time. And I don't think it's going to be me." His smile is a gigantic billboard of relief and pleasure; it's a cue for everyone to laugh, and suddenly all the inmates are chuckling. The laughter spreads around the room—a wave of good cheer from the inmates, a burst of released tension. I'm swept up in it too. I laugh happily along with everyone else.

"Wait!" says Slash, as if he's been struck by a brilliant idea. "Wait wait

wait wait wait." He searches the room for inspiration, and then turns to Laird. "Can you like cross your heart and swear on your mother's..." but then he stops himself short. He slaps his palm on his forehead. "Aw, I'm sorry," he says. "Can you check that? I'm only kidding with you, man. I'm only kidding." Laird has been taunted before in life, apparently. He's not saying anything, but he hasn't panicked yet and he hasn't asked me to help. He's going to go this alone.

The class continued in this vein for an hour. I tried to interrupt, but I didn't try all that hard because I knew I'd be shouted down. Finally, a guard came and cleared the room. On the next day, the same tumultuous group had signed up for class.

JAIL DIARY, JANUARY 6, 2000

Slash is smiling to himself as Laird sits down next to me. Despite his ordeal yesterday, Laird has come back to class, remarkably enough. It's not for me, however, that he has returned. I'm sure he's come because this is where the cool people are hanging out now: Rhino, Slash, Joey B., Frenchie, Steve. As soon as Laird lands in his chair, Slash picks up where he left off yesterday.

"She's your mother, for god's sake, kid. I just don't get that. I mean she's your own goddamn mother. What are you going to do? 'Hi Mom. Ka-*boom*'? I mean come on! Ka-*boom!*" Slash laughs incredulously and invents new shotgun noises. Ka-*pow! bam!* Take that, bitch! Other people are laughing. I'm laughing a bit.

Now Slash's brows are curling into outrage. His own code of morals has been offended. This is an outrage. But we also understand that he has a sense of humor about things. He waves at the other students to quiet down. "Shuttup, *please!*" His face twists into incredulous skepticism. "What the fucking fuck are kids coming to these days. Jeeezus!"

Laird is through with denials. His jaw is locked; either he'll endure or I'll intervene. Fortunately, Jim has cued in to what's going on and he pokes his nose through the door. His walkie-talkie is broadcasting a conversation occurring among the guards upstairs. Jim has discovered a need to rummage through the children's books behind a blackboard. His own classroom is empty, and he's aware that all of his students have lately been coming to the library to bother Laird.

Now that he's here, he's in charge, I think to myself. That means that I'm not at fault anymore. But in fact he isn't in charge, he's merely looking through the children's books. His silence tells me that I'm supposed to be teaching, and not simpering along as Slash cues the class with jokes.

"This is a class on American Literature," I say. "If people are not here for that reason, they should leave."

"Yes, sir, Theo," says Slash and draws himself up in his chair. He offers me a smart salute and a smile. I'm not his friend anymore. I'm a high school assistant teacher, Mr. Waldo. Mr. Waldo has some lessons he wants to teach. He has a job. The students seem to recognize this; even Slash understands. If Mr. Waldo insists, he should be left alone because he's only doing what teachers do. And it's all he knows.

I lean my elbows forward onto the table and ask the air if anyone has had a chance to read the story on the syllabus for yesterday. It's today's story, too, because we didn't have a chance to get to any work yesterday.

My regular students raise their hands. Thank god for that.

"I read it like a long time ago," a new person says. "Like in high school. The guy gets locked in the basement or...right?"

"Okay, fine," I say. I can't find my class notes. "So I guess the other people will follow along as you can, okay?" The twelve new inmates look away. "What I wanted to talk about anyway was, to begin with, the coat of arms...and then some of the conventions and the habits of Gothic writers." What am I saying? This group of inmates could care less about Gothic writing. Anyway, they've got a good Gothic story sitting in front of them. They've just got to draw it out.

"What's a coat of arms?" someone asks.

"I know what a coat of arms is!" Laird exclaims. "My family has a coat of arms. It's a family emblem. I'm Scottish. I forget what mine looks like, though." His comments are lost. People are turning to their neighbors or looking at me now and it seems that they're beginning to sense that the fun is over.

"We're going to finish up with our reading of 'The Cask of

Amontillado,' okay?" I ask. No one has yet interrupted me. I take advantage to move rapidly forward. "Those of you who've read the story will know that Montresor, that his family seat, his palazzo, has been built over a series of catacombs. Now, in ancient Rome, the catacombs were where people buried their dead. You see, and so your ancestors might just be buried beneath..."

My students are packing in their goods for the day. As I'm talking, I see them turning to one another, as if the program they've tuned in for is going off the air, and now there's nothing to watch. They're disappointed. I've taken over. They all must act like students now; they owe that courtesy to me. They run their fingers through their hair; they smile. They look over at Laird. They know to obey prison rules, and the rules say that they have to let me teach my class. I can't get very far, however, in my teaching, because I keep looking at Slash mouthing words to Laird and I keep seeing Laird out of the corner of my eye. He doesn't know if he should laugh with Slash or take offense or simply leave the room. As I'm rambling about Poe's biography, I watch Laird's face perform a spastic dance: smile, scowl, blanche.

When a guard finally comes to remove the prisoners from my classroom, I touch Laird on the arm as he's leaving.

"I'm sorry for this," I say.

"It's okay."

"I'd like to have a class that actually works. You know? I'd like to have something that you can look forward to."

"Oh, I think I'm going to like your class, once you get it under control."

"Do you have anything to read, now?"

"My dad left me a copy of *Antigone*. You know *Antigone?*"

He pronounces the word *Antigone* too casually, as if his parents frequently leave tragedies out for him to peruse during school.

"Have you read it yet?"

I suspect that Laird's dad, Bill, a high school English teacher, is sending his son a message.

"Have you read it yet?" I ask again.

"Of course," he says. "It's a great play. I've got the Jean Anouilh version."

I doubt he's telling the truth, though. If he has read it, I doubt he's understood very much of it. I had to read it when I was his age and I got nothing out of it, zero. But maybe Laird is different. Maybe his experience in life has taught him something about what's described in that play: family disaster—the kids turned against the parents, the parents turned against the kids, everything turned over to the machinery of the state.

I ask Laird if he's been able to make any sense of it yet. "No, I haven't, to be perfectly honest," he says, brightly.

I ask him if he's on good terms at all with his dad now, if he's been able to patch things together somehow. "I'm the only flesh and blood he has left. He still loves me. We're just all like going to try to work this one out, I guess. It's kind of a traumatic thing, you know?"

He sounds optimistic but I'm not so sure he has reason to be. From the rumors I've heard, Bill Stanard has given the police all the information they need to get a first-degree murder conviction.

PART TWO

CHAPTER EIGHT

Teaching

Over the next four weeks in jail, I taught in a small, self-enclosed carnival. I came every day vaguely prepared for my lecture and the inmates came every day intently prepared to make merry. They closed the door, propped their feet on the table, and waited for Laird. Strangely, he came every day, each time smiling and unbowed. The inmates weren't just after Laird, though: anyone in need of instruction in "respect"—anyone new and young that is—was encouraged to come and when he did, was loudly welcomed into the mix.

The inmates wouldn't have said "carnival." They would have said "zoo." If you ask an inmate in the Vermont jails—probably this is true of any jail—how the prisoner society organizes itself he will offer an earful on survival of the fittest, on how hawks eat sparrows, cats eat mice, sharks minnows, and so on. In Woodstock, there was supposed to be an animal hierarchy by which the jail was ruled, and every inmate, as in bigger, more horrible institutions, was supposed to do his part to uphold nature's balance. I never once saw the balance of nature enforced with a show of physical strength. But I did see it, especially in my classroom that January, belabored until I was sick to death of it. The essential idea, one that could be picked up from any TV show or movie—it's laid out in detail in the books of Edward Bunker—is that jail is a "respect" culture. The large animals sleep and slumber most of the time up at the top of the hierarchy, but when they are not given their due, they rise in great fury and tear the flesh, or cause the flesh to be torn, of those lower down.

I decided not to wake the slumbering beasts. That meant not interrupting them, or causing them displeasure, or otherwise showing disrespect. When Rhino and Slash and any of the other alpha inmates were around, I deferred, mousily, to them. I hated myself for it, but didn't know how to turn things around.

I probably should have just kicked out the bad guys. But I had reasons not do that. First, I wanted to teach all comers. I felt it would have been a failure to cull my preferred few from the jungle-carnival and lock out the rest. Second, I was learning a lot from Slash and from Rhino, too. I liked them and wanted to learn more. I had come to jail in the first place to get to know a rougher element of the Vermont population and here they were, acting predictably rough. I wasn't surprised and wasn't about to give up on them. So, despite advice from Jim, and despite a series of invitations from Slash and Rhino themselves ("Are you gonna kick me out? Well go ahead then, Theo," said Slash. "Next time you see me I'll be on your front porch with a fucking Molotov cocktail"), I refused to kick anybody out.

Thus, a sort of low-level chaos descended over my class in January. I couldn't get any academic work done at all—I was permitted ten minutes of lecturing and was then basically told to shut my fucking mouth, which, after some fighting words from me, I basically did. Perhaps for this reason—my vanishing—the course became unusually popular that January. It became a spot where the inmates from the different cell blocks could meet and exchange their views. The guards kept an eye on us by entering and making random inspections of our two windows and of the bathroom, and Jim poked his nose into the room once or twice a class to let us know he was there. As long as there were no corpses served up to the administration afterward, we were considered to be doing okay.

In fact, the inmates were doing fine, and in my role as inmate wannabe, I was doing fine, too, but the class itself was on the skids. Many of the students who came were not even aware that there was a syllabus. Others shredded it into strips as we talked and left them trailing on the floor afterward like palm fronds or hay or festive ribbons. I picked them up before Jim could see and hid them in the bottom of the trash.

In the beginning of February, a profile of Laird's family, or ex-family, was published in the *Valley News*. It was a two-part series that ran on the front page, above the fold. It was written by their star reporter and columnist, Jim Kenyon. I read it carefully, and discovered some interesting gossip there.

Under the headline "Father of Murder Suspect, Husband of Victim

Says His Son Had Been Troubled But Mostly by Problems Typical of Teenagers," I learned that it cost $26,000 a year to send Laird to school at Gould. One of Laird's previous schools, the Indian Mountain School in Lakeville, Connecticut, had cost $23,000. I learned that in 1984, the Stanards sold their horse farm in Middletown, Rhode Island, for $300,000.

There was some discussion of the troubled teen himself. Mention was made of his having stolen his mom's credit card, his poor grades, and the "marks" on his wrists. This was a side of Laird I didn't see in jail at all—poor grades and credit card theft and suicidal despair were not part of his self-presentation—but he had turned into a model child the moment he was arrested. It wasn't hard for me to imagine him as a bit of a slacker in school, a slacker with a credit card and a bag of attention-getting tricks. According to the article, Laird had been sent home immediately from school in October 1999, after he showed what he contended were scars from a suicide attempt to a school friend. He had then been duly vetted by his family doctor at Mary Hitchcock Hospital in Hanover, New Hampshire, and declared fit to return to school.

Over the Thanksgiving holiday, I learned, Laird had told his parents that he wanted to drop out of Gould. He had formulated a plan: he would go to the public high school in Woodstock for the remainder of the year. If that wasn't agreeable to his parents, he would go to a private school across the New Hampshire border, Kimball Union Academy. Bill and Paula Stanard had demurred. Bill told the reporter that he'd assured Laird he could do what he wanted to do once he turned eighteen (his birthday was coming up in June 2000). For the time being, however, his parents were his legal guardians. They had a moral—not merely a legal—obligation to guide him according to their best judgment. In their view, his interests lay in finishing the year out at Gould. Laird had apparently accepted his parents' decision gracefully. He never mentioned the matter again.

Laird's equanimity might have been a clue that all was not well. I learned later that he had been known to people at Gould as a kid who lost his temper easily, a kid who let himself seethe and storm at even minor provocations. When he had a falling out with Elizabeth during the Christmas dance, his anger had caused an embarrassing moment among the teenagers. Elizabeth had refused to dance with him. Worse, she disappeared sometime during the evening, though she had been his date. When she reappeared, Laird was almost out of control; his face was red with adolescent fury. He screamed at her in front of the other teenagers. Everyone was embarrassed. Eventually, Laird calmed down.

I later heard this story from one of Laird's teachers at Gould: during a camping trip at the very beginning of Laird's time at Gould, a fellow student made an ironic remark about an item of camping equipment belonging to Laird. The students were gathered by a campfire preparing dinner. The remark—something about Laird's drinking cup—provoked a public tantrum. Laird was indignant. He stormed off into the woods. He refused to return. "It was almost like when a kid says, 'All right, I'm going to hold my breath until everyone apologizes,'" the teacher recalled. "He was going to sort of punish himself out there until everyone got with his program." The other kids were actually quite willing to apologize. Two young women, fellow students, trekked out to coax Laird in from the woods. Finally, as dinner was getting cold, a visit from a teacher did the trick. But Laird's prickly behavior lingered in the mind of the teacher. The instructor identified him as a teenager whose feelings were so prone to injury, so unpredictable and delicate, that he was destined to have a rough time of it in the topsy-turvy world of his fellow teenagers.

It seems that Laird took refuge in the company of his teachers at Gould. He waylaid them with stories about Web sites he had built, e-businesses he was founding (this was September 1999), and the foreign lands he had had occasion to visit. He was carving out a distinguished career for himself by himself, according to his line of talk. His parents and his peers didn't know this. Nor did they care, he suggested.

These aspects of Laird's character—his self-dramatizing loneliness, his penchant for public displays of passion—were scarcely limned in the Kenyon article. The newspaper seemed to have abridged Laird into a tiny handful of anecdotes passed on by mystified onlookers.

To be fair, there was a good reason for the scarcity of firsthand information: Laird was in jail and not available for interviews. Still, the reporter had spent time with Laird's dad, had gone to Bethel, Maine, home of Gould Academy, to figure out what people said of Laird there (the interviewees didn't know Laird well, it seemed, but then no one did) and had poked around West Windsor some, asking questions of neighbors. After four thousand words, Laird remained somebody's strange son, now lost to the world: a cipher gone underground.

The next installment of the article brought more news about "Old Money Families." The correspondent noted that Bill Stanard had belonged to the Ivy Club at Princeton ("'To get into Ivy, the oldest, most expensive, and most patrician eating club at Princeton University, candidates must sit for 10 one-on-one interviews...' *The New York Times* wrote last year."), and that Paula's parents had sold their 900-acre farm near Lake Sunapee in New Hampshire in the early eighties for $600,000. This contrasted, said the reporter, with the spartan family home in West Windsor, which Paula had named Penniworth, in honor of Yankee flint. Kenyon, the reporter, wrote: "But something was always missing from Penniworth, some townspeople have observed, during the fifteen years the Stanards have lived there. No bicycles on the lawn; no swings hanging from a tree in the yard; no crayon drawings taped to the windows."

I asked Laird about this.

"Oh, isn't he so full of shit, that guy? If I had anything, it was a ton of kid crap," Laird laughed.

I wasn't much persuaded by all the money talk either. In Kenyon's write up, the townspeople in nearby Brownsville made wise observations about what was missing in their neighbor's family life while the family itself, a chilly aristocratic group, spent their time up on the hill with their horses. When there was time left over, they used it to wonder about which private school Laird should attend next. The one thing they never considered, the reporter pointed out, was sending him to public school.

It seemed to me that a Sunday-morning homily might be gathered together from the hints that Kenyon had sprinkled, objectively, as journalists should, over his two-day profile. Delivered from the pulpit, it might have run something liken this: "People of the Upper Valley, it is beyond my ken to judge. And yet a thought has occurred to me: they had too much money. I'll say it again. Much too much money. Would that those Stanards had had the common sense of native Vermonters. Or the warmth. You see, people can be rich and yet impoverished. So they were punished by the hand of their very own only child. Meanness begat meanness. *Be not deceived, dear friends,"* he would warn. *"For whatsoever a man soweth, that shall he also reap."*

I, for one, came away from the articles thinking mostly about Bill. In one of the photographs, he sat in the light of a window before a tall bookshelf. He wore a Portuguese fisherman's sweater that, I guessed, had probably been knit for him by his wife (the text mentioned a second, half-knitted sweater stored in a basket by the chair). Like his son, it seemed to me, he was currently embarked on a wide-ranging, seemingly aimless, seemingly earnest voyage. The reporter wrote:

> If there is an answer to the questions posed by his wife's death, Stanard believes it might be found on the bookshelves of his 19th-century home: Shakespeare, Eugene O'Neill, perhaps the writings of a Buddhist monk.
>
> "Sometimes I have an answer and it lasts for about ten minutes, and then it sort of disappears," Stanard said. "I've tried all the obvious ones promised by organized religions. Evil with a capital E. All the ones offered by psychologists where they talk about people who are so devoid of emotion, who can absolutely do things that (seem) horrific to us" because they overreact to minor problems.
>
> "That doesn't fit either."

I studied the photograph of Bill each time I picked up the paper. Above Sunday's headline ("I Don't Have an Answer Yet") he turned in his chair and gestured to somebody outside of the camera frame. His eyes were wide, his hands outstretched. It seemed to me that this was the real story. There was no more wife and no more kid; there hadn't been anyone else in the family. Now the dad was by himself arguing with his house full of ghosts. They were visible to him, perhaps, but not to us.

In jail, the one thing we all appreciated about those series of articles was their description of Laird's ongoing education. Naturally, it made no mention of the people who were really giving him his education—Slash and Rhino and the silken-haired wife-batterer, Freddie Stockwell—but it did say that Laird was taking, among other things, American Literature and "advanced computer technology" in jail. Will and Laird and I got a good chuckle out of this: advanced computer technology was not in our university course catalog. If such a class had been offered, Laird would have had to teach it, since he knew more about our old 386s than anyone else. But there was some accuracy, however faint, in the American Literature part of the paragraph. Neither Will nor Slash nor Rhino seemed to agree with me at that point in the history of our class, but I saw a grain of truth there—perhaps only a stunted, ingrown grain—but anyway, something. And now, after a month of chaos in class, I wanted to cultivate the grain and make it thrive.

CHAPTER NINE

Darling

JAIL DIARY, FEBRUARY 10, 2000

Today was the beginning of *Huck Finn*. Eight criminals in class. When they sat down half of them reached into their clothing to retrieve the newspaper sections they had smuggled out of the current events room next door. Staring into the *Rutland Herald* is their way of saying Leave Me the Hell Alone. My way of responding is to leave them alone, at least for a little while. The remaining students were polite if not actually interested. They picked up the dog-eared copies of *Huck Finn* I had piled at the center of the table, leafed through them for a few moments, and returned them to the table. Usually, at the beginning of class, the inmates are willing to play along with me; they're relieved to have been released from their cell blocks and glad to have an outsider to talk to. Not today. Judging from the faces of the inmates, it looked like it might have been an angry night up in the cell block. Joe Emmons had been in a fight, apparently, and had taken a blow to the eye: a nightstick or a broom or who knows what had released a jet of blood into the white space around his pupil. His eye looked like a horror shop eyeball—ghastly but comical. When I saw him in the hallway a few hours before class, he told me that he'd been in trouble and had to spend the night in the hole. He seemed dazed and angry. "Sucks being you," muttered a guard in response to one of Joe's complaints (something about a pain in his hand). The guard's patience had apparently run out. In class, Joe didn't smile but neither was he upset. He seemed ready to resume the life of the civil daytime Joe, a curly-headed former school bus driver. He wants to learn to write beautiful, heart-softening letters to his wife. In the past, I've given him some help with his letters. Lately, he's begun sending them off to his roommate's wife, who, he says, he's known for a long time. This, I gather, is what got him in trouble.

I'm usually granted a grace period of a minute or so in the beginning of class to make my literature pitch. After that, things can quickly fall apart. Today, the goal was to give the class some necessary background for *Huck Finn*—its setting, its author—and to cajole the inmates into reading the first few chapters out loud. The larger goal was to seize control of the class. I've finally had it with being pushed around by Slash and Rhino. I've let them take advantage of my forgive-everything, college-kid persona for almost two months now. I'm sick of it. I want a change.

Those few classes in which we've actually had an intelligent, informed discussion about books have occurred when I've resolved not to be nice. If I don't smile at everyone, if I cut people off, if I slap the table with my books or my fist or my foot, I tend to get better results. Then, when they're paying attention, I can talk to the inmates as if they're a group of bright college kids in a seminar. This was my plan of attack today. I aimed to be formal and humorless and nervous. I arrived in class pretending to be in a foul mood; I pretended as though I were in a great hurry to get my work done. Never mind that it's a joke to pretend that anyone who works here or lives here is in a hurry. Everyone was faintly amused by my busyness. A county jail is the existential opposite of hurry: it's flesh piling up at the depot. It's purgatory. We all know that. I didn't care. In the end, I don't think anyone was fooled by my being brusque and professorial except, perhaps, me. And that only for a little while. I lost the touch after a few moments. But the show encouraged me and now I'm resolving now to do it more.

The Adventures of Huckleberry Finn is the first novel I've tried in class, the first excursion into a dialect and the first prolonged excursion into the nineteenth century. It's bound to discourage some people straightaway. That's fine with me. I want to discourage people. I want an air of special purpose in the room, of elitism and election. If some hurt feelings result, so much the better. Today, I did what all the thugs in jail do when they want to make themselves feel special: they pick on the weak. By so doing, they claw their way up the hierarchy a little bit; you're not a bitch or a patsy or a punk anymore if you can find somebody else to play the role for you. I found Richard Darling.

For the last week, an inmate who dresses every day in his own private uniform of denim—jackets and jeans—has been coming to class to stare at the goings on. He has wide, beautiful blue eyes that nicely match his baby-blue jean jacket. He's a tall, skin-and-bones kid sometimes called Darling by the other inmates and sometimes called Turtle (but never Richard, his first name) because he was arrested once for shooting a turtle with his bow and arrow. He was living outside, on the banks of the Connecticut River in Windsor. He was hungry, so the story went. He shot the turtle with his arrow and hoisted the impaled creature onto his head. Yelling "I'm going to eat him," he marched down a residential street near the river. The police were called.

This was several years ago. Now he is older, nineteen at least.

Darling Turtle is a sad case and I'm not sure I can deal with him. I understand from the other inmates that he's never had a family of his own, and that he's been in institutions of one kind or another since he turned thirteen. Before that, he was passed from foster family to foster family. The other inmates occasionally—very occasionally—try to be nice to him, but they don't have the touch of nice people. It's like watching soldiers pirouette. They try for a second, stumble, and give up. Plus, Darling isn't easy to like. He's rumored to be a jail snitch, for one thing. Even if the rumors are false, they have made life difficult for him. No one wants to say anything that he might overhear or misconstrue or understand accurately. It doesn't help that Darling is also a sexed-up kid who plunges his hands down his pants during class and makes a point of catching your eye as he's doing it. The routine bothers everyone, including me, but asking him to stop gives him a jolt of pleasure. In the past I've told him he can't act like that in class. A chastened, sad look comes over him. His blue eyes widen (with excitement, apparently); he sits upright in his chair and ten minutes later, he's busy flopping his hand flirtatiously from lap to hair to lips to pants. He wants you to watch. He doesn't want you to watch. It's a nursery game. I'm not interested.

Today, feeling only slightly guilty, I decided to nominate him to be our class punk.

"Darling," I said, before beginning my *Huck Finn* speech. "Sorry to be a jerk. Everyone in here has passed an admissions test. You haven't passed it. You've got to pass the test to get into the class."

"No, I don't," he said. "There's no test in here."

"Oh yes, there is," I assured him. "Yup, sorry. It was a while ago."

I looked at the other students, who were looking approvingly at me. "They pretty much all passed," I said.

"Un-hunh. We passed it, Darling," said a pot dealer from Brattleboro named Tim. He's a wiseass. He's in his forties and is still playing the class clown. To indicate how near he'd been to failing my test, he raised his hand to his eye and, with thumb and forefinger, made the sign for "tiny little bit." He squinted through his fingers at Darling. "Just...fucking *barely* passed," he sighed. "Theo asked some pretty hard fucking questions. Theo can be pretty much of a hard-ass, if you don't know that already."

"I am," I said, staring at Darling. "I did. Hard-ass questions I asked until they could hardly write anymore. I put it all on the test, you know."

"Yup," said Tim. "The first question was like: 'Have you ever killed a turtle?' If you got that one wrong you were out right away."

Will jumped in: "The next question was like: 'If you did kill a turtle, you were pretty dumb to get yourself arrested for it, weren't you?' If you answered that at all, you got it wrong. And you probably would have had to answer it, I guess."

Ignoring Will and Tim, I went on about my test: "The truth is that everyone here has a certain reading level and a certain familiarity with the material covered in the course, which is American literature. I'm going to do another test in a few weeks. You have to take that. Maybe study some first, okay?" I offered him a copy of *Huck Finn.*

Darling wasn't moving. I held the book out toward him like a treat. Evidently, he thought I was joking. He tilted his chair back against the bookshelf and turned his face up to the fluorescent light tray in the ceiling. An army of pimples marched down his neck and into his shirt. I tossed the book into his lap.

"Can one of you guys tell him to leave?" I asked the class. Now that I was picking on someone, the inmates were only too happy to join in. They had an officially sanctioned target.

"Get the fuck out of here Darling," said Slash.

Hmm, I thought. Pick on the weak. This feels good. This is definitely working.

Darling sat up straight. Slash asked again. Darling reached for the book in his lap. It took him an age to gather his legs beneath him and stand up. He moped over to the doorway. He opened the door and hung his hand on the top of the door frame. He gave me an angry look. "I heard you were a fucking snapper," he said. "Is that why you're here?"

Trying to turn the tables, was he? No chance, Darling, I thought. I said nothing. He was on his way out and I wanted him to go quietly.

"What, did you start messing with the students at your last job? You snapped some little kid, didn't you? And that's why they put you here?"

"Go on, Darling," I urged in a flat voice. "Out." He couldn't shut the door on himself. It was against his nature. He looked around at the other students. Everyone was quiet; Will and Tim were thumbing through their paperback *Huck Finn*s. Slash had lost interest in Darling. He was probably losing interest in the class, too, if he had any to begin with.

Darling wrinkled his brow. He scratched his tummy. "There's not a fucking test in here, is there?" he wondered. "Is there really a test just to be in here?" He seemed to want an honest answer. Darling has been signing up for my class every day for a solid week. He has been punctual and has at least taken the reading assignments back to his cell, which is more that I can say for a few others. And Darling is a true descendent of Huck—a misused, incorrigible, scorned kid. This is one more episode in his lifelong standoff with "sivilization." The book—hours spent listening to the voice of Huck Finn—might ground Darling, might give him a kind of company he's never had.

"Yes, there is a test," I lied. "You didn't take it. So good-bye. Okay?" I felt a twinge of excitement when he shut the door. The remaining inmates didn't bat an eye. One more loser, treated to his just desserts: smiling contempt. They hardly noticed what had happened. I, however, was pleased with myself. I can't believe I did that, I thought to myself. And: I can't believe he actually left! When he finally clicked the door closed, I got up and locked the thing shut.

If he comes back, I'll kick him out again.

This was the beginning of a good period for me in jail. I had material to teach that seemed distantly relevant to the lives of the students; I had decent students; I felt I could talk openly with them. It seemed as though they were reading fairly regularly and possibly even learning... well, something. Slash, Will, Laird, Tobin, sometimes Frenchie and sometimes Emmons: they were the outlines of a class, a blueprint from which I meant to cause a structure to rise. Not everyone came every day. Laird, for instance, had taken to sleeping away his days, and when he did come down to school, he would sometimes play with the computers rather than come to class.

On the day I kicked Darling out of class, a new academic seriousness settled in among the remaining students: Laird announced that he'd read *Huck Finn* before and had studied it at his prep schools. Some of the other students—Tim and Will and Slash—not wanting to be outdone, professed a similar familiarity with the text. (It always surprised me how inmates felt responsible for knowing *Huck Finn;* they didn't necessarily feel responsible for killing the people they'd killed or robbing those they'd robbed, but they did feel a moral obligation about *Huckleberry Finn.* He was part of their patrimony; they wouldn't cop to having seen the movie or having read the comic book. I didn't believe the students in this, as in many of their claims, but I was glad they felt obliged to lie in this instance.)

My goal in the first *Huck Finn* lecture was to offer the students a sense of the time and place in which Mark Twain set *The Adventures of Huckleberry Finn.* I explained that it was written in the 1880s in Connecticut, but set some forty years earlier, before the Civil War, before the transcontinental railroad, and before industrialization had had time to create large-scale urban problems. I said that it was set in the time and the place of the author's youth—the Mississippi basin—but written with an awareness of what the country had lost over the intervening forty years: some of the mystery of a new continent, some of its early promise, some of its innocence. The circumstances of the book's creation leant themselves to a golden-hued view of the past: you should keep that in mind, I said.

Yet Twain's youthful paradise was also full of menace, as the real Missouri had been. I talked for a while about the western frontier in the 1840s; how at the time the nation extended west through the Ohio Valley and then petered out, for practical purposes, in a violent, rolling swamp of mud, namely the Mississippi River. Travelers wrote about it as if it were the river on the outskirts of hell. It was supposed to teem with snakes and animal carcasses and man-eating crocodiles. It was often advertised by travelogue-writing visitors from Europe as a force that could suck down whole forests when it felt like it and flood a region the size of Ireland in a morning. In its southern latitudes, it was known to exhale a deadly strain of malaria. And everywhere, it tended to drink down those who were unlucky enough to fall in: this because the waves were thought to be the heaviest waves on earth, made up exclusively of silt. They shrouded swimmers in quicksand and never gave them up.

In short, I wanted to impress the inmates with what a primeval wilderness the place was, and how, for a long time, it lorded its power over the humans who settled along its borders. Of course, I said, in the 1840s, on the far shore of the Mississippi was a hidden nation of Indians and mountains and wild beasts—the Territory Ahead. I wanted to suggest that Huck Finn's personal strength, as well as his enduring power over the American imagination, derives from his close association with this landscape: its vastness, its mysteries, its eternal, coursing flow.

I asked Will to read the opening two pages of the book. Huck introduces himself in the book's first sentence, then sketches the ending of events in *The Adventures of Tom Sawyer*, and begins, in the section we concentrated on in class, to describe civilized life as administered by Miss Watson and the Widow Douglas.

I thought the inmates might first be interested to find that the Woodstock jail was submitting them to a civilizing process that hadn't changed much in its essentials in 150 years. The process was popular among the old biddies in Saint Petersburg in the 1840s and was creaking away tolerably well in jail in Woodstock in the year 2000.

In Saint Petersburg much stress was laid on proper comportment at meal times, on well-meaning but rudimentary school exercises, and on plodding Bible reading sessions. The whole process was numbingly slow. In Woodstock, a similar regimen was in place, although nowadays there's less faith in Bible reading, at least among the officials, and more importance attached to good behavior at meal times. There were a few other similarities that I felt were worth discussing: the urge to chuck it all and be bad, the similar urge to slip away to somewhere, anywhere—good place, bad place, middling place—but here. I made these points on my own. The inmates were silent except for some snorting and coughing, a reaction I took for nonplussed agreement.

I didn't want them to sit quietly through the larger, more important point. "What is the result of this education in civilization for Huck," I asked. "Anyone...? Slash?"

Slash said that he had a good idea about what the fucking educational program of the Vermont DOC did. It ruined people's lives. It brainwashed them. He went on for a little while about that—the failed psychological engineering, the naiveté of the therapists, the enraged inmates who emerged—and his speech derailed my *Huck Finn* lecture for a time. Slash was sometimes my ally and sometimes my antagonist in class. If I told him to shut up, I would be showing disrespect, and that couldn't be tolerated. He'd curse me and stalk out. Or something worse could have happened, I didn't know what. If he was in a good mood, however, he would sometimes grin a tight, angry grin at me, promise me that he had a long memory and would remember my disrespect. In order to avoid a fight, I let him talk, as I usually did, and looked around the table at the other inmates.

Tim had unfolded the *Valley News* and was perusing the article about Laird's dad. Laird had been in jail for almost six weeks by then. His fifteen minutes of notoriety were up, it seemed, and now there were just nagging follow-up stories in the paper: the Kenyon profile of Bill Stanard, an announcement that the police had recovered the shotgun used in the crime, a report about a status conference at the Windsor County District Court. I didn't want to allow the class to be distracted by any such news and I asked Tim to put away the paper.

"The result of Huck's education," I said, "is a deep boredom. As time goes by, the boredom worsens into something like depression. Do you guys know this feeling?" I read the inmates a sentence in which Huck says that after an evening passed with Miss Watson and her spelling book, he retreated to his room, so "lonesome" he "most wished [he] was dead."

The antidote in *Huck Finn* to civilized death is wild nature. Our first look at the other world in *Huck Finn* comes in paragraphs on page three of the book. They describe Huck's retreat to his room, his lighting of a candle, and his settling down in a chair by his bedroom window. After Miss Watson and the widow have gone to bed, Huck cocks his ear on the world of natural powers and portents that surrounds St. Petersburg. I had Tim begin with this passage. I asked him to read loudly so that everything he said could be understood in all corners of the room. He cleared his throat and read slowly but with good volume:

> The leaves rustled in the woods ever so mournful; and I heard an owl, away off, who-whooing about somebody that was dead, and a whippowill and a dog crying about somebody that was going to die; and the wind was trying to whisper something to me and I couldn't make out what it was, and so it made the cold shivers run over me. Then away out in the woods, I heard that sound that a ghost makes when it wants to tell about something that's on its mind and can't make itself understood, and so can't rest easy in its grave and has to go about that way every night grieving.

As Tim read, the inmates obediently followed along in their books. Even the older people had put away their newspapers—perhaps following Tim's lead—and were staring dully into their Penguin paperbacks. Great, I thought, this is working. They're paying attention to a book. Wonderful. It seemed like a cheap trick. What a surprise! I thought. This is working.

I asked the class if the forest in their experience really was like that. Did the trees rustle with barely decipherable messages? Is it likely that owls making a racket might eventually seem a sound pregnant with meaning? Tim, who's apparently spent a lot of time in the woods hiding from the police and tending his pot, said that you hear every last tiny thing when you've been out there in the woods for a while, particularly when you have the feeling that there are cops out there looking for you. Did he feel that the woods could really be *interpreted* as Huck was doing? The woods tell you a lot, a tremendous amount, Tim said. "They talk to you more than people in here do," he offered. "Or maybe they just tell you what you want to hear more often." By his nodding, Slash seemed to agree.

The main idea I wanted to impart for the class was that there is, in *Huck Finn*, a neighboring world in which regenerative, quickening powers circulate. To reverse the slow death imposed by "sivilization," Twain and Huck recommend a plunge into the soul-rescuing Mississippi. I meant to suggest to the inmates that they could, if they tried, do something similar. Obviously, they couldn't go rushing out to the Ottaquechee, though it was awfully close—it twists along behind the rec yard and is visible from the jail's northern windows. But they could do something. The inmates were not altogether as cut off as they assumed they were. I meant to harp on the deadening routine of jail—eat, sleep, eat, sleep, and so on—and I meant to contrast this with the unpredictable life of someone who loses himself in books. Or in an art project. Or perhaps in inspired observation of the details of his daily life in jail. All of these things might enrich; all of these things counter the samenesses of jail.

"I know that traveling the Mississippi by book is not quite the same thing as traveling it in real life," I began. "I know you guys can't even get outside to the damn Quechee River. I'm sorry about that. And I know everyone here would like to be somewhere else—"

"I just love Huck Finn," Laird piped up. Despite his habit of sleeping away his days (which earned him a punishment of early evening lock-in in his cell, which meant more sleep), Laird seemed especially lively on this day. It was obvious to me that he had once liked school. He seemed to be trying to bring that sensation back. He wasn't always a screw-up—he'd won an award in ninth grade at the Indian Mountain School in Lakeville, Connecticut—the McMillan Prize—for being an all-around good kid. He'd coached little kids in soccer. He'd been a junior counselor at a summer camp in New Hampshire in the summer of '99. He'd been hired on by one of his teachers from IMS. Something of this successful early adolescent persona—it must have been in eclipse lately—seemed to be reemerging. In class, he was a picture of good-natured, likeable subservience. His glasses twinkled in the light. He wore the fleece vest with the insignia of his ski team stitched across the breast. He had hardly taken it off in six weeks. His cheeks were still apple red from his days as a skier, and he was still, after all, a strong believer in the hearty smile, the can-do attitude.

I didn't want to lose the point: Huck's harbingers of doom—the owl, the whippoorwill, the crying of the dog—are really harbingers of the life outside that's awaiting Huck. "Evidently," I said, "the destiny of our hero, his calling, his spirit—whatever—is doing roughly what Miss Watson had done earlier with her spelling book, namely taking a set at him, and working him middling hard. Huck's job is to listen. If he does, he'll be let go out into the world. He'll be transcending his cooped-up little family life in Saint Petersburg."

This was the beginning of my *Huck Finn* lecture, the one I had labored over at the Norman Williams Public Library in Woodstock; the one that had done such reliable service when I was a literature TA in my former life. It was part motivational speech, part History Channel documentary. It was supposed to flow gradually into the promise of the landscape, the enduring appeal of going West, the pleasurable terror that early travelers found in so much moving, rolling mud...and so forth. I had adapted it for use in the jail. Inmates, particularly Will and Emmons and Rhino and probably most everyone else as well, expressed their freedom by entangling themselves in the law—by ripping away at its rigging. Huck's freedom is a different kind—it takes the form of a spiritual journey, of an exploration of the land, and the currents that drive through it. He comes into his own when he gets out onto the river. Perhaps the inmates could consider that definition of freedom. It was almost the reverse of theirs. If nothing else, it ought to have provided an interesting contrast.

On that day, I began making this speech and faltered. The more I talked, the more I could see the expressions on people's faces drooping toward incredulity and boredom. "Freedom on the inside? Free spirit? Maybe so, but not for me," said Slash's face. Emmons and Will were staring blankly. Slash had a point. No one was visibly embarking on any journey at all, spiritual or otherwise. Slash had been in jail since 1997. He was looking at an undetermined amount of time on probation when he was released. The rest of the inmates, I guessed, would be similarly entangled in the rigging of the system. That entanglement would probably continue; probably it would worsen.

I listened to myself talk and wondered at what I was saying. Laird interrupted after a few moments.

"I'm probably going to be moving out West when I get out," he said. "Always wanted to go. Now I guess because of my situation, I have the opportunity, you know? I mean when I get out."

"Bull fucking shit," said Slash.

"What situation?" someone asked.

"Well, I can't go back to Gould. And I guess I'm not going to go home right away. I mean when I get bail. I don't even know if my dad wants me there."

"Is that so?" said Slash.

"Yeah, so the Wild West," Will said. "Perfect for you."

"Yeah, gunslinger. Go West," said Slash.

Tim interrupted with a song: "I want to ride to the ridge where the west commences." He couldn't remember the next line. "Something something something can't stand fences," he sang.

Laird smiled. "Yeah," he said. "I'm going to be skiing out West, I guess. Ski bum, man."

I tried to get myself back on track but Tim was going on with the song and suddenly Laird was laughing. And then everyone was laughing. My lecture faded. We had other things we wanted to talk about, it turned out: a woman in the news who'd driven her boyfriend into a tree while she was drunk. Slash knew her. We laughed about that for a while. A guy who killed himself in a sporting goods store in Rutland with a rifle he had pretended he was going to buy. We laughed about the poor shopkeeper and listened while Slash imagined what the clerk might have said to the dead man: "Couldn't you have done it outside? Couldn't you have brought a fucking sheet, at least? Jesus!"

After a while a guard came and knocked on the door. "Rover's here," he said, but no one moved. Everyone was having such fun and it seemed, strangely, that for once the inmates didn't want to rush out of class. They dawdled and joked for a little while longer until the guard had to knock again.

CHAPTER TEN

Huck Finn

JAIL DIARY, FEBRUARY 16, 2000
During the past week, the students have read through chapter eight in *Huckleberry Finn*. Today, Wednesday, I had my best *Huck Finn* class so far. I've been trying lately to show that life after the escape from family life at the Widow Douglas's is not all boyish idyll for Huck. It's not an endless fishing excursion in the company of the loyal slave, Jim. It's not even really an escape from family life. It is, however, a departure into life, into its turbulence and violence and strangeness.

In class, we've been over chapter five, in which Huck's father, Pap, reappears in St. Petersburg after a mysterious absence in the wilderness, and chapter six in which Pap spirits Huck across the river to a cabin on the Illinois shore. There, the two of them resume their version of family life—lolling and fishing and sleeping in the woods—which Miss Watson and the widow had been trying to educate out of Huck. For several months it's a pleasant, jolly life, says Huck, but "by and by, pap got too handy with his hick'ry and I couldn't stand it. I was all over welts."

For today's class, I planned a discussion of what occurs in the cabin (various episodes of domestic violence), Huck's escape (also violent), and the world-assessing calm that descends over the narrative when Huck finally manages to extricate himself. I didn't want this last point to be lost on the students: Family life ends for Huck, but immediately thereafter he falls asleep, and immediately after that he delivers himself out into the currents of the river. Thus begins a new, more perilous, more serious portion of the book. It doesn't last very long because the demands of the plot get the better of the author, but for a little while, Huck is a wide-eyed master of his domain, a sovereign Adam in possession of a gun and some fish hooks. He wanders around Jackson's Island, pulling catfish from the murk, haggling them open with his saw, and preparing dinner for himself. All the while, he's making steady progress toward his famous brand of unknowing moral courage.

I wanted the students to discover all of this on their own: without the lecture, without the flattening summary. Today, as always, I had to push them a bit to get things going. And today, as usual, the class was in no mood to be pushed. It seems that Slash is working himself into a fit over his upcoming parole hearing. His PO has said to him that she thinks he's a danger to the community. He feels he's a boon to the community. Now the parole board must decide. This is the oldest story in prison life, and I'm surprised that the parole process hasn't been sussed out by the inmates to the point where it no longer holds any mystery for anyone. I thought parole boards were as predictable as the days of the week. They're not, it seems. They could ignore the PO or they could send Slash back to Virginia. They could hold him for a year or let him go tomorrow. He's in a state.

Just as I was sitting down, Slash pulled his chair in next to mine and burned his angriest, most outraged stare into my eyes.

"She said I was a potential reoffender," he hissed. "That fat fucking whore said I was danger to the community. Can you fucking believe that?" I could believe it, but didn't say anything.

"She" is Donna, his parole officer and tormentor. He seethed when I told him I'd like him to try to concentrate on the book for forty minutes. Then we could have a break and discuss his hearing if he still wanted to go over it.

"Forty minutes for class, okay?" I pleaded. "And then the floor is yours." It was a thin bribe and Slash had no interest in it. He was insulted by the offer and muttered something nasty at me that I couldn't hear.

Joe likes it when Slash is unhappy. I can see him grinning out of the corner of my eye as Slash launches into his I-can't-stand-another-minute-in-here routine. So, for that matter, can Slash. As soon as Slash noticed that Joe was enjoying his misery, he tore into Joe.

"What a fat fuck you are, Joe," he said glumly. "Too dumb to stay out of your wife's fucking apartment. Too fat to cut your fucking wrists. Try harder! Scratchy scratchy, scratchy with a fucking razor. Please."

Joe would not rise to the bait. At one point he raised an eyebrow and offered to take Slash on upstairs in the cell block. "You're too fucking filthy to fight. Take a shower and then maybe. You're too much of a fat gorilla to fight anyone, Joe. You know that."

"As you all know," I interrupted, "things have lately been getting worse for Huck. Right? Everyone knows this?" I described how his dad has been threatening to remove him to still another cabin farther away in the woods and how the widow has been sending people around to kidnap Huck back into civilization. Now Huck has been locked into the cabin on the Illinois shore with Pap.

So that everyone would have, if they didn't have enough of it already, the sense of steadily enclosing menace that this chapter produces, I had Will read the passage in which Pap, in his delirium, imagines himself to be set upon by entangling snakes.

"There was Pap, looking wild and skipping around every which way and yelling about snakes. He said they were crawling up his legs; and then he would give a jump and scream and say that one had bit him on the cheek," Will read.

When this vision subsides, Death comes for him, or at least this is what he sees, and in his drunkenness he retaliates. Mistaking Huck for Death, he lurches after Huck in the darkened cabin:

> By and by, he rolled out and jumped up on his feet and he see me and went for me. He chased me round and round the place with a clasp knife calling me Angel of Death and saying he would kill me and then I couldn't come for him no more. I begged and told him I was only Huck, but he laughed such a screetchy laugh, and he roared and cussed and kept on chasing me up. Once, when I turned short and dodged under his arm, he made a grab and got me by the jacket between the shoulders and I thought I was gone; but I skid out of the jacket quick as lightning and saved myself.

Everywhere there is death in this book, I said. It's something that burns in people's imaginations, even in Huck's. In this scene, Pap is on the verge of killing, because he can't get death off the brain.

I meant to segue here to a more general discussion of how, in a society preoccupied with spiritualism, and gunfighting, and with a cultlike reverence for the dead, the innocent, especially children, may well find themselves herded off into the grave. Many of the kids in the book, like the forlorn Stephen Dowling Botts and the doomed Buck Grangerford, to say nothing of Huck himself, find themselves targeted.

"I think we're being invited to make judgments about this Pike County—okay, the Mississippi society—okay, the American society, based on how it treats its kids," I said. "I think this book means to be a wide-ranging indictment. And I think it means to propose an alternative. Do you guys get that?"

Slash was rubbing his chin. Finally, Rhino had something to say.

"I want to read this part here," he said. "This part is great." He skipped ahead a few lines down the page and began reading. "Does this remind you of anyone?" he asked.

I had a sense of what was coming and asked him to stop.

"Lemme just read this, please," he said.

"No," I insisted.

He went ahead anyway.

"This is the part I like. Check this out, right? After Pap falls asleep, right? So who does this remind you of?"

"Slash," I said. "Let's get everyone to quiet down."

"No can do," he said. "Man's reading his homework, right?"

Rhino read: "By and by I got the old split-bottom chair and clumb up as easy as I could, not to make any noise and got down the gun." He was laughing but he kept on reading. "I slipped the ramrod down it to make sure it was loaded, and then I laid it across the turnip barrel, pointing towards pap, and set down behind it to wait for pap to stir.... And then I pulled the motherfucking trigger. Boom! The motherfucker's head blew into a million pieces."

He was laughing happily in deep rolling chuckles. "By and by I says to myself, Holy shit! Know what I mean?" He let his eyes fall on Laird.

"Oh wait," he apologized in a treacly voice, full of fake, mocking sorrow. "I guess the book doesn't really go like that. I read that somewhere else like the *Rutland Herald* or something."

Laird locked his jaw and stared at me. I think we were all embarrassed. An interval of quiet descended over the class, and I think eventually even Rhino was embarrassed. No one knows what to say when people stick their needles into Laird. Yes, he did a terrible thing, but he doesn't make a satisfying pin cushion. He won't take offense and he won't retaliate. He just sits there looking frightened and aggrieved.

Laird won't even look at Rhino or Slash when they're harassing him. He kept his eyes fastened on a point somewhere in the middle of my chest. So it was my turn to think of something to say. I flipped the page of the book and picked up with the next chapter. But it was time to go, thankfully, and I heaved a heavy sigh of relief when I heard the guard banging on the door. So, for that matter, did everyone, I think. I will have to leave the resolution of this scene—the world-assessing calm part of it—for tomorrow.

JAIL DIARY, FEBRUARY 17, 2000

Huck's escape from Pap's cabin frightened me when I was a kid. It's the nightmare sequel to the nightmare Angel of Death scene, though this time, Huck seizes control of events. He also seizes control of his father's store of possessions: the gun, the ax, the cookware, the fishlines, the matches, "everything that was worth a cent," says Huck. It's a wise bit of thievery under the circumstances because it undoes Pap and makes Huck into a wealthy man, relatively speaking. Henceforth, Huck will be a man of means and Pap will be the penniless fugitive, stalked by ambient threats. Perhaps there was a moral somewhere in here for my students: out of disastrous family life comes a new beginning. Or: you must turn the tables for yourselves. Or: the barest rudiments are enough for a new life... or something.

I almost asked Duane Placey, the guy who'd done in his wife's boyfriend, to read the passage I had in mind but immediately thought better of it. Something in a news article about him I read once a while ago sprung into my mind as I looked at the paragraph in question and I decided instead to read the bit myself. In this scene, Huck is putting the final touches on his long-dreamed-of exodus from his life as a persecuted kid in Pike County. He's shot a pig and dragged the carcass back to camp. I read:

> I took the axe and smashed in the door—I beat it and hacked it considerable a-doing it. I fetched the pig in and took him back nearly to the table and hacked into his throat with the axe, and laid him down on the ground to bleed—I say ground because it was ground—hard packed and no boards. Well, next I took an old sack and put a lot of big rocks in it,—all I could drag—and I started it from the pig and dragged it to the door, and through the woods down to the river and dumped it in...

As I read, I could hear the sound of the deliberate, ritualistic rhythms that Twain wrote into this passage. I'd forgotten how incantatory, how nearly musical the writing becomes at this point in the story. "I put..., I took, I fetched...Well, next I took...," says Huck. I kept thinking as I read about how mysterious this passage is, how it seems that Huck's been overtaken by a deep, Zen-like single-mindedness. Where does it come from? In class, we haven't yet met such a purposeful, solemn Huck. The students were quiet as I read, and I tried to give the passage the slow, strange, gory pace that I hear when I happen across the lines myself. A few sentences down, Huck pulls hair from his head and plasters the strands across the back of the ax using some of the spare pig's blood. Everyone was listening to every word, and I couldn't help thinking that the presence of people in the room who'd recently lost control, who'd submitted themselves to an inner voice not too long ago gave those lines a special believability. "Who's in control now?" I asked the students, without having much idea of the answer: "Why's Huck doing this? What's the purpose?"

"To make it look like someone else killed him?" Laird asked. "Like he's been killed by robbers or something?"

"Yes, that," I said. "But there was more to it."

"He's like doing it so deliberately?" Laird wondered. "Is that it?"

I didn't know how to respond. Laird was anxious to give me the correct answer. I think he was anxious to *know* the correct answer.

"He's done it before? Is that it?" Laird asked. "So he knows exactly how to do it?"

Everyone was looking at me for the verdict. Where does Huck's pig-axing plan come from, and what's its real purpose? And the blood smearing? The sack of rocks? Its burial in the Mississippi? I did have a sort of answer scribbled in my notes from previous go-rounds with other classes: Huck has an instinctual feel for how to give his life with Pap a graceful, purposeful ending. *Like a priest, a ceremony, a death rite,* I had penciled into the margin of my book. The explanation, however, wasn't on the tip of my tongue. The students stared at me. Duane was utterly blank—he could have been watching a TV program; he could have been staring at a menu in a restaurant. Laird was anxious to get to the bottom of things. I tried to explain, but made a muddle. I could see Laird wondering: "He thinks Huck's a priest? Huck's doing a ritual? What for? Maybe Theo doesn't actually know what he's talking about?" I burrowed further into my explanation: Yes, Huck is dispatching himself into a new existence. And yes, there's something ceremonious about the procedure.

"It's hard work," I said, "and the kid's normally a shirker. Suddenly here he's all business. You see?" I wanted them to see that a mysterious, unknowable urge for self-revival had taken hold of Huck. I couldn't tell if the silence of the students meant that they were bowled over by the truth of what I was saying or just bowled over by too much teacherly talking. By Will's crinkled brow and Slash's narrowed eyes, I guessed that some of the students—the smart ones—were paying some attention. And Laird, who must know something by now about surviving disaster, was anxious to pursue the game. He wanted more explanation, more talking. His expression said, Let's follow this along, I'm liking this.

I think all the students wanted me to push forward, and so that's what I did.

The passages I had marked out for today's class—the centerpiece of my lesson plan—were the lines describing the new life that ensues after the violence with Pap. When the massacre in the cabin is complete—the blood appropriately smeared across the floor, and Pap is still away searching the Missouri shore for whiskey or whiskey money, Huck loads his worldly goods into a canoe. It's tied to a willow on the bank. He no sooner climbs in himself than he falls asleep. He wakes up in the dark, is frightened for a moment, and then he looks out across the water. I had Duane read what happens next:

> The river looked miles and miles across. The moon was so bright and I could a counted the drift logs that went a slipping along, bright and still, hundreds of yards out from the shore.
> Everything was dead quiet, and it looked late, and *smelt* late. You know what I mean—I don't know the words to put it in.

Duane Placey is not the best reader—he stumbled over the words and produced, apparently by accident, a sound filled with an appropriate mixture of slowness and vexation. I wanted to congratulate him on a reading so aptly done but Tim interrupted.

"You see, he got something from the pig," said Tim. "He inherited the pig's sniffing nostrils. What a wicked sense of smell a pig has. Did you ever notice that?" We had to joke around for a while about the murdered pig and his snout because Tim can take nothing seriously.

After a few minutes of this I started to push the class back toward the book. Laird wanted to help. "So, what's the point, Theo?" he asked. "You're saying about this new beginning thing, the Garden of Eden thing?"

"That's coming," I said, "but first something changes in Huck himself. What's changed? What do *you* think it is, Laird?"

"He can see across the river? He sees further? He's not locked up in the cabin anymore, so he's freer."

"Obviously. Duh," Will said. "So what?"

I wanted the students to read this scene the way I read it, as an awakening of Huck's famous night vision, his radar-like capacity to navigate through the darkness. This is a skill the students badly need and it'll help, I think, to see someone, even if it's a fictional someone, putting such a skill to use. Moments after he opens his eyes, Huck unties himself from the willow on the bank: "The next minute I was

a-spinning down stream soft but quick in the shade of the bank..."
After a few miles, the boat finds the deep current toward the middle
of the river:

> I got out amongst the driftwood and then laid down and let her
> float. I laid there and had a good rest, and a smoke out of my pipe,
> looking away into the sky, not a cloud in it. The sky looks ever so
> deep when you lay on your back in the moonshine. I never
> knowed it before. And how far a body can hear on such nights!

The voices of people talking at a ferry landing come floating across
the water—he makes out every word in their yokel discussion—they
filter gently into his memory, and then the sounds subside into
mumbles and laughter. Off he goes, deeper into the current, with his
pots and his ax and his fishing line. The scene is a lovely
transcendence by raft and river; it's the most vivid of any escape
scene in the book and probably the most vivid of any we are ever
going to read in the class. It emphasizes the prevalence of darkness
but also insists on a few countervailing points of light—stars, moon,
village lanterns in the distance. I wanted the students to follow it
carefully. And then I wanted them to see Huck touching down on
Jackson's Island. They were meant to experience the sense of
opportunity and newness that overcomes the story at this point and
to see that it comes at least in part from Huck's having tapped into
his mysterious inner radar. Perhaps it's a faculty he had to develop.
Perhaps it evolved to meet an environmental need: the kid has had a
difficult life. I shared some of these thoughts with the students and
read a few more sentences that were supposed to illustrate the
awakening of Huck's senses: The way he sees Jackson's Island
looming up in the night like a ghostly steamboat, the way he watches
a monstrous big lumber raft come creeping down the river, and hears
an oarsman cry out, "Stern oars, there! Heave her head to stabbord!"
The raft washes by in the night, knowing nothing of Huck.

Slash was taking in the pith of the lecture while he was thumbing
through his legal papers. He was not persuaded.

"Don't tell me to wake up my senses in here, Theo," he said. "If
you try to smell more shit in here, what you're gonna end up

smelling is more shit. Believe me. I lie awake at night upstairs in bed
and it doesn't smell late. It smells like ass."

"Yes, yes, I'm sure," I agreed.

I had Laird read a passage in the next chapter that describes what
Huck does during his first few days on Jackson's Island. He watches a
ferry boat from St. Petersburg searching for his dead body. It gives
him up for lost and goes home. He sets up camp, and takes to
counting the stars and the driftwood. "And so on for three days and
nights," says Huck. Laird read:

> No difference, just the same thing. But the next day I went
> exploring around down through the island. I was boss of it; it all
> belonged to me, so to say, and I wanted to know all about it; but
> mainly I wanted to put in the time. I found plenty of
> strawberries, ripe and prime; and green summer grapes, and
> green razberries; and the green blackberries was just beginning to
> show. They would all come handy by and by, I judged.

This is the Huck-as-Adam sequence, the part of the book when its
easiest to see America as a Garden of Eden and Huck as a mythical
First Child, at play in the fields of the Lord. In this section, he plays
some, but he's also taking dominion over the land and its plants, and
relaxing into the warm embrace of Mother Earth. Soon enough, he
finds himself tripping over a good-sized serpent.

Anyway, Huck's transcendence has evidently taken him backward
through time; it's washed away the absurdity and trivia of everyday
life—Pap, chuckling yokels—and deposited him in his own private,
alluvial year zero. Here, in Huck's fresh new world, every decision opens
out into the realm of philosophy: how should Huck spend his time?
There are fellow creatures on the island: how should he approach them?
There is a snake in his garden: what should be done? In order to get the
students talking about these questions, I asked the class what they
thought Huck meant by saying he mainly wanted to "put in the time."

"He's basically trying to do his bid," said Duane. "He's got a lot of
time out there to kill and he wants to get down to killing it. It
seemed like a reasonable answer to me, minus the jail-shaped way of
looking at things."

"So Huck's in limbo?" I asked. "He's waiting for whatever comes next?" Dwyane nodded. Someone else objected that Huck has not been sentenced to do time.

"He's running away from home, basically. And that's forever. He's not doing time. He's just living. He's damn lucky," said Joe. Joe wished he could get the hell out of Vermont and never have to come back. He was going to have to go back to his hometown when he got out in order to do probation.

I eventually sided with Joe. I pointed out that Huck is directed now not by his father's comings and goings or the widow's schedule—or any other social routine. That's life in St. Petersburg, I said, and life here in Woodstock, but it's not what life is like out on Jackson's Island. Out there, Huck is directed by the promptings of his imagination and by a personal sense of what's important. His sense is telling him simple things: to learn how the land lies on his island, to figure out who else is there with him, to collect food, and to store things away for later.

"Totally," Laird agreed. His eyes widened as if he'd just gotten a hold of a wonderful idea. "This is totally sometimes the way I feel. I mean I have so much time now that I didn't used to have. I can hate it or I can love it, you know? And in a way it's up to me what I do with it. I feel that way sometimes. A lot of the time I feel that way. You know?" He looked around the table to see if any of his fellow inmates would back up his enthusiasm. No, they wouldn't. Their empty faces offered him nothing.

"So that's what he means by 'putting in the time'? Sort of, allowing the time to pass?" I asked.

"Yes!" Laird announced, smiling. "That's it!"

I didn't know whether to trust Laird or not. His speech sounded suspiciously like a teacher-pleasing pitch. It sounded like something he might say to a judge at sentencing: *I've reconciled myself to my lot, your Honor. I know now how to live a humble life.* But who knows? If he is trying to say what I want to hear, he might also be trying to talk himself into a good attitude at the same time. This would be a positive, hopeful sign. For all I know, he doesn't need to do any self-persuasion at all. In the novel, an episode of violence engenders a magical awakening. The sequence of events caused no one in class, not even Slash, to raise an eyebrow. Perhaps it's not such a strange idea; perhaps this sort of thing happens in jails a lot.

JAIL DIARY, FEBRUARY 21, 2000

Laird has evidently been thinking about life on Jackson's Island, because he picked up the subject on his own today, almost without prompting from me. We had moved on from the raspberries and summer grapes. We were talking about Huck's homestead on the island, which is really just a fire pit next to a tent of blankets. We talked of how, after establishing this "home," Huck climbs a tree to get a better view of the island.

"In a way, this is an afterlife for Huck," I pointed out. "At least he's passed on from the old world of civilization. The people back in St. Petersburg assume he's been murdered. They've already given up sounding the river for his corpse. When he climbs up into his observation tower, his tree," I said, "he stays up there for two hours, listening, and taking in the lay of the land. It's a brand-new world."

"Okay, I get it," Laird said. "I think I get it. It's more than new; it's like the beginning of the world, basically, and Huck can sort of control things because he's the only person living in it? Because he's sort of the first person or whatever?"

"Yes, exactly." I said. "The beginning of the world."

What was true? He launched into a mini-speech, heavily colored, it seemed to me, by the sci-fi movies he likes to watch. The gist of it was that the world moves in cycles. The old people are in charge and then the young are in charge. Right now, we are going through a period in which the old people hold sway. But that would change. When the old guard presses down too hard on all the people coming along behind them—the foot soldiers and the rebels and so on— battles ensued. Civil war. Then the old order would give way to the new. And gradually, you'd find a whole race of new people in charge of everything. That was all for the good.

"Do you know that expression 'The phoenix always rises stronger from the ashes'?" he asked. "That's true. That's something I've always believed."

Will agreed. He said that he liked the book and had not expected that he would find what he's been finding in *Huck Finn.* So that was all good. He then announced that what we needed was a revolution all across the country, a second American revolution. "It's gonna happen," he mumbled—perhaps with a little less conviction than normal. There's a thin, rote quality to Will's political philosophy; he sometimes sounds as if he's trying to remember the words to his speeches. I wonder that the real world hasn't intervened somehow to alter his philosophy. But Will has a remarkable capacity to overlook the data streaming in from the real world: he prefers the real world of *There Comes a Pale Horse,* evidently, with its nexus of powerful bankers and Jews and dreaded Internationalists. Today, Will launched into his speech about imminent social upheaval apparently out of habit. His voice dragged at first and his eyes moved tiredly around the room. But then he picked himself up. Will still believes, or wishes anyway, to be seen as as a believer in the idea that revolution is inevitable. It will come one day and will return us all to the innocence and freedom of a premoral society. He dragged us across this stretch of teenage apocalypticism, with which I'm familiar enough by now, while I got agitated. All students, not just Will, are constantly on the lookout for an occasion to lay down their philosophies. When they find their moment, they start applying their ideas around the room in a thick paste. That instinct kills a class; it smothers the books and their ideas. It holds up the kids' private amalgam of lore and newspaper factoids and prophecy as the truest, highest level of class discussion. Meanwhile, the book under consideration chokes and dies.

Slash finally interrupted Will. "The only thing that's inevitable for you is a fucking ten-year bid, dude. And claustrophobia," he said. "That's what's inevitable for you. Why don't you take a fucking shower?"

Will said that he took a shower this morning. He felt great. What about Slash?

The class was coming to an end at that point; I was relieved. I didn't want to ruin the good rapport the kids were developing with the book and with me for that matter, so I listened to their argument for a while and waited for the rover, a guard who moves the inmates to and fro, to come. The daylight from our two windows was draining out of the room and I knew the rover would arrive momentarily.

JAIL DIARY, FEBRUARY 24, 2000

We read more of *Huck Finn* today, but I've had enough of him for the time being. I'll write instead about what happened at the end of class—something interesting.

After all the students had left the library, I was standing by the tables in the main schoolroom, looking over my attendance sheet. Laird shouldered into a group of inmates next to me and tugged on my shoulder. We moved out of the crowd to a slightly more private spot near the computers. "I've got something to tell you that has to do with my case," he whispered. "I can't tell you now. Too many people around." Okay, I said. I must have looked a little surprised. I could see Jim eyeing me from across the room. The rover was looking at me too, and we were all being looked at by the jail's closed-circuit TV.

Laird's is an especially high-profile case; whispering to him might be interpreted the wrong way. The number-one rule for teachers is to stay out of the students' private business; that's privileged information and it belongs to the prosecutors. A meddling teacher can easily meddle his way into trouble: a subpoena, or even a rumor of kibbitzing could get me fired. I know this and yet it was hard for me to separate myself away from Laird. I think he saw that. "My dad wants to talk to you," he whispered. His dad is an English teacher like me, and someone whose response to Laird's crime seems to be a lot like my response. He'd like to get Laird reading. He'd like Laird to get to know himself better. These are the presents that Laird has gotten from his dad so far: in addition to *Antigone*, Robert Pinksy's translation of Dante's *Inferno*, a memoir about a gay man's coming out, and the J. D. Salinger collection *Nine Stories*. Salinger is an across-the-Connecticut-River neighbor of the Stanards. Laird says that he loves Holden Caulfield. He also says he loves the story "Teddy," about a precocious American Buddhist boy on an ocean liner.

It seems like Laird's dad is more and more part of the picture now, a good sign. He's coming to the visiting hours on Wednesday evenings, and, according to Laird, is promising to donate some old Macintosh computers to the jail school. Judging by the gift of the coming out memoir—Paul Monette's *Becoming a Man: Half a Life Story*—it seems to me that Bill is hoping to help Laird come to terms with his sexuality. My guess is that Laird is already at ease on that score. There's nothing like Rhino grinding his hips at you and miming a sex act he once performed on a hapless prisoner in New Hampshire to sour you on the fashionable idea of being "bi." In Laird's first week or so, he had some liberal, supportive things to say in current events class about civil unions in Vermont and Bill Bradley's stand on gay rights, but people scowled at him. Laird got the message. He dropped his open-minded views in a heartbeat. The Woodstock jail, it's turned out, is a fiercely homophobic society. Laird has fallen into line. He's now taken to referring to a young woman with whom he spent his free time at Gould as his "girl," and his "woman," designations which sound ludicrously macho in his mouth. We've heard that he and his "girl" have been planning to get married (surely an exaggeration) and that his "woman" gets the best of everything, thanks to his never-ending largesse. "Whatever my girl wants, wherever she is, she gets it," he says, which happens to be the formulation all the other prisoners use to describe how chivalrous they really are to the women in their lives. Of course in Laird's case it's obvious that he's boasting about lavishing away his parents' money on people. I have a picture in mind of his friends accepting his gifts and tittering about him behind his back.

JAIL DIARY, WEDNESDAY, MARCH I, 2000
I've been getting a bit closer to Laird over the past week. He's been obsessing lately about the foster son in West Burke who executed his foster mother at point blank range. Scott Favreau's crime neatly recapitulates Laird's: the family gun, the family car, the wild-eyed plan that was falling apart even before the trigger was pulled. And of course the dead mother, shot to death as she was busy trying to be a mom. These are the salient details. They must bring something powerful home to Laird. Well, do they? I've heard him lately applying a spin to

Favreau's crime that hasn't occured to me: the victim, forty-four-year-old Victoria Campbell-Beer, was a tyrant. She'd been abusive to Favreau's accomplice (her stepdaughter) and to Favreau himself. The teenagers put an end to an intolerable situation; they "laid down the law" as Laird says. He and I have been talking about this. He's also told me some things about his life at Gould Academy in Bethel, Maine.

He's told me about his relationship with his "fiancée," and her circle of friends; a circle that was really, he maintains, a tribe of wiccans and lesbians and witches. They were all drifting toward college except for Laird, who, as a junior, was less concerned with college and more directly interested in being part of the clique. (Me: "But are you interested in witchcraft and stuff yourself?" Laird: "Not at all.") He's also told me about his mom briefly, and about his ambition to be an actor. We steal our conversations from lulls in the current events class and from the ten-minute interval between classes. Our discussions are furtive and semiprivate, like trysts in a schoolyard. They take place in whispers in the library behind the moveable blackboard, and occasionally in the main schoolroom, down at the far end of the current events table, as we're pretending to read the newspapers. He hisses into my ear and I try not to look interested. Every few seconds he stops talking to peer around the room. When we're in the library, we step out from behind the blackboard after a few moments, and I watch his eyes scanning up and down, over and beneath. Then he picks up his monologue again.

There are two intertwining strands to this performance: the abundance of cash in his family coffers, and his enduring innocence. All the strands in his tattered narratives, it seems to me, stem from these two great cords. But is there any strength to them? I'm certain he's not innocent. That cord is an airy nothing, a lie even he knows will give way. And his family money? The Stanard family may be richer than any other family whose son is locked up in jail but that's not saying much. People in Woodstock who know the Stanards say that if they're very rich, they're keeping it very quiet. The *Valley News* says that in 1985 they paid $27,500 for their house in West Windsor, a modest sum even for fifteen years ago. Now Laird's bail has been set at $1.5 million. "My dad has the $750,000 in cash," says Laird, waving casually at the figure like a TV stockbroker, "he's just got to sell a few bonds to come up with the rest. The money's definitely, definitely no problem." So he assures the class, but for the time being no bail has been posted. The family, I'm guessing, doesn't trust Laird to remain within the jurisdiction. Perhaps they don't want him free.

Regardless, in the long run, says Laird, he will have an easy time of it the courts. Why? I ask. Because he has an excellent lawyer, the best money can buy. The mere fact of his family money, he thinks, will finally work in his favor because the lawyers and the judges are also wealthy people and when push comes to shove, they will look out for their own. So he assumes.

But his money, it seems, has also been a burden to him. He's starting to wonder if Elizabeth wasn't interested in him exclusively for his money, and for the convenience of the credit card he had removed from his mother's purse. He thinks all that money might have made his parents corrupt: they tried to buy a solution to Laird's problems by sending him away to boarding school. "But you can't buy your way out of a problem like I had," he observes accurately enough.

He also wonders sometimes if the money hasn't corrupted him. He's told me that he had $200 in cash in his pockets on the night of the killing. That sum he'd collected from billfolds—not his—lying around the house. Plus, he had a credit card. He needed all that money because he was planning to go to Maine to see Elizabeth. And after that, he didn't know where he was going to go. It would be a while, he assumed, before he'd be in control of his parent's money.

The other theme to which he returns is his innocence.

"I didn't do it, I *swear*, Theo," he says. "I don't know who did it but I swear to god. I swear to god. I didn't do it." He's said this over and over again, and by now, now that we've been talking about this for a week, he's getting used to hurrying past the thesis sentence and lurching toward the tangled evidence itself. There are, unsurprisingly, dozens of strands to the story of how he came to be accused of this crime. In our conversations, he anxiously ravels them together. Then he undoes something just a bit—a wink telling me that he's kind of,

well, smile, lying. "Whatever I say doesn't go out of this room, right?"
he asks. I nod vaguely. As I watch him knitting up his story and tearing
at it and knitting it up again, I'm learning something about the world
he inhabited last fall before the shootings. Here's what I've heard.

Yesterday Laird had an urgent secret to disclose. It concerned
Elizabeth, his sometime, would-be girlfriend at Gould. It's not the
murder that's been on his mind, it turns out, but Elizabeth. We stood
behind the blackboard, his face reddening, the words tumbling out
of his mouth in a great gush of indignation and hurt: "I did
everything for her! She was like my best friend I've ever had. We were
supposed to get married. We were going to go to the same college!"
They had had the deepest talks he's ever had with anyone in his life.
He'd stopped doing his homework so that he could help her with
hers. He'd stayed up late every night instant-messaging her as she sat
in her dorm room across campus. They'd planned out a future
together. Like all hopeful high school sweethearts, it practically went
without saying that they were to be married. That's how close they
were. But now, he said, she's been talking to the police. He can't
believe it. Why would she do that? He was stunned by the thought.
He said that she hated authority, and took her own direction in life,
just like him. So why would she ever say anything to the police?

I didn't know. He stared at me for a moment as if I had the answer
and then turned back to the happier subject of his marriage. I have
great difficulty seeing him as a bridegroom but no difficulty seeing
him as college student. Now both of those notions are as fantastic as
his protestations of innocence. "We still are supposed to get married,
as far as I know."

He wishes anyway that Elizabeth would come to visit. He said
that he thinks of her all the time. I asked him if he didn't think it
would be best, now that things were as they were, to let her go, to let
her get on with her life. He agreed, or seemed to agree, that that was
necessary and then he said, "I really wish she'd come for a visit or
something, though. I miss her. I mean a *lot*."

Like a lot of schoolboy crushes, this one seems as though it might
have lead a vigorous fantasy life. It might well never have existed at
all. The picture I got as I talked to Laird was of a new boy at school,

lonely and looking for friends. He'd found a circle of them—older girls in the senior class. Unlike the typical Gould kids who were outdoorsy and bright eyed and relentlessly healthy, Laird's friends liked to sneak away into the woods to smoke cigarettes. They were not virtuoso skiers or soccer players or lacrosse players. Nor were they bound for the better colleges. They were, he said affectionately, the "freaks" of the school. They wore black clothing and combat boots. Some of them were lesbians, he said, or at least that's what they went around telling people. That was fine with him. I had the impression that to be a lesbian, in Laird's eyes, was to be different, discriminating, above the fray. I also had the impression that he wished he could have been one himself. How much quicker then, would he have been admitted into that circle of older girls, with their unusual tastes and attitudes and desires. He might have been able to set about satisfying those desires. As it was, however, Laird seemed merely a rueful and frustrated admirer of his friends; their errand boy more than their boy toy.

At home, he could, and did, apparently, make a bolder assertion of his identity. Somehow, in the fall of last year, he managed to persuade his parents to believe that he was "bi." I'm guessing that he was shocked and disappointed to find that his parents were not shocked and disappointed by the news.

There were other things that Laird liked about Elizabeth: She was unafraid of adults. She was moody. She was a year older, and on her way to college. She'd been at Gould for two years and knew everyone; she was fiercely loyal to her friends and had a close relationship with her mother. She had real toughness—a steely, cold-eyed kind that had truly impressed him.

When a blood drive was being run at school, she urged him to donate. He claimed that she liked the sight and the smell of blood; according to him, she wanted to see him up there on the table with a needle in his arm. She was curious to know if he could handle it. As the blood was draining from his vein, she sat in a chair opposite him, urging him to pump his fist, to engorge the line, to foul up the system. He did it. Nothing much happened. But there were others, an athletic faculty member nearby, for instance, who had all but passed out. Laird felt vindicated. He'd *done* it. He was thrilled. Elizabeth, he thought, had thoroughly enjoyed the whole scene, though probably she had wanted to see him turn ashen and collapse under the stress.

"That's what kind of a girl she is," he said, brightening with the memory.

That wasn't the only provocative, spur-of-the-moment project they had undertaken together. Laird liked to respond to her dares, to prove himself the equal of her imagination. He gamely misbehaved in the local shops around Bethel, Maine. He stole things. He made jokes in front of the counter people; he knocked groceries off the shelves accidentally on purpose. At the Sunday River ski area, he did an entire run with his pants down by his knees, his fanny hanging out in the snowy air.

She hadn't dared him to do anything having to do with his parents, I asked. There was never anything like that, was there?

"No! No way! I'm not saying that!"

The newspapers have reported that just after he was arrested, an Elizabeth Burton, seventeen, a student at Gould Academy, told the police that Laird had said to her that he was planning to kill his parents. "Why would she say a thing like that?" I asked. He shrugged. He's already answered this question in front of the police and his lawyer, apparently. An automatic look came over his face. "I don't know," he said blandly. "I don't know." And then, in a quieter voice: "I think she was mad at me. She must have been really, really pissed or something... I don't know. Ask her." A lot will depend, if he goes to trial, on the question of how much preparation he did, exactly, before the crime. Three weeks worth, as Elizabeth has it, would be a lot.

JAIL DIARY, MARCH 3, 2000
Surprisingly, Laird wants to talk to me about his feelings for his mom. Earlier in the week, on Monday, he told me that he loved her a lot, much more than he loved his dad. "Why would I want to hurt my mom? If anything, it was my dad who..." Pause.

"Who what?"

"Just kidding." Smile.

"Okay."

If his mom were still alive, he says now, she could get him out of trouble. She'd do whatever was necessary. She's always done that in the past. Whatever it takes. "I loved my mom," he said to me today in the library, again behind the moving blackboard. "She was the only one who really was sort of always looking out for me. She did everything for me. And I did a lot for her." He comforted her when a close family friend died; he helped her through some of the problems she was having with his dad; he used to sit out on the porch in Windsor with her and smoke cigarettes late into the night. "She probably didn't even want to be married," he said. "She had all the money she needed on her own." After the family friend died, there wasn't anyone for her to lean on but her son, Laird said. So obviously he didn't want to kill her. "Though maybe," he confessed, "I might have said something like that to Elizabeth or something. Like all kids say when they're mad at their parents."

One of the reasons he's here in jail, he told me today, is that he's just given up on acting. He won't act as though everything is perfect. He won't go around playing the innocent as his dad does. Other people can carry on pretending, but for him the jig is up. "My dad is acting all sad and innocent now and everything but I can guarantee you: he hasn't shed a tear over this. And he turned me in! It's all on my dad's words! This whole thing, the entire case! Why do you think he did that?" I didn't know why Bill had done that. "Because…! Because…!" Laird stammered. He was too agitated to go on. He had to pause and rewind: back to the forensic evidence. The tests the police did on the night of the crime up at the barracks in Bethel, Vermont, he said, came back negative. Blowback: negative. Gunpowder residue: negative. Fingernail scrapings: negative. "So the evidence speaks for itself. So I don't need to act anymore. I'm going to let the police do whatever they have to do make their show. And Dad can make whatever show he wants to make, too. I'm through with all this acting shit."

But this decision to quit didn't come easily. Acting, he said earnestly, was one of his best skills. I asked him about that and he launched into a scattered history of his life on stage: "A year ago, two years ago, I really wanted to be a professional actor. I still do, sort of."

He said he'd like to work on Broadway someday. He's been in a lot of different school productions: *The Importance of Being Earnest, Our Town,* some Shakespeare. He's been a stage manager several times before; and at the Indian Mountain School, he practically lived in the theater. He was the drama teacher's favorite student. That's who hired him to work at the summer camp. He loves performing, and loves to show off his talents to people who can appreciate them.

He loved Elizabeth, among other reasons, because she had been an approving audience for him. She'd been difficult to impress but when she was impressed, it really meant something. It meant that he was getting closer to her. To him, he said, it seemed that they were falling more and more in love.

Laird fell silent after that remark and stared hard into a row of library books. "I'm in the worst trouble of my life, I need like Johnnie Cochran or something. I'm going to be on trial for my life! I didn't think anyone was going to accuse me, you know? Say that I did it, say that it was me.... If they did I was just going to look at them and say...Whatever! No way!"

One of the things that stopped me from committing crimes when I was seventeen was that I was too afraid of getting caught. I told him this.

"I didn't think I *would* get caught," he pleaded, his voice rising into his register of mystified indignation. "I thought the police we're like going to pat me on the back and say, 'There, there, kid.' You see? So...And now I've got a really big problem," he concluded. "All of this"—he motioned toward the current events room, and the cell blocks above us. A guard's walkie-talkie was approaching and we could hear it crackling and striding toward the library door.

"Plus, none of my friends are coming to visit. I'd really like it if Elizabeth came to visit. So I just sit in my cell. I just sort of sit there like an idiot. And at night I just sort of lie there."

Before the shooting, sometime in October, Laird wrote a poem for Elizabeth. I think it may have something to do with why he killed his mom. He gave it to me yesterday in class.

He says he's still writing poems for her. This one, he says, he did in early November, about a month before the shooting:

> I can imitate your pain yet
> I cannot share yours.
> I feel that
> Sometimes I have failed you.
> I want to do everything.
> Yet I know I can't.

The failure, the *imitation* of pain, the wanting to do everything. Some of this background is starting to make sense to me. I want to do everything. *Yet I know I can't.* Maybe a voice inside him said: *Yes, Laird, go ahead.* Yes, you can have real pain. You know you can do it. *Just do it.*

JAIL DIARY, MARCH 6, 2000

I've been looking through my bookshelves lately because I have to begin thinking about what I'll teach now that *Huck Finn* is soon to be finished. It's going to be set in the twentieth century and is going to give us a view of territory—crime, family, blood—that's closer to where we live now.

In reading through the end of Truman Capote's true-crime book, *In Cold Blood,* last weekend, I noticed that one of the murderers, Perry Smith, also sees himself, in his dreams, as an actor whose audience has abandoned him, has left him in a frightening well of silence. Toward the end of the book, as his execution is drawing near, and he's starving himself to death in jail, he dreams of himself in Las Vegas singing "You Are My Sunshine" and accompanying himself variously with a banjo, a harmonica, and a guitar. At the end of his act, he climbs to the top of a platform and peers outward:

> There was no applause; none and yet thousands of patrons
> packed the vast and gaudy room—a strange audience. Mostly
> men and mostly negroes. Staring at them, the perspiring
> entertainer at last understood their silence, for suddenly he knew
> that these were phantoms, the ghosts of the legally annihilated,
> the hanged, the gassed, the electrocuted . . .

There's a bit of this in Laird's memory of life before jail. He's still got the script and the music he used to perform running through his head. He's still doing his show: I love my mother! I love Elizabeth! I'm a good kid! But now there's no one to listen to the routine.

And Laird, like Perry, has a terrible impulse toward self-betrayal: "I swear to god, Theo. I'm innocent." But then: *"I thought the police would pat me on the back."*

"Elizabeth and I are supposed to get married." But then: *"That's all finished because I sacrificed myself for her."*

"I've given up acting." Then: *"The greatest performance of my life will be my trial. I need Johnnie Cochran."*

And worst of all: "My mom would have gotten me out of this.... *But my dad told the police on me. He turned me in."* His face flushed when he said that, as if he was remembering again how it was really his dad and not the police who'd pointed the finger of blame at him. Without the normal physical evidence—the gunpowder and the blowback tests—the police have had to rely on eyewitness testimony. Bill is the state's star witness. Laird seems to think it's his dad's fault that he's in jail. He seems to think that the problem with his crime was that he left a witness around to turn him in.

JAIL DIARY, MARCH 7, 2000
In every gathering of inmates there are a few old shadows—people who might have arrived here in transport from the Bastille or Alactraz or some other long-ago prison. In Woodstock, these people are mostly old drunks—they've been in and out of jail their whole lives—in many cases more of their lives have been lived in than out. You can tell how accustomed they are to incarceration by how well they provision themselves for a trip to the schoolrooms: they carry plastic coffee mugs, document folders, candy and pencils and folded-up newspaper sections. They wear heavy wristwatches and string dogtag necklaces that hang down into their clothing. Today in class two such men ambled in and took their seats. I've seen them around a bit before, but don't know what they've done or where they came from or when they'll be getting out.

Old men like this cast a pall over every group. They're like ghosts of Christmases yet to come. When they come floating into the room, everyone shrivels, especially the teenagers.

Today the class was filled with young people who might well be spending the next several decades behind bars. Frenchie is charged with aggravated sexual assault; the state says he kidnapped a young woman, held her forcibly in his car and in motel rooms, and raped her. Jim Vandriel, nineteen—recently transferred from the Rutland holding tank to ours—is here on a first-degree murder charge. He's accused of stabbing a tattoo artist to death. Will Emerson only robbed a convenience store, but it's his third felony. They only give you so many strikes, particularly when the third one involves a gun, as Will's did. Joey Bergeron is a car thief, but he can't seem to stay out of jail; when they do let him go, he violates his probation or runs away from his work crew. The authorities have apparently charged him with a new crime lately, namely escape, for which you can do ten years if you're convicted.

In the beginning of class, I watched these teenagers and twenty-somethings laboriously avoiding eye contact with the shadows. The young folk grimaced. They picked at their teeth. They spat into plastic cups. They smiled at one another.

The old men were merely grumpy. They needed to shave and to drink some coffee. Instead of hovering over the table as many new people do, they dropped into the chairs nearest the door. They coughed. After a moment, they laid out their newspapers and their coffee cups as if they were making two private table settings.

I, for one, was overjoyed to have them. When shadows talk in public—if they talk—the teenagers tend to shut up. Despite themselves, they are anxious to have a look into the future and if the old people can crack open the door a bit, the teenagers are not above looking inside.

Today, as the elder, frailer old man relaxed into his chair, we could hear a deep bubbling coming from inside his chest: something viscous—some phlegm or pneumonia or maybe just some coffee—was cooking away inside his abdomen. He'd wrapped himself in an ancient hunting jacket and layer after layer of flannel shirts. His name, according to the sign-in sheet, was Richard: he said he was from Bellows Falls. The other old gentleman—also clad in flannel, also wheezing—told us that he was waiting for a spot in a drying-out facility in New Hampshire. He had to wait in jail rather than at home because of an agreement he'd made with a prosecutor.

Today was the day I finished with *Huck Finn*. It was another good, auspicious class after several lousy, inauspicious ones. I decided to end our discussion of the book not with Huck lighting out for the territory ahead, but with several paragraphs in the middle of the story dealing with the passage of time. So I had everyone turn backward to a dreamy, lyrical section of the book, just before the Duke and the Dauphin arrive to drag the book off toward Vaudeville. There's a period of calm here before the frenzy of theater-acting, revivalism, and lecture-slinging.

I gave our visitors some spare copies of the book. Richard, the sicker older guy, said that he couldn't read. His glasses were locked inside his cell. He said he'd just follow along verbally.

"Fine," I said. "Good idea. That's basically how we've been following along, too."

I told the class what I meant to accomplish today and asked everyone to turn to chapter nineteen. As the class was settling down, I read from the beginning of the chapter. Huck has just escaped from the murderous Grangerford-Shepherdson feud and has lit out once again on the river.

"'Here is the way we put in the time,'" I read. "'It was a monstrous big river down there—sometimes a mile and a half wide; we run nights and laid up and hid daytimes; soon as night was most gone, we stopped navigating and tied up—nearly always in the dead water near a towhead...'"

The theme of today's class was the gentle, unstoppable, forward movement of time. I've noticed that a lot of the kids here fall into a deep depression once they see what they've done to themselves. With the newspapers accusing them, a trial in the offing, and victims demanding justice, they don't know what to do. I'm told that Laird has been huddling in a ball on his bunk lately. It seems he's been missing a lot of school.

Most of the kids come to school because the jail says they must.

And often they don't come: "What are they gonna do if I don't come?" Laird asks, reasonably enough. "Put me in jail?" Laird was put on a suicide watch during his first week, but his cheery smiles and reassurances got it lifted right away. Now, instead of being suicidally depressed, I suspect that he's just manically depressed, which probably amounts to the same thing.

"I'm way bipolar," he says happily. "Always have been."

He's been in class for the past several days, however, and today seemed to me like a good time for some proselytizing on the subject of time's healing powers.

"You tell 'em, you old men!" I was tempted to shout. "Tell them that things will work themselves out. Tell them that one actually moves forward in life, despite the interminable samenesses of jail routine." But I wasn't sure the old men would go along with me, so I stuck with my *Huck Finn* lecture plan.

I read out loud about Huck's days and nights on the monstrous, wide southerly section of the river. I paused occasionally to ask the students questions, and obligingly, politely, they answered. The lines I ended up focusing on describe Huck and Jim at twilight, watching from the shore as the days turn into night, and the nights into day. Their routine has them tying up the raft in the early morning, after their night of traveling, and setting out their fishing lines:

> Next we slid into the river and had a swim so as to freshen up and cool off; then we set down on the sandy bottom where the water was about knee deep and watched the daylight come. Not a sound anywheres—perfectly still—just like the whole world was asleep, only sometimes a bull frog a cluttering maybe.

There's some more fishing, and some cooking up of breakfast, and then Huck and Jim retreat into the woods, where they laze off to sleep. The verb tense is the habitual past: "we *would* take some fish off the lines . . . and afterwards we *would* watch the lonesomeness of the river . . . sometimes we'*d* have the whole river to ourselves." And so on.

To the inmates I said that this unschedule-like schedule is the moral opposite of the world's routine. I got a little mixed up, but what I was trying to say was that it happens also to be a temporal opposite:

the world wakes, he sleeps; it moves, he is still; it works, he is idle.... I hoped the inmates basically understood what I was trying to say. By the steady eye contact I was getting from Laird and Will, I judged that at least some of them were making sense of the words on the page.

"Living in his opposite realm," I said, "Huck has experienced more than his share of loneliness and nighttime dangers." I gave some examples: there have been sawyers, whirlpools, towheads, and steamboats; there will be a whole parade of floating rogues and trigger-happy villagers to come. The whole point here—one I didn't want to foul up with too much explanation—was this: "This living out of sync," I said, "is not a curse; it's not a tragedy; it's a sort of exile, fine. But exile in Huck's case allows for something important to happen, for a necessary distance to open up between the kid and the world. This distance is the best thing that ever happened to Huck. It's what brings him to himself; it's what pushes him toward his destiny." To give the idea some deeper illustration, I turned back to the book and read a passage that describes what Huck and Jim see as they watch the sun rise over the Illinois shore:

> The first thing to see, [says Huck] looking out over the water, was a kind of dull line—this was the woods on t'other side—you couldn't make nothing else out; then a pale place in the sky; then more paleness spreading around—then the river softened up away off and warn't black anymore; but gray; you could see little dark spots drifting along ever so far away—trading scows and such things—and long black streaks—rafts; ... and you see the mist curl up over the water, and the east reddens up, and the river, and you make out a log cabin in the edge of the woods, away on the bank on t'other side of the river...

"I think the idea is that you may slow down but you see more. Is that it?" asked Will.

"Sort of," I said. No one else wanted to say anything. So I talked for a minute about the clarifying effect of watching, just watching, the world go about its business. I said that there might also be a clarifying effect to be gleaned from sitting as the sun rises over the world. And I mentioned the abiding force of the river current, which

sweeps all things living and dead forward into the future. I was trying
to suggest that nature, at least in Twain's understanding, has a way of
taking care of its own.

I talked for a little while longer, but wasn't sure if everyone was
following me. Eventually, I asked for help from one of our visiting
codgers. "Have you ever camped out sort of on a riverbank? Or slept
in a boat?" I asked.

"When I'm fishing," Richard said. And then he lapsed into a
coughing fit. When he recovered he said, "One thing I know: God is
working his purpose out."

The whole class was silent.

"Hymn," he explained.

The teenagers shifted in their chairs. Bergeron cracked a smile.
Frenchie smiled with him.

"God is working his purpose out: one of my hymns," Richard
explained.

"Okay, man," I said. "Can you forget about God for a second?"

He mumbled into his beard in response.

"Will you tell them that all the wasted time in jail isn't always
wasted time?" I asked. "That you can take advantage of it, too?"

He shook his head. He kept coughing into his sleeve. I kept
burying his responses in a storm of gurgling chest noises. It was nice
to have a visiting prophet in class, but this one was a distinctly
equivocal, noncommittal one. No, he wouldn't say that he'd taken
advantage of his time in jail. Yes, he agreed, he'd been on a journey.
But where had it taken him? I asked. He didn't know. He couldn't
say. He peered into my eyes and then coughed up his lungs, and then
wiped his mouth with his sleeve. Then he lapsed into his normal
mood of sorrowful recollection. I think the teenagers were a bit
spooked by the way he could so easily lose track of himself. I was.

I looked around the room to see if anyone else wanted to weigh in
before I ended class.

"I know what you're saying though, Theo," Laird volunteered. He
has the prep-school instinct of waiting till a teacher falters, and then
stepping in to perform a rescue at just the right time. "Our time is

different now," he said. "So I guess we are maybe going to be a little bit out of the mainstream for a while. Is that what you're saying?"

I said it was.

"And it'll help us to like see the world from a distance?"

"Yes," I said.

"Laird's definitely gonna need to take the long view," said Will. "So are some other people around here," he said, eyeing the very silent Jim Vandriel. "But I guess so do I. Or I will. I guess I'm going away for a while too, so yeah."

It turned out that Richard, the shadow, had some more advice to dispense. Just as the class was ending, a stream of Polonius-like counsel issued from his lips. "Stay away from the screws [the guards, that is]. Try not to get no disciplinary reports written up about you. Try to save your money. Don't let nobody take your shit." We were quiet as the old man dispensed his advice—none of it new—all of it apparently reassuring.

All in all, I think it was a nice way to end the book. With the old man's advice sifting through the air, with no one paying especially close attention since the advice was outdated, elderly person advice, we watched and smiled toward him. It was snowing outside and we could hear the trucks rolling by outside in the snow. They sailed quietly by like a fleet of ships, all of them moving about the same speed, all of them groaning a bit as they made the hard turn in front of the jail, all of them purposeful and busy.

Later, in the stairway leading up to the cell blocks, I asked some of the kids in class how they'd liked the book. "It wasn't so bad," said Frenchie, though I don't think he read all that much of it, "not too bad at all," he clucked.

"We need more time in this class," said Will.

"Yeah, you should have it like a couple of times a day," Laird said.

"We need to be able to get something out of it though," Will said, "something we can like put on our records or something."

CHAPTER ELEVEN

Deeper In

> I subsequently came to understand that in addition to depravation of
> freedom, in addition to forced labor, there is, in a convict's life, one
> more torment, one that is almost more powerful than all the others.
> This is *forced communal existence.*
> —Dostoyevsky, *Memoirs from the House of the Dead,* 1860

JAIL DIARY, MARCH 14, 2000

Now that I've been in jail for four full months, I'm one of the long-
term Woodstock denizens. The average criminal around here slinks
in like a stray cat: he bathes, eats, naps, and barbers himself into a
state of gentlemanly presentability. He stays a few more nights,
watches as much TV as is humanly possible, combs his hair one final
time, and is gone. He's off to another state to face other charges
elsewhere; or he's off to begin a sentence at one of the state prisons,
or he's loosed back out to wander the streets. Sometimes the
criminals come in, sniff the air for a few hours, and leave: it's a
mysterious process—these coming and goings—and since I'm not
part of the decision-making apparatus, I am in the dark as to how it
works. I know that a lot of the criminals here are not full-time
professional outlaws, but rather restaurant cooks and welfare dads
and Jiffy Lube employees. They got in trouble years ago for offenses
they can hardly remember now: check kiting or drunk driving or
fighting with their wives. Then, on probation, they deteriorated.
Some of them went over the edge: crack, Oxycontin, heroin,
whatever they could get their hands on. Now, they're caught in
never-ending battles with their POs. "One more dirty UA and off

you go to the Woodstock lockup," says the PO. Then the judge
warns and then whatever family there is warns and finally the PO
makes a speech: "Don't pee dirty. If you pee dirty you're in trouble.
And by the way, Mr. Johnson, remember what I said about peeing
dirty." At the next opportunity, Mr. Johnson will have turned in a
pee sample that's loaded with pot and crack and cigarettes and
alcohol—and off he goes to Woodstock. When he gets here, he
mopes into the current events room, tail tucked mischievously
between his legs. He finds a chair under the flickering security light,
turns to his neighbors and sighs: "Here on sanctions. Fucking Phil
Damone. Got any shampoo?" Damone is one of the POs in
Brattleboro, a scourge to half the population of the Woodstock
Regional Correctional Facility, and a powerful force for order in
southern Vermont—so it seems, anyway, from here.

"Fucking Damone," the neighbor says back. "You got him too?
Fuck that fucking cocksucker. Fuck Damone. Fuck."

Having been here for four months, I hardly bother to make
friends with these short-termers, these jail tourists. I need people
who're likely to stick around a while. I need intelligent people who're
likely to do the reading in class. I've already lost some of my best
students. Where has Duane Bedell, the farmer from Addison, gone?
He's vanished, but I have no idea where to. No one else seems to
know either. And Steve, the folksinger? Very absent these days.
Apparently, he's on the verge of being shipped to Virginia.

I am on the look-out, then, for the long-termers. But the long-
termers tend to be a nastier kind of criminal with complicated legal
cases that require tons of evidence gathering and innumerable status
conferences in court. I'm not sure I want those people in class.

I'm personally much more interested in the nicer kind of criminal:
the people who have families, who belong to a particular place, and
are possibly capable of regret. People like this turn up regularly—
about once a week. They arrive in the current events class stunned,
sometimes swaying uncertainly in the air, sometimes trembling as
they seat themselves and perspiring as the other inmates stare. A few
weeks ago, a fellow named Dave slunk into the current events room
on the heels of the other felons: orderly mustache, cobalt blue

sweater—made for him by his wife, as it turned out—deep-set dark eyes. He's a carpenter, owns his own business, and smiles sweetly when he talks about his kids. I've talked to him a few times in the library. It seems he's had a drinking problem for many years. It seems he's lately been out of work. It seems he's taken to hanging out with his daughter's friends and that recently he made a bad mistake. "I caressed a fifteen-year-old girl at one of my daughter's parties," he said. This is his second such offense, the first one having taken place in '92. He could be going away for ten years now, maybe twenty. He doesn't weep or plead for sympathy—in fact he strives for direct, stand-up-guy self-criticism—but the other inmates are openly disgusted by him, and the whole experience of being charged and sent off to jail is trying his soul, as he says piously. In fact, the soul and its owner have waived their right to a trial since Dave has accepted a plea bargain. The soul is guilty, it seems. It's now being shriven here in jail. No one talks to him. His wife and kids will have nothing to do with him. His business is gone. Every day his voice gets thinner, his face paler. Every day his gaze seems a little more lost. Having him in class is like watching someone succumb to a ferocious case of Alzheimer's—a sturdy being is falling apart before my eyes— but what can I do? Nothing. I try to make his day a little brighter by teaching well. Otherwise, I don't say much.

Most of the jail's new arrivals aren't as straightforward and self-aware as Dave is. They are garden-variety losers and bums who actively repel sympathy. But people like Dave, people who've lately been brought low by the world, have kept me interested in coming to jail every day. They're like frazzled soldiers who've blundered in from the battlefield. They don't quite know if the worst is over yet— they've survived the shock of an arrest, an arraignment, some initial press, some bargaining with the lawyers—but what else is looming in the future? They don't have a clue. Neither do I.

Toward the middle of March, Dave was shipped away to another jail. Laird's presence, which had attracted a lot of students to class initially, wasn't the draw it had once been. The inmates had gotten all the dirty details from him that he was going to divulge, and now they were leaving him to his own devices. His own interests tended toward comic books and *Star Wars* and Harry Potter. He often brought his own reading material to class during this time and conspicuously lost himself in it. I let him be. Emmons had been let go on bail. I thought I'd never see him again, though as it turned out, he was back before the end of the month. Will Emerson, the purple-haired punk who'd robbed a Sunoco station, wasn't always the most faithful reader of my assignments. Often, he came to class with nothing new to say.

In March, the days seemed awfully long to me, though as a part-timer, I was only in jail for four or five hours at a time. In my boredom, I started to miss the talkative, semirepentant people like Dave, the carpenter, and Duane, the farmer from Addison. I'd felt a connection with those inmates, especially with Duane. I'd felt some of his indignation, some of his smallness in the massive vice grip of the system, and of course his longing to get back to his farm. Though he was accused of a more hideous crime than the one he admitted to me, he'd spoken eloquently, I thought, about his life as the chief hired man on a large family farm. He'd also acknowledged being a lout toward his spouse; he'd been irascible and had smoked too much pot and had let himself get drunk a few too many times. His father had been the same way, he said, with his mom, though back then there hadn't been the pot. Anyway, he'd given me a colorful, and, I thought, a true picture of his life in Addison. I wanted more of that kind of connection with the inmates. I wanted to know how they had once lived out there in the Vermont countryside (on a farm? beneath a bridge? in a trailer? in an apartment?) and what they had lost when they were taken away.

Scott French came on like a guy who was itching to tell me his secrets. In the hallways and in current events, he winked at me. He muttered. He whispered into his friends' ears while keeping his eyes fastened on mine. Once, halfway through March, he tapped me politely on the shoulder as I was reading the newspaper. He leaned over and burbled into my ear: "You want to know what Laird does upstairs? You do?" he asked. "You should spend a few days with me up in the block. You want to know what we really do up there? Get yourself arrested and come on up," he suggested. Then he winked: "We'll make a man out of you, Theo. If you want."

After that conversation, I made an appointment with Frenchie. He and his friend, Chubba, a dazed druggie from Brattleboro, appeared in the doorway at the appointed time. Chubba obligingly locked the door, while Frenchie eased his bottom onto the table in front of my chair.

"How long do you think you'll be in jail?" I asked him.

"Eighty years," he said, "thirty-five to eighty, or thereabouts." I took a deep breath. He was in his early twenties. It was the kidnapping charge that was going to kill him, he said. But the girl had wanted to come with him, he insisted. "I ain't no fuckin' kidnapper, dude," he promised, shaking his head. I wanted to agree with him. He was a pudgy, blank-eyed, short kid who wore his hair done up in a pompadour. He seemed too weak, too sleazy, too lacking in initiative to do anything really harmful. Later, I found out that he'd held a sixteen-year-old runaway hostage in his car and had held her in various apartments around the state. He was accused of beating the runaway and forcing her to perform oral and anal sex. In Newport, Vermont, on the Canadian border, he'd finally fallen asleep, at which point the girl escaped. "So after about an hour of waiting," she wrote in her affidavit, "I slowly got up and sat down on the coffee table to put my shoes on. I then went out the door, went to the car, and grabbed my stuff. I kept looking over my shoulders to make sure he wasn't going to get me. I then went up Central Street and proceeded to the police station to turn myself in." It was late on the afternoon of April 14, 1999.

Frenchie had his rap down: "Is it kidnapping if the girl waits for you outside the bathroom at Wal-Mart? They have that on videotape. Is it kidnapping if she follows you out from a store and gets in your car while you're already in it? They have that on tape." His lawyer was too lazy to go out and find the tape. Anyway, the girl was a lying little bitch. She wasn't kidnapped and if she was raped it was only in a technical, legal sense since she was below the age of consent when he had had sex with her. If I had any doubts, I could ask Chubba, his buddy, about her willingness. Chubba had been there the whole time, and had seen just how victimized this poor little bitch had been. She was the violent one, not Frenchie. She had the sex problem, not Frenchie. Chubba grinned and gave me a sleepy, babyish nod.

I didn't hold out much hope for Frenchie as a student because he made a point of ignoring me during class and he often left the readings I gave him on the library table. I wanted to hear more, however, about his life on the outside. He spoke in suggestive, vaguely ominous platitudes about the life he'd lead as a free teenage troublemaker-businessman in southern Vermont. He was in the sales business, he said. The trick in sales was to buy low, get high, and sell. Or sometimes it was to buy a girl, get her high, and sell her. The trick was to figure out how to keep your merchandise alive and well for as long possible. It wasn't like he was in the frozen foods business or anything where you could just store whatever you wanted to sell in the back of a truck.

When I pressed him on how exactly he made his money, he asked me if I'd ever been to the bus station in White River Junction. What about the truck stop in Wells River? Yes, I'd been there, too. Did I ever guess that sometimes people went to the bus station for reasons other than taking a bus?

"No, not really." He sighed. Did I ever guess that sometimes truckers needed a little company on the road? Did I hang out in Bellows Falls much? Springfield? Hinsdale? He told me to think of him as a traveling salesman. Those were the places he traveled to on business. He had been accused by a prosecutor, he said, of stalking his victims in certain areas near the bus station in White River Junction, and near the liquor stores in Brattleboro. But he never needed to stalk anyone. He just hung out on Eliot Street near the grocery store and in the Harmony parking lot in Brattleboro; people came to him, not the other way around. He wasn't a hunter; he didn't snatch his living from the street. He was a farmer. He was an employee of the land. His job was to look after the fresh little things coming up.

Frenchie came to class a few more times early with Chubba in tow. He liked to bring his motorcycle magazines and study them as I asked him questions. A lot of the stories he told seemed frankly incredible to me, but the settings emitted the flavor of places that had once, apparently, been quite real to him. So I liked to listen to him for his grasp of the geography around the Connecticut River Valley in which he once scratched out a living. There was an earnestness in some of the stories and an instructive undercurrent to them. He wanted me to see how easy everything had been for him, and could be for me, too, if I chose to learn from him. After a while, it began to feel like he was giving me career advice.

I heard from him about an old apartment building next to the railroad tracks just south of White River Junction where a mom and her two teenage daughters made a living selling heroin. A room off the kitchen had gone up in flames one night and Frenchie had had to douse the place

with fire extinguisher foam. The mom had a nice car and a home enter-
tainment center. But she had never been able to get the fire smell from her
house: it reeked of cooked sofa cushions and charcoal. That's one of the
places Frenchie had met his girlfriends. From there, he'd recruited them
into his business.

I also heard about a trailer up on a frozen dirt road in the Northeast
Kingdom in which a hermit had shot himself with a hunting rifle. Only
Frenchie and a few of his friends knew of the death. How was that? News
got around. A birdie told him. He had cousins all over the place. He and
his friends had borrowed the man's television and his winter clothing. The
man was, for all Frenchie knew, still there—probably very cold by now,
certainly bored without his TV.

In Brattleboro, somewhere off of Canal Street, in the basement of an
apartment house, there was a former laundry room, now a storage vault,
that overflowed with electronics: DVD players, Gameboys, VCRs, car
stereos. It was becoming a regular community depot. People left things
there when they were in a hurry to leave things somewhere and picked
stuff up when they needed new stuff. Of course, you had to have a key and
had to know how to get down there.

I heard about a farmhouse somewhere not far from Springfield, Vermont, in which two old grannies lay in their beds all day long insensate,
nearly dead. They could hear Frenchie arrive and they could hear him stalking through their house, but they never raised a fuss. He assumed that they
were dying. He visited them frequently, knocking on the door and smiling
like a grandson with tins full of cookies. He prowled around the place, stealing curtains, antique clocks, a painting of a farmhouse, and a clock radio.
Once he ate a meal in the kitchen. Another time, he sat down to watch
some TV with the old ladies and had, mostly by himself, a conversation.

When Frenchie told his stories, he spoke in his flat, affectless voice,
inclining his head gently to the left and gently to the right, rarely looking
me in the eye.

In his stories, he appeared as a black-hearted traveler, a reaper, who
went around casting his hooded eye at old people, picking at corpses, and
preying on little girls. Now, as a result, he was in possession of an instinc-
tive, animalish memory for the lay of the land. If I wanted to know how

things really were in the world, if I wanted to see the real conditions of real life, with all the natural gore exposed, I'd have to ask him to show me.

"What about the other kids in the jail?" I asked finally. He'd been talking for three days about life on the outside to me. I'd listened. Wasn't he going to bring some of the kids from upstairs down into class?

I was interested in one kid in particular named Jim Vandriel. Frenchie did persuade him to come to class a few times, and then he came a few times on his own, so some of his recruiting did actually work.

I knew about Vandriel because he was Laird's cellmate and because his case had been written about in the *Rutland Herald*. He seemed like a bright, thoughtful kid. At least he seemed this way from a distance. And it seemed to me as though the kid could probably use some help.

In the *Rutland Herald,* Jim was James Vandriel, eighteen, of West Rutland, charged with first-degree murder. He and a friend had killed the owner of a tattoo parlor and head shop. I knew from newspaper reports that the murder had occurred in November 1997, that the victim's name was Dwayne Bernier, and that Vandriel's friend was thought by police to have been the leader of the two. Vandriel himself was said to be cooperating with the state's attorney.

At the time of the crime, Vandriel had been sixteen and his accomplice, a seemingly well-behaved old expert in karate named Eric Marallo, had been seventeen. In the summer of 1999, the police, acting on a tip, arrested Eric, and soon after that, arrested and brought charges against Vandriel.

In person, Jimmy had the sunken face and empty eyes of a weary, time-oppressed prisoner. He'd been in for about six months when I first met him but seemed as though he'd been locked up since grade school. His black hair hung in a damp curtain around his shoulders. He spoke in a voice so quiet that it could be heard only if you happened to be sitting with your chair pressed up against his. He wore a plaid golfer's cap to school, and liked to devour the daily edition of the *Rutland Herald* off in his private corner of the basement.

Though it hadn't been reported in the paper, the other inmates seemed to know that Bernier had been stabbed in the face with a hunting knife, that his eyes had been penetrated with a drill bit, and that after his death, he had been bludgeoned with a stool. Laird and Will and Frenchie seemed to agree that Vandriel had been a witness to these events, but not the prime mover behind them. He had emerged from the tattooist's shop splattered in blood, and sick to the point of dizziness.

The story coming from Vandriel and his friends seemed to describe a conscience-wracked kid who'd seen a bad thing, had kept quiet, but was stepping up to take responsibility now. In this version, he and his friend Eric had once been wild, naive kids who had wanted to get the hell out of Rutland and meant to do it by stealing money and salable goods. They wanted to fix up Eric's car or, failing that, they wanted bus tickets for Arizona. They had chosen the tattooist's shop, the Dragon's Leyr, as a target because, unlike the other head shops in Rutland County, it wasn't downtown but hidden away in the woods in East Wallingford, five miles south of Rutland. They felt they could get away with whatever they had to get away with as long as they were carrying out the operation way off in a stand of pine forest in East Wallingford. It happened that that was where Bernier had his shop.

According to Laird, once Bernier was dead, Vandriel had watched Marallo search through the victim's bloody pockets and had watched him remove a pulp of stained bills. He had watched as Marallo wiped down the counters in the tattoo shop with his shirt sleeve and had helped burn the clothing they were wearing in his parent's woodstove a few hours after the crime. There had also been a fourteen-year-old kid present at the scene of the crime—he was a good kid and didn't deserve to have his life ruined over his part in the whole thing, which was insignificant. Because Eric did a good job of keeping everyone in fear, and also because of the cops' persistent laziness, the crime had gone unsolved for two long years. During this time, Jimmy had gotten a regular job at a convenience store and was beginning to think about college.

In other versions of the story—when it was told by the inmates who'd met up with Marallo in the Rutland jail, or who had known him out in the street—it was Vandriel who'd been the assailant and Marallo who'd watched the attack in shock. In those versions, Marallo had tried to intercede and had been stabbed (by accident) for his efforts. Vandriel had held the victim down after he fell and had told him to shut up as he pleaded for his life. He had taken to the victim with a drill bit and a hunting knife after his death.

In still other versions of the tale, however, the fourteen-year-old had been actively involved in the plan to kill Bernier. He hadn't taken part in the attack, but he'd known it was going to happen, had watched it happen, and had kept it a secret for two years. He was getting off scot-free.

Some of the inmates were predictably incensed about that. They themselves were being charged as accessories to crimes less serious than murder and were looking at long sentences for having waited in cars and for having helped after the fact. What happened to equal justice, to justice for all?

On one occasion in the current events class, Vandriel tried to put the rumors to rest. He was going to take a plea, he said, but it wasn't the real truth he was pleading to. Only he and Marallo knew what that truth was. Marallo was a liar. The fourteen-year-old was free and deserved to remain free. So Vandriel, out of the generosity of his heart, was going to be taking a fall. That was all we needed to know. It seemed like a vaguely plausible story to me, if I allowed for the customary self-ennobling that was common in jail, but then the other rumors—rumors that turned out to be false—had had a similar ring, at least in my ears.

Of all the kids in jail school, I had the most confidence in Will Emerson. His hair was dyed a dark, shining purple when he first came into jail. Laird's was dyed a deep orange-cidery shade. When they sat together at the current events table, before the dye faded, they lent the room a pretty, autumnal hue. Will had been kicked out of high school in 1997 and had been living in Springfield, Vermont, occasionally, and on the road, occasionally, since then. He was twenty-one.

In jail, Will was a good friend to Laird, and did not make a big deal out of Laird's having murdered his mom. When the other prisoners gaped at Laird, or spoke loudly in favor of the death penalty, Will was instantly forgiving. "If I was on your jury, I'd think you did it," he said to Laird one day during the current events class. "Just from the way you are, I guess, your way of reacting. But that doesn't mean I think you're a bad person or anything." Laird didn't notice the compliment. He was shocked to discover that he appeared guilty, even to the other prisoners, who, he presumed, wouldn't be on the lookout for guilt.

Will was full of practical advice on how to live in the bombed-out, crumbling world that Laird had foreseen, but not actually visited in person. His first lesson was that, on arriving in a new town, or a friendly old one, for that matter, it was a good idea to camp in the vicinity of a box store: an Ames or a Wal-mart or a Target. The security at enormous stores like that was lousy, the merchandise could be resold easily, and big corporate chain stores expected to be burglarized, so there was no sense in *not* stealing from them. They made up for the lost revenue by charging regular customers a little extra with every purchase. Plus, they had insurance. Plus, they could go bankrupt and have all of their debts forgiven. All the laws and bylaws, in short, favored them. The first time I heard this theory of life, I responded with a speech of my own to the students who were present in class: if people like Will didn't go around stealing things all the time, I said, the price of stuff wouldn't be what it was. It was Will's fault that prices were artificially high. He gave me a sympathetic smile and nodded his head in amusement as I talked, as if he was surprised that I could be, in this day and age, quite that naive. Things didn't work that way, he explained in a fake rueful voice, grinning and pursing his lips. "Sorry, dude, to bring the news," he said. "I'm in jail now. There's less crime out there, right? Are things any cheaper out there? Do you think Mr. Ames or Mr. Wal-Mart is suddenly going to cut you a deal? I don't think so."

I shrugged. "Maybe," I said. There were other criminals listening who giggled at my stupidity. The consensus of the class was that you had to keep the box stores in check somehow, otherwise they'd swallow every-thing. Robbery was the nicest, cleanest way to do it.

Will's second lesson was that Vermont, despite its faults, was an excel-lent market for drugs. There were plenty of customers and, comparatively speaking, few dealers. Anyone with a tiny bit of initiative could drive down the highway to Springfield, Massachusetts, or Hartford, Connecti-cut, or New York City and return with $10,000 worth of pot in seven hours. It sort of made other jobs less attractive.

I first started to get to know Will the day I had the students write paragraph-long descriptions of their hometowns. They were supposed to write for fifteen minutes and then read their paragraphs out loud during the remaining forty-five. In his essay, Will's Springfield was drawn up as a sterile, futureless city where the teenagers got away, literally, with murder. The police were apparently too dumb to figure out what was happening, but all the teenagers knew that a certain Jen had been raped and murdered by a certain Adam. The kids laughed about what an idiot Adam was, and what bigger idiots the police were. Will had taken advantage of the general permissiveness to make Springfield into the seat of a bustling drug-dealing business. He had also done everything he could to make it the shoplifting capital of southern Vermont. Somehow the merchants there were duller or more indifferent or more intimidated than merchants elsewhere in the world, it seemed. He had no explanation for it.

In Will's essay, and afterward in our discussions about Springfield, he introduced himself as the director of a small underground economy. He brokered pills and pot, and swapped these for cash and different kinds of pills. Because guns came with the territory, sometimes he bought and sold guns. According to his paragraph-long essay, he was a Robin Hood—his phrase—for the younger teenagers who were just learning to get by on their own. Those who were in want could apply to Will and he would supply. The kids had apparently stitched together a Sherwood Forest from patches of the local geography: a deserted mill building, the backyard of an ex-factory, an abandoned house, and, naturally, the school parking lot. These places belonged exclusively to the teenagers. Over time, the kids' Springfield-preserve had become an asylum for the underaged, the daring, and the ambitious criminals-to-be of the upper Connecticut River Valley.

Later, after class, I asked Will to tell me more about his hometown. Before his eighteenth birthday, he said, before he was subject to adult penalties, and before he cared about getting into trouble, he had involved the merchants of the town in a sprawling game of cowboys and Indians. It was a sort of perpetual hide-and-seek contest that was designed expressly for people like him: kids with no money and lots of impish courage. In fact, it *was* he who designed it. He played as much as he could, and always for the love of the game, rather than for the products that he spirited away in the pockets of his trench coat and cargo pants. Later on, as he got older and developed a record with the police, every outing subjected him to greater and more enduring adult-sized penalties. So the game, of its own accord, refined itself into an extreme sport. It involved fleeing at high speeds on foot, on skateboards, on bikes, and, finally, by car. There was a tremendous rush to be had when you leaped from the grasp of a rent-a-cop, and, of course, a bigger rush still when you left the real cops befuddled and yelling into dark ravines.

Over the past few years, Will told me, he had developed a fondness for mental contests: chess matches played in the maze-like floor plans of giant warehouse stores. When it came to matching wits, Will always won. Always.

Well, he won most of the time anyway. One of his favorite games was played like this: He liked to stroll along at the bottom of a wall of products, ogling them, fingering them, climbing the shelves sometimes in order to reach expensive things, and, of course, eyeing the security guard. Eventually, someone—a man in a tie, a woman in a store apron—would collar him and drag him to an office. The security guard would find, to his embarrassment, that Will's pockets were empty, that the store had made a mistake and insulted the integrity of a decent customer-schoolboy. Meanwhile, Will's friend would have made away with pounds and pounds of electronic equipment, with CDs, with Christmasy baubles and videocassettes, and candy, and dozens of other things that happened to fall into his pockets.

On other occasions, Will's friend would be the decoy and he would be the thief. To show who was cleverer than whom, Will liked to make off with the personal items of the employees: their time cards, their coats, their sunglasses. Sometimes, days later, he'd return the stuff he'd taken. He'd show up in the store and merchandise and funny hats would miraculously alight on the shelves. Then, just to honor the spirit of the game, he'd take something else.

After a while of listening to these stories, I got the point: in a factory town that had given up the ghost a generation ago the only creative thing to do was to make trouble. I didn't believe it. Three-quarters of his high school classmates had made legal, sensible escapes and most of those who remained didn't bide their time by doing crimes. Plus, Springfield wasn't as forsaken as he made it out to be. At least in his family, it seemed, there had been computers and books and trips to the nearby mountains. But Will didn't want to talk about the distant past. He preferred to talk instead about how he had married two of his favorite things, crime and sport, into one high-stakes adventure game.

"If doing crimes is your extreme sport, why don't you just turn up the notch a bit on a regular extreme sport," I asked, finally. He could have decided, it seemed to me, to do a rock climb without a rope, or to surf handrails on his skateboard, or to leap into rivers from bridge railings.

"I do all that. It's not quite the same thing as doing crimes," he said. Nothing was quite as exciting for him as getting away with a crime.

During his first two months in jail, he elaborated almost obsessively on his original paragraph-long essay. He knew I would listen, and so he volunteered, especially when other people were talking about their former lives, to describe the freedoms he had enjoyed as a lawless little kid. On and on the stories went. They clouded and mingled in my head, as I'm sure they had in his.

The last burglary he could remember doing was the time, during the previous summer, when he walked out of a store with a canoe on his head. He wanted to go fishing, he told us, the store had the canoe, he took it, he had a wonderful time, and he meant to bring it back. Unfortunately, winter had sneaked up on him and though he had had definite plans to go bring the canoe back, at least to the delivery entrance of the store, he'd been arrested before he could carry through with them.

The more Will talked about his boyhood in Springfield, the more I wondered about his most recent crime: an armed robbery at a truck stop off of I-91. Finally, after he'd been talking and bragging enough to make me tired of his stories, I asked him directly. "What was the idea with the gun and the robbery Will? Tell me about that," I said. He sighed and smiled his mischievous, naughty-boy smile. The story really began, he said, when he decided to move to Florida.

He had been waiting for his probation to expire, and when it did, he meant to go south, basically forever. He might enroll in a community college down there, might publish his 'zine, and might just vanish into an inaccessible swamp. He would read his favorite books and lie on the floor of a flat-bottom boat; he would drive it off into the ocean every once in a while, meet a connection, and return with product.

On the Saturday night after Christmas in 1999, Will and his friend Rodney drove to Benny's Sunoco. It was 3:30 AM. The store's safe and cash register were supposed to be crammed with holiday money. The plan was for Rodney, who thought of himself as an urban, gangster-rap kid, to hold the gun on the clerk, while Will would empty the till and raid the safe. Since Will's brother had worked at Benny's, the thieves had some inside information. For instance, the safe, which usually contained about $5,000, was never locked. The security camera, which was supposed to deter or at least record a robbery, never worked. The clerk carried a gun, but would never use it. Actually, they weren't certain about that. They weren't certain about anything, really. The surest thing about the plan was the store's location: an empty stretch of road outside of the empty town of Chester, Vermont, five miles north of Springfield. Nothing ever stirred in Chester, but at 3:30 AM, in the middle of winter, Chester might as well have been at the bottom of a frozen lake. The only people who would be about were the ancient Quebecois lumber haulers who stopped at the truck stop for coffee and gas. Will knew that they could be watched and avoided. He was sure he'd have at least several minutes of privacy in which to remove the money, apologize to the clerk, and scoot away in the getaway car. The police, for their part, would have to scramble up to Chester from Springfield. They would come flashing and sirening onto the scene just as Will was settling down in his apartment to count the money.

It was an excellent plan, Will assumed. In the execution, however, everything fell apart. Rodney, it turned out, was not much of a robber. At the last minute, he decided he didn't want to hold the gun. He didn't even want to go in the store. He said he'd wait outside in the car, but in fact he didn't wait. He took off. A wise decision as he avoided a criminal charge in this way. Inside the store, the safe was locked, contrary to rumor, and when Will had the clerk open the register, there were only forty dollars inside, which Will decided against taking, on the theory that if he took nothing, and hurt no one, the police might decide that the incident was a wash. When Will came out, he had the .38 Special in his pocket but no money and no getaway car. The police were on their way. He hid in the woods, having nowhere else to go, and watched as the cops pulled in. He nearly froze to death in his hiding spot because he was wearing only a sweatshirt. Fortunately it was not such a cold night after all. The next morning, back in Springfield, his mother overheard him arguing with Rodney. The two of them were discussing Rodney's ungangsterish behavior of the night before. Will's mom telephoned the police to report that she suspected her son of having committed a robbery. A few days later, Rodney was picked up and taken in for questioning. Evidently, for reasons Will couldn't understand, he agreed to help the police. They asked Rodney to wear a wire, and to drive Will to a spot in the woods where the gun and some clothing had been stashed. He agreed. The last Will saw of him, he was watching from his car as the police took Will into custody.

This was Will's third felony, which meant that he now had three strikes against him. In theory, because the third felony was a violent one, he had struck out. He had to decide if he would take a plea or go to trial. At trial, he could conceivably get thirty years. With a plea agreement, he might get seven to fifteen.

To the other prisoners, the crime was a comedy. Everyone had a good belly laugh over his mistakes. He chose an idiot-bonehead accomplice, didn't manage to make off with even a candy bar, and didn't really manage to make off at all, since his buddy abandoned him at the gas pumps. And then there was the clerk. Will made the mistake of telling everyone that he had been so frightened during the crime that he lost control of his bowels. He left a trail of excrement on the linoleum gas station floor. *Too fucking funny!* said the other prisoners. The next morning, his mom turned him in, and the day after that, his friend turned him in, and now he was going to be in jail for a good long time. Will had told everyone the story and everyone thought it was *too fucking funny!* The other prisoners patted their bellies and shook their heads when someone brought it up. "Gonna have to suck it up," said one middle-aged codger when Will first told the story. "Oh boy, are you going to have to suck it up. Three strikes and you're out! Life, man! Welcome to your life!" The prisoner was one of those graying, decrepit jailbirds whose alcoholism had been putting him in jail every few months for decades. He looked at Will through his watery eyes, shook his head in slow admiration and began to giggle and cough and cry. He lost control of his breathing after a moment and had to be pounded on the back. Eventually he collapsed in a puddle on the library table. I couldn't tell if he was shedding tears of happiness or sickness or was just emitting extra water from his eyes. I was laughing a little bit, too, feeling the silly hopelessness of it all. When the drunk recovered himself, he wanted Will to tell the story of the clerk and the vanishing accomplice over again because one of his buddies was on his way to join us and had missed the best parts. Because Will was an obliging, genial kid, he shrugged his shoulders. When the drunk's friend turned up, Will started talking.

If Will had been able to shut himself up a bit more often, his time in jail might have unfolded in the orderly, systematic, industrial way that time is supposed to unfold in jail. You wait, you get sentenced, eventually you enter a rehab program, you come up for parole, and, provided you're not a monster, they eventually give it to you. But Will wanted to have no business with systems. He loved airing his views, especially if there was a chance of causing a stir, and it didn't matter to him that too much talking in jail always prolongs sentences and always arouses the contempt of whoever's listening.

Most prisoners allow their brains to relax into a mushy stew of inattention and depression after a few weeks. I admired Will for his refusal to allow himself to degenerate like that. He wanted to be noticed, and I took it as a measure of his mixed-up sadness and pride that he made a spectacle of himself, boasting and refusing to be sorry for anything, even as he knew that he was making his future much tougher that way.

It wasn't hard for me to imagine him carrying on in the same vein before a judge, thereby inviting the judge to sentence him to decades in jail. I wanted to get through to him somehow before that happened. I wanted to persuade him to take some interest in his future, and to steer himself away from the worst the system could dole out.

Though he was peaceable enough discussing *Huck Finn* in the library, he almost got himself expelled from the current events class one day in early February. He'd been sassing Jim all along and had crossed the line one too many times. Through a quirk in the rules, an expulsion from Jim's class would have meant his being barred from the school altogether. Jim mentioned this to me and the next day, I tried to talk Will into an apology. What will you do if you don't come down here during the day? I asked. Where do you think you'll go?

"The day room, maybe," he said, or maybe to his cell. Or he'd go to outdoor rec more often. Maybe he'd just meditate on his bunk. So far, he said, he hadn't found the Woodstock jail to be punitive at all. It had just been dull and pointless. He was ready for a change in the routine. He wanted to see what they might have in store for him: the hole, early lock-in, no canteen privileges. "What else can they do? I mean, I look at the big picture, I'm at the very beginning of something, of a big turn in my life. It could be jail, it could be a trial, it could be escape or acquittal or who knows what it'll be. I'm standing just before the curve. And here I go. That's my attitude. So a little time in the hole or whatever—a little bit of getting kicked out of school. That's not really going to bother me. I'm standing right before the big bend in the road, you know?" I groaned. I could see where we were headed. He went on: "Fine. I can sleep fourteen hours a day. That's more than half my total sentence right there." He looked over the titles of the books on the library shelves and smiled. He said that he might just find a way out of jail somehow and go live in Florida, which, in his experience, was practically a giant refugee camp for fugitives. It was a more lawless place than any place he'd been to in his life. *That* would change him.

I groaned again. But at least we were having a reasoned, quiet discussion in which he was outlining his views. I took some comfort in that and assumed that, like any twenty-year-old kid, his views might be changed. He needed perhaps a good reason to change them, and I hoped that my class might help in supplying that.

Will and Laird were the ones I knew best, but there were lots of other kids in the Woodstock jail whose cases I'd been following in the news. Many of them were like Will in that they refused to acknowledge they'd been fazed by their arrests. They refused to acknowledge even that living in jail was going to change their lives all that much. They seemed well prepared to carry on their battle against authority, and to me that opened up a vision of ever-narrowing cages, of futile self-punishment.

Some of the kids seemed friendly and promising enough. There was Steve, the folksinger guy, about whom I knew little because he rarely came to class. I knew he could sing well. And there was Darling Turtle. He began drifting back into the classroom in March, in spite of my banishment. His pimples had expanded across his neck and forehead, but he was otherwise the same quiet, gangly kid. Perhaps he wasn't so unpromising after all. Anyway, I declined to kick him out a second time.

Elsewhere in the jail, lurking in the cafeteria, or slumping in the hallways, there were many others: a handsome kid from Brattleboro who had slashed at his girlfriend with a razor. A college kid who had shot his friend to death by accident. A nineteen-year-old drunk driver who had crashed his car into his friend's car and had hurried from the scene as the friend slowly bled to death.

Every week or so the jail gathered in bewildered and benumbed survivors of crimes like this. Every week the newspapers wrote articles that

induced similar feelings—numbed indifference—in the newspaper readers around the current events class.

I decided that a meaningful class in jail should offer its students meaningful credit. As it was, I wasn't even giving out grades, much less college
credit in class. I was scarcely taking attendance. There was a stick at my dis-
posal—expulsion from the jail school (I didn't want to use it)—and no car-
rots. I sent a proposal to the Community College of Vermont: I would
recruit a roster of experts in the humanities. The class would be a sort of
Introduction to Western Literature with a focus on the struggle to build a
liberal society (we would read something from Thomas Paine, some of *The
Autobiography of Thomas Jefferson*, Lincoln's speeches, and chapters from
Frederick Douglass, among other things). I talked to a soon-to-be-retired
professor at Dartmouth who agreed to come by and lecture. I thought I
would ask an uncle of mine, also a professor, to come by and lecture.

Before hearing back from CCV, I told the inmates about my plan.

I poured out the details as I stood in a stairwell, surrounded by a small
crowd of students, waiting to be admitted to the school.

"Do it," urged Laird. "You gotta do it." He said his dad would come
by to help. He offered some other names. When I mentioned college
credit—free college credit—the ears of the younger kids pricked up. They
turned their heads smartly toward me.

As I waited for CCV to write back, the idea developed in my head. I
knew in a general way that the jails in Vermont were filling up with young
people. I knew that more high school kids were in jail in Vermont now
than ever before in the state's history. I also knew that the universities were
churning out unemployed and underemployed Ph.D.s. Could there be a
University Within Walls, a Teach for Incarcerated America? Why not?

I put the idea to the inmates in class. They loved it. "Bring on those
graduate students," they said. They were of course especially keen to have
women student teachers.

I also told my regular students during this time that I'd been taking
notes about their conversations. In addition, I said, I had been poking
around into the details of their crimes. Yes, behind their backs; yes, without
their permission. When I went home at night, I had been writing down
what I learned. On my computer, a narrative with characters and dialogue
and a particular point of view—mine—was taking shape. I said that writ-

ing about the jail was making my experience real. It made our exchanges in class linger in my mind, made me see the funniness and sadness of our dull county lock-up, and forced me into close scrutiny of every new character who turned up. The literature we were reading was doing the same thing, but in a different way. I hoped an interesting book would result.

The inmates were pleased by the news. Will looked at Laird. Laird looked at Will. They smiled. "We knew it," they said at once. Did I want their help? Bill Stanard could help me, Laird volunteered instantly. Laird's family had a lot of connections in the publishing world. I gave him a skeptical look, not because of the unlikeliness of the claim but because I was skeptical of everything Laird said.

Will was all for a book. Will was for anything in which he could have a leading role. Would he actually have a leading role? he wondered. Yes, he would, I assured him.

Actually, he said, his role in my book didn't matter all that much because he wanted to write his own book; in fact he was already writing his own book. It was going to be about the way that the government was selling young people down the river; it would call those young people to arms. It was going to be a sort of manifesto for the new youth movement. Stylistically, it would resemble the *Anarchist's Cook Book,* being a scattered collection of explosive street wisdom. From a literary point of view, it would be more like *Fear and Loathing in Las Vegas,* with gonzo traveling and daring and drug experiences written into every page. He already had about 200 pages of it in his cell. The whole thing was scribbled into piles of blue notebooks. His eyes found Laird's. "You've seen my notebooks, right?" he asked.

Laird nodded. "So am I writing a book," Laird chipped in. "Me and my dad are writing one together. It's about all this," he said, gesturing vaguely over his shoulder as if waving at the past few months.

And Darling? Darling also had a memoir afoot; it was spiced with poetry and philosophical ruminations and recollections of his childhood. He wasn't going to let anyone see it, though.

Suddenly, we were a society of authors. Of course we were writing books. What else were we going to do with all this time on our hands and all this rich, unexploited literary material at our feet? What thoughtful person wouldn't be turning the situation to advantage? There was fun and profit in writing a book after all, not to mention a chance to wrench the world around to our points of view.

When the news of our literary ambitions was out in the open, we were quiet for a few moments. We didn't know enough about writerly shop talk to launch ourselves into a round of professionals' gossip. The time was right but we didn't know what to say. I personally did not feel like pointing out the obvious: not one of us had ever published so much as a single word. We had scarcely wanted to until lately. I had had two or three opinion pieces rejected by op-ed editors at the *Chronicle of Higher Education*. I had tried once to publish an article about the Tour de France but my major point—I'm not too bothered if they all take drugs—did not manage to interest any of the publications to whom I sent my essay. I didn't want to acknowledge it, particularly not in public, but my writing career had petered out after those efforts.

The students had less experience than I did. They hardly read before jail; still less had they written.

There was so little reality to our fantasy that talking about it was as easy as dreaming.

"Make sure you put in how little we learn in jail school," Will suggested as he nodded at the bookshelves and the dry erase board. "Make sure to put in how fucking bored we are in here. Will you put that in?" I agreed to put that in.

He was putting quite a bit in his manuscript about boredom; the whole thing, he said, was a sort of ode to boredom.

"Make sure to put in how Rhino and Slash are the real teachers around here," Laird urged. I agreed that I would.

"What are you putting in your book, Laird?" I asked.

"Everything," he said. "I'm putting in my whole story. I'm putting in everything that really happened at home, in my family. It's going to be for kids like me. And for parents too."

"Good," I said. "Excellent. I can't wait to read it." I never heard another word about it. I'm still waiting though and still vaguely optimistic.

In the three weeks following the end of *Huck Finn*, my class continued to pursue the theme of children leaving families, and children at large on the American continent. We read about the descendants of Huck in Hemingway and in Ray Carver. We read a Flannery O'Connor story about a family lost and then found in the wilderness called "A Good Man Is Hard to Find." We read the James Baldwin story "Sonny's Blues"; to my disappointment, the students didn't read it well. I made all the old points—the protective family, the salvation of the blues, the troubles that were passed down from father to son and son to father. Since no one had read the story, the students stared at me blankly. I read passages out loud to them and they submitted to my "teaching." I needed some new material.

My instinct was for something more directly relevant to the lives of the contemporary down and out: the druggies and wanderers and starry-eyed hipsters like Emerson. I wanted material that would catch my students where they lived. It had to address what was happening in their lives frankly and without flinching. I didn't want anything that was too obviously about life behind bars. I considered and rejected the idea of any novel set in jail. The inmates generally felt they knew all there was to know about life behind bars anyway. At that time, I was interested in writing that would help us understand the appeal of losing control. I wanted to find narrative prose that would permit us to look calmly at moments of great danger. I liked the idea of a slow voyage into violence.

JAIL DIARY, MARCH 20, 2000

Today, a story about descent. "A Distant Episode" is about a haughty Westerner who gets swallowed up by the East. It's a classic Paul Bowles story: frightening, musical, and mean. I made everyone give exacting attention to a sequence in which the main character, a professor, stands in the darkness at the top of an escarpment in the desert. He's been lead through the stinking suburbs of a dingy city somewhere in North Africa; his guide has taken his money and has hobbled off rudely into the night. From somewhere in the void beneath his feet the professor hears the piping of a flute.

Slash and Laird and Will were thumbing through their texts. Rhino was leafing through a car racing magazine. Laird looked up from his reading. "This is the part where he gets nailed, right?" he remarked absently.

It was. Up to this point in the story, Bowles has been quietly escorting his professor researcher into the presence of an obscenely savage, nomadic tribe, the Reguiba. "The Reguiba is a cloud across the face of the sun," warn the local Arabs. "When the Reguiba appears, the righteous man turns away."

At the top of his precipice, the professor mumbles absently to himself ("Is this a situation or a predicament?") and notices that there is nothing to give the landscape scale—no more houses, no visible trees. The bottom of the cliff seems miles away. "Then he spat over the edge of the cliff," writes Bowles.

> Then he made water over it and listened intently, like a child. This gave him the impetus to start down the path into the abyss. Curiously enough, he was not dizzy. But prudently he kept from peering to his right over the edge.

"What an idiot," Will said.

"Anyone ever done this?" I asked. The inmates were silent. Mike Tobin was giving me a funny grin. "I mean everyone here has gone looking for adventure in unfamiliar places among unfamiliar people," I explained, "right?"

"Sure," said Tobin sheepishly. "I know what that's about." Rhino said he was himself a savage tribe. He *gave* people adventures when they came to jail.

I read on: "'It was a steady and steep downward climb. The monotony of it put him into a frame of mind not unlike that which had been induced by the bus ride.'"

He begins humming to himself—the name of a café where he'd had tea earlier in the evening—Hassan Ramani, Hassan Ramani— over and over.

"He's in a trance," Will offered. "The flute or something?"

"And the walking?" asked Darling.

I wanted the students to see the professor listening at the void, and to watch him giving in to the strain of music in its depths. It is an exotic, distant, imperiling melody. It seduces and enchants.

"What's the real danger here for this professor?" I asked. "The music, the landscape that disorients, the foreignness of the place and the people—what kind of dangers are these?"

"The danger is he won't be able to handle it," Will said. He began telling a story. The point of his tale was that he had friends who liked to drive their cars fast and to take lots of pharmaceuticals while they pushed up the speedometer. One of them had been killed in this way. Others had gotten themselves arrested. "You have to know how to handle things that intoxicate you; you have to know how to mix your drugs right," he explained. "You can't just go wandering off without knowing what you're wandering into."

The danger of taking risks, as he saw it, was that you could get caught by the police. There was an outside chance of getting killed, though that didn't really apply to him, since he knew how to mix and handle his drugs. The benefit of taking risks, however, was that you might elude the police and drive extremely fast. There's tons of fun in that for him, evidently.

"Fair enough," I agreed. I was hoping to persuade the class to look into the beneficial aspects of losing control. "A Distant Episode" is by no means a cautionary tale. Danger is helpful, Bowles suggests. Sometimes terror is just what the doctor ordered.

When the professor descends to the bottom of the cliff, he is immediately set on by a ferocious dog. It's too dark for him to see what's happening. More dogs attack, then he's assaulted by a group of men who kick him savagely in the head. A Reguiba tribesman thrusts a gun against the skin of his back. He loses consciousness. When he wakes, he opens his mouth to breathe. His tongue is promptly amputated.

The rest of the story deals with the professor settling, uncomfortably at first, and then with greater and greater ease, into the nomadic world of the Reguiba. He learns obscene dances and delights the women and children of the tribe by rushing at them in feigned anger. He becomes a sort of filthy-minded community puppet. Toward the end, the Reguiba tire of the professor's dance "program" and sell him off, after a year, to an Arab in a nearby city. The Arab locks him into an empty room in the back of his house but by then, by the time he's returned to civilization, the professor has lapsed into a deep madness. When his eye falls on a calendar stuck to the Arab's mud wall, his first vision of civilization in a year, the grid of words and numbers overwhelms him with a horrible discordant noise. It was an "imminent and mighty" sound, says Bowles, like "the

tiny inkmarks of which a symphony is composed." It drives him
crazier still. He begins to seethe and sweat.

In Bowles's view, this madness is nothing less than a spiritual gift.
"Much madness is divinest sense," writes Emily Dickinson, "much
sense, Madness." It's this kind of sensible craziness that's infected the
professor. Having lost his tongue, he has gained a powerful acuity in
his hearing; he can hear a calendar; it shocks him with a fitting dread
of himself and of the ordered civilization from which he came.
Whereas before he took no notice of this power, or used it casually to
advance his aims, he now perceives it as yet another force that
seduces and betrays. It's the force that brings professors out into the
desert to spit and pee on nomadic tribes. The solution, the story
hints in the end, is to be your own man, to make your own music.

In the last pages, a fit of insanity descends on the professor; he
throws himself at the walls of the Arab's room. Bowles writes:

> he attacked the door into the street which resisted for a while
> and finally broke. He climbed through the opening made by the
> boards he had ripped apart, and, still bellowing and shaking his
> arms in the air to make as loud a jangle as possible, he began to
> gallop along the quiet street toward the gateway of the town. A
> few people looked at him with great curiosity.

When I've taught the story in the past, I've pushed the discussion
away from sympathy with the professor and his amputated tongue.
I've tried to urge students toward a reckoning with the moral value of
thinking for oneself, even if this thinking is sometimes irrational.
"To listen to yourself, to really hear—this is what you owe yourself—
and everyone else, for that matter," I've said.

In jail, I thought that this lesson would be easily taught. After all,
lots of inmates—not just Frenchie—work hard to persuade people
that they're nuts. When they do come off as insane, the other inmates
respect them for having defeated all of those smiling shrinks and cops
and lawyers who come walking through the current events room.

As it turned out, the inmates were barely able to listen to my
reading of the story. They dragged the discussion off in a direction I
hadn't anticipated at all.

I read the last lines of the story out loud—the professor jangles and bellows off into the desert—and turned to look at the inmates for their reaction. There was an interval of silence and then Slash sighed: "So many lunatics like that around here," he said, staring at Tobin. "So many sick, sick fucks."

Tobin smiled apologetically.

"Slash," I said.

"The man's got a point," said Rhino.

Tobin shrugged his shoulders. "It's okay," he said softly.

Slash persisted: The problem with the professor was that he was basically institutionalized, he said. His face reddened. "Which means that you live with fucking lunatics."

He told us about people he'd known in other jails who'd descended into madnesses much, much worse than anything this professor went through. Example followed example. The craziness of locked-up people breeds craziness in everyone—even the guards. This was the theme on which he embroidered for several minutes. Worst of all, the craziness of incarcerated people spreads every day, via released inmates, out from the jail and through society, where it preys on other people, young people, and victimizes them. That, of course, leads to more crime.

The lines on his forehead twisted in exasperation. His eyes lingered contemptuously on Tobin and then turned to me. He pointed his index finger into the air in front of my nose. "How would you like to be locked up with thugs and fucking apes? And snappers? Imagine every night locked in with a maniac on every side—below you, above you. What would that do to you?"

"Obviously..." I hesitated.

"You'd go fucking nuts, obviously."

He absorbed the Bowles story easily into his argument. It was a parable about barbarism. It was a cautionary tale. The author had it right: take a normal person, put him in with fucking animals and sure enough, he'll turn into a fucking animal. "Bingo!" he yelled and stretched his face into a mocking, aren't-I-a-genius mask. The author's only mistake, he said, was that he didn't adequately show the kinds of depravity that result from being locked down with animals.

"Look at Ernie Sinclair," Slash insisted. "Look at Hazard Campbell. Look at Rhino." Rhino patted his belly. Slash went on: a roster of the insane and pathetically institutionalized among the Woodstock population was produced. "How did they get that way?" he asked.

"If it comes to that, if it really comes to being like institutionalized, I'll just commit suicide," Laird promised.

"It will come to that. Believe me," Slash assured him.

"Jail is just discombobulating, you know," said Will sadly. "It does fuck you up. Over time, I mean."

He also didn't want to be around for his institutionalization. "If I see it happening and if I'm not getting out for a while, I'll definitely string up," he promised.

After a few moments, the class had settled into a dead-end agreement: it's better to kill yourself—have a friend do it if you're not tough enough—than it is to let the system have its way with you.

Having arrived at this truth, we didn't know where to go. We sat there silently, staring at Tobin and Rhino and watching the windows.

"I've done a lot of time in my life," Tobin said finally, grinning. "And it's not been all that bad. I'm pretty happy about it, actually. It's okay for some people." He paused and then said: "I mean, look at me. I'm okay with myself. I turned out okay, I think." He was joking, I thought, but I wasn't sure.

CHAPTER TWELVE

Drifting

JAIL DIARY, MARCH 21, 2000

Slash is enraged over his parole thing, as usual. And yet sometimes
Slash's rages make for fabulous classes. I left the jail after school today
trembling and elated, as if I'd just survived a car wreck. I felt as
though I were blithely skipping away from roadside death. I think we
all felt this way—as though they we'd been guided through jagged
steel and broken glass—and the sensation was so pleasant and
unfamiliar that we lingered much longer than usual in the library.
The kids had to be hurried out of their chairs and even then they
dawdled, almost daring the guard to call for help.

In the actual class session, the students didn't say very much, so
perhaps I'm reading a lot into things. But no, actually, I think I'm
not. Will and Laird and Tim sat motionless in class today, eyes
glazing with water, reading softly, and breathing in long slow drafts
of air as if they were trying to medicate themselves with the words on
the page. "Lighten up, kids," I wanted to say, but I also felt as though
the students were doing something very private and separate from
me—it wasn't my business to tell them how to react—and so I didn't.
I just clammed up and let Laird and Will and Tim—our readers
today—read on to the end of the story. Toward the end, I was nearly
in tears myself. No wonder priests and cops have such good luck
recruiting in jails. People here are defenseless when something
touches them; they basically give up at the faintest hint of warmth.
They're so surprised they hardly know what to do.

Denis Johnson, I discovered today, works wonders. Today he was

a spiritual guide for the students, a lazy-eyed, tripping advice-giver—
and the kids soaked up every word they read.

I was supposed to show a movie—a documentary about Paul
Bowles followed by a bribe (a *Sopranos* episode)—but I couldn't get a
hold of either. I didn't have any reading scheduled on the syllabus so
I grabbed a copy of Johnson's *Jesus' Son*—a collection of short stories
narrated by a heroin addict—-and passed out Xeroxed copies of
"Emergency," which describes the movements of two drugged-up
hospital workers at the end of their shift.

There is a loose association with families and travel in these
stories. Most of all, I've wanted to teach them because the characters
in Denis Johnson could easily turn up on my class roster: they are
junkies, wanderers, people in search of home, people who feel
themselves at the ends of their lives.

Because of the no-movie debacle I had to beg and plead to get the
kids to even look at the Xeroxes. I opened a canvas bag of inmate
treats that I sometimes bring to the jail—it's filled with packets of
mints and gum and pens—and passed a goodie to each inmate. Then
I pushed the reading practically into their laps. Perhaps because they
felt they were owed the longer lasting pleasure of a video—or maybe
it was the appearance of certain girls on-screen they wanted, or
certain songs on the soundtrack—the candy didn't help. I had to
assure everyone, several times, that the story was full of pills, and
tripping, and blood—lots of blood, I said.

"What kind of pills are they taking?" Will asked.

"It doesn't say—random pills," I explained, "is that okay with you?"

"It's got violence in it, though," he wondered.

"Yes, yes! It does," I promised.

Will eventually picked up the Xerox and read through the first
paragraph to himself. His eyes smiled consent. "Okay," he said. "I
can like this."

In the story, a hospital orderly, Georgie, has filled himself with
pills he's stolen from a cabinet in the OR. He's obsessed by the pools
of blood he sees on the floor and can't understand why there should
be so much liquid—goop, he says—sloshing beneath his feet. He

runs his mop over the tiles in long, sweeping arcs, though apparently the goop is only visible to him. Still, he's horrified by it and rubs passionately at the floor, trembling and weeping. "What am I *crying* for?" he wonders when the narrator (a sweet, air-headed druggie named Fuckhead) asks. Georgie is too stunned or too stoned to answer: "Jesus. Wow, oh boy, perfect," he mutters.

Things get moving in the story when a patient with a knife sticking out of his eye socket strolls into the hospital: "'Who brought you in?'" a nurse said. "'Nobody. I just walked down. It's only three blocks.'"

The image—the knife in the eye, the conversational tone of the victim—settled my class into quiet attention. The kids wanted to know if the knife was part of the hallucination (no), if someone could really survive a wound like that, and if a person did have such an injury, what parts of his brain would be affected. We had an intense, focused, nearly scientific conversation about these details. Acts of passion—especially the dreamy, ethereal, bloody kind that Denis Johnson describes—work on the students, it turns out, like a lullaby.

Over the next few minutes we followed the hospital staff as they worried about how to extract the knife from the patient's brain. We read a little bit and discussed; read a bit more and broke off again to talk. Will recalled something he'd read or been taught about a nineteenth-century railroad worker in Cavendish, Vermont, whose brain was penetrated by a three-foot iron bar during an explosion. The man recovered and went back to work a few months later. Slash recalled a black guy in a jail in New Jersey who'd tried to commit suicide, had succeeded in piercing through a lobe or two in his brain, and had been given extra time in the hole, after his recovery, for self-mutilation.

In "Emergency," the eye-knife catastrophe stuns the hospital staff into a state of petrified inaction. The nurses and doctors scuff their shoes on the floor and stare. "I'm just going to watch this one," concedes the doctor on duty. "I know my limits. . . . We've got to get a team here, an entire team." When Georgie, the orderly, is instructed to prep the patient, he wanders off to the bathroom to sing songs and bathe his hands in running water. A discussion among the rest of the staff ensues:

Everybody had a different idea about how exactly to approach the problem of removing the knife from Terrence Weber's brain but when Georgie came in from prepping the patient—from shaving the patient's eyebrow and disinfecting the area around the wound—he seemed to be holding the hunting knife in his hand.

The talk just dropped off a cliff.

As he read this section out loud to the class, Will started to giggle and squirm in his chair. "He just pulled it out?" he asked.

"That's what it says, I guess," he concluded. And then everyone in the room was chuckling warmly—a tide of surprise and pleasure was washing through the library.

It was an old jail story after all: the nightmare crisis—suicide, self-mutilation—that turns into a joke, the fabulous, timely escape, unbelievable yet true!—that really does set you free. There was nothing new to a jailbird in any of this. And of course you don't really have to be an inmate to have such fantasies. Without trying at all, I have three or four similarly colored inklings a day—some on behalf of the prisoners, some strictly private affairs in which I'm the one who's relieved of my problems.

Right away the students wanted to talk about the factualness of the knife-pulling: Could it have happened like this? Did it actually happen? And also: What kind of brain damage did the patient really suffer? He must have had some. Did he just walk out again the next day or what?

It was a funny thing to see the students suddenly so in love with facts. Normally, we'd just as soon drop them into a deep hole. Facts don't do what you want them to, say the Talking Heads—that's a living creed for the residents of the Woodstock jail. I suspect that Laird has been planning in his hopeful, daffy way to desert the new facts of his life, to wander back through the recent past and turn up in his parents' living room. He feels he's overdue for such an exit by now. And so for that matter do Vandriel and Will and Frenchie and the other kids who're in deep trouble.

In the story—it sort of happened this way in our class too, for that matter—the removal of the knife frees people from impending doom. A shiny new dispensation materializes on the scene. Suddenly life's possibilities are waving gaily from every window and balcony and passing car. Georgie lays the knife on a medical chart. On the next page, he and the narrator are staggering bleary eyed and stoned out into the hospital parking lot. They've forgotten that it's summer, says Fuckhead. They've forgotten what morning looks like: "We lay down on a stretch of dusty plywood, in the back of the truck with the daylight knocking against our eyelids and the fragrance of alfalfa thickening on our tongues."

"Dude!" Laird exclaimed under his breath. "Dude," he muttered again. "What the...?" He scooched his chair up to the table and offered to read a bit out loud himself. In an instant, he was focusing his eyes and breathing quietly—everyone was breathing softly in that slow, sleep-like way that normally, in a classroom, accompanies the spooling of a VCR tape.

The rest of the story takes Fuckhead and Georgie on a funny, sad, druggie tour through an unspecified patch of Midwestern countryside. This is their new dispensation, and it's quite a bit happier than the hospital. The place is a carnival of improbabilities: an LSD guru conducts a seminar amid a pack of journalists at a fair, a pregnant jackrabbit dives into the path of the truck, and, later, a freak summer snowstorm comes barreling across the plains.

The pregnant rabbit is killed of course. Georgie insists on rescuing the babies, and the narrator, gentle drug addict that he is, tucks them into his shirt to keep them warm. "Little feet! Eyelids! Even whiskers!" he exclaims breathlessly. Later he forgets about them. His weight presses against them as he sleeps, and they are killed. He burbles his apologies. It's all he can muster; no one in the book can muster much more. Face-to-face with the strangeness of the world, the characters manage to be, by turns, aghast, tearful, awed, and, on every occasion, helpless. To add to their problems, they are constantly getting themselves lost.

Yet it's in all of this, says Johnson, that the mystery and wondrousness and sorrows of life inhere; we should be so lucky to go on voyages like this. An orange pickup, unhappy rabbit babies, the snow and sunshine on the windshield—these are the things the writer is desperate to salvage from his not-too-reliable memory of that time.

Before we ended for the day, I wanted to make sure the students understood all of this. Their lives have been rich in sorrow and strangeness; they're wealthy at least in these departments. I felt like congratulating them for having accomplished, well...something. I felt like urging them, anyway, to embrace what they have. But somewhere in the last fifteen minutes of class, Slash slunk in from one of his meetings with his probation officer. He shuffled toward his chair and collapsed. He jammed his cap over his eyes.

"Late as usual, man," I said and smiled. I slipped him a copy of the story and told him where we were in it. As soon as I saw his eyes, I could tell that something was badly wrong. His whole face was swollen; his eyes were bulging from his head and the skin around them had turned a lurid crimson. He stuffed his forehead into his baseball cap again and settled his arms across his chest. I thought he might stay submerged there for a while but he was too excited by whatever he'd been through not to call attention to himself. He stared at his arms for an instant and then lifted his head to stare at me. I didn't want to turn away from him since he was obviously asking me to pay him some attention. Yet it was difficult to look him in the eye. He was slowly shaking his head back and forth, as if he meant to deny some horrible fact, and as he turned his head, little globules of water were dropping onto his cheeks.

"What's wrong, man?" I asked. "Slash...?"

The other kids looked away. No one said anything. The other students were mortified—Slash in tears—it was too embarrassing to watch. It was too embarrassing even for anyone to speak. In our silence we could hear the clanging of doors upstairs and the crackling of Jim's radio in the room next door.

He turned away, wiped his snotty nose on his shirt, and turned back to look at me again. Then he sunk deeper into his chair and buried his face in his jacket. "Just keep talking," he mumbled. "Just keep going on. I'm okay," he said.

I hesitated. At first I felt like laughing or making a joke to break the tension but a wisecrack, it seemed, could easily have been taken the wrong way.

"Nothing we can do for you, man?" I asked after a few more seconds.

"Nope," he said. "Nothing." There were more tears and more sniffling. The whole thing was absurd. We were having a decent, functioning class and then within seconds, we were engulfed by Slash's bottomless sorrow and rage—the tragedy of his life— whatever it consists of. This is what I know: He was a carpenter once, and had developed a good reputation as a competent builder in the mountain towns of southern Vermont. He worked for himself and only when he wanted to. He was a snowboarding teacher in the winter. He was good friends with Jake Burton, the millionaire inventor of the snowboard. His girlfriend is said by the other inmates (who see her in the visiting room) to be extremely beautiful. She's an English major at Marlboro College. Four years ago he was on the news for something, something violent and frightening that he won't talk about. He's been in jail since then.

"Just do your thing," he urged. "You're fine. Just keep talking."

He pushed the Xerox paper across the table toward me and folded his arms again on his chest.

One person crying will effect the others, or anyway it did somehow today. Perhaps the other inmates have had too much faith in Slash's toughness, in his steely contempt for everything and everyone. To see it collapse was a little unnerving. Prisoners aren't supposed to cry on occasions like this. It must mean that Slash is really losing it.

Finally Laird picked up the packet of Xeroxed papers. I asked him to read out loud through the rest of the story. We listened as Fuckhead stumbled across another half dozen prairie miracles: he happens on a deserted drive-in movie theater, mistakes it for a cemetery, and gapes across the field of graves: "Just beyond the curtains of snow, the sky was torn away and the angels were descending out of a brilliant blue summer, their huge faces streaked with light and full of pity." The characters seem to be caught in a merry-go-round of portentous signs and crises that demand their immediate attention. But toward the end, the narrator concedes that all of this happened ages ago, in the early seventies, and that his memory has turned fuzzy since then: "Or maybe that wasn't the time it snowed," he guesses.

> Maybe it was the time we slept in the truck and I rolled over on the bunnies and flattened them. It doesn't matter. What's important for me to remember now is that early the next morning the snow was melted off the windshield and the daylight woke me up.

That turn in the story was the reason I wanted to teach the story in the first place. "So it was twenty-five years ago," I prompted. "You see? You get it?"

"I get it, I think," said Emmons.

"Explain," I said. He tried. He couldn't. I tried.

"There's such dark stress on doom and signs of catastrophe in the story," I said. "Let's list the really dark ominous stuff that happens," I urged. We made the list: the knifed patient, the blizzard, the killing of the rabbit, the freakish weather.

"But then it turns out that all of this stuff happened a long time ago in the past," I said. "You see? So all of those crises just kind of played themselves out naturally. You see?"

People did not see, evidently. At least I think they did not. But it didn't seem to matter all that much. Slash wasn't paying attention of course, but we weren't paying attention to him. We were watching Laird read from the book. I for one was thinking about the powerful warmth outside and the goodness of spring—which is coming along for everyone and that I honestly think will bring relief.

As I listened to Laird's voice, I could hear some of the other kids sniffling. I made brief eye contact with Will and Tobin: they gave me embarrassed grins and looked down at the table. Everyone was kind of crying together toward the end—over what, I honestly had no idea—the trippy freedom of the heroin addicts, the shock of seeing Slash fall apart, the imminence of warm weather—probably a little bit of each. Probably each kid was crying for himself.

I think also, underneath, that we were just flat-out pleased to be upset over something, even if it was just stupid Slash and a stupid short story: something was finally happening in jail. The frozen sea within was cracking. Great! When it was time to go, after the last kid had filed out, I stood up too suddenly and a wave of nausea and dizzyness knocked me back into my chair. I stood up again, minutes later, with my head tingling, my stomach turning, and without making eye contact with any of the guards. I pushed my way through the electronic doors and out onto the street.

The students have finally given their dumbass tragedies a voice— not that they poured their hearts out—but each private disaster amounted to something today. And they all mingled sloppily, together in a jail soup. It was a fine afternoon. I do think now that the kids are salvaging something from their little wrecks... their concentration, the respect they gave Slash, their respect for the book, their willingness to carry on through the whole exercise—all of this suggests progress to me.

JAIL DIARY, APRIL 3, 2000

At the moment, I'm planning a new syllabus—this time on menace and violence in the American landscape. It's a put-the-mirror-up-to-nature project. I'm going to ask the students to look at violent characters in American literature over the coming weeks, and I mean for them to take a pitiless look at themselves while they're at it. It might not work of course, in which case I'll be, essentially, a pusher of junk on junkies, a mole for the bad guys. If jail is an expensive way to make bad people worse, I'll be a freelancer, coming in from outside the jail, doing a little extra in my private way, on the cheap. That's not, of course, what I have in mind. I've been feeling lately that I may as well confront the kids head on. I plan to read more Stephen King, Denis Johnson—and some new stuff: Cormac McCarthy, and Flannery O'Connor's novel *The Violent Bear It Away.* I'm scheduling in some movies, too: *Reservoir Dogs,* as per Laird's request, and *Taxi Driver,* a huge favorite among the inmates. I may also show a Mad Max movie because there's such heavy demand for it. I won't do *Terminator II,* even though I know that would bring them in in droves.

Something happened in the last half of class today to undo my confidence in the kids more than a little bit. The students let me in on Laird's escape plan, ridiculous notion that it is. I didn't know whether to laugh or cry or get angry or what. I sat there dazed, shaking my head and giggling a bit as if a gypsy were forecasting bad news, as if my little syllabus were fluttering away in the wind.

There are two things everyone knows about escapes. First, they are ludicrous fairy-tale ideas that never work. Second, people who believe in them are almost beyond hope. Despite massive evidence to the contrary, would-be escapees still believe that they can outfox the system, ditch the past, run off merrily on the lam, and pick up life, in a different place, more or less where they left off. They suppose that the police will quit looking for them after a while and that their encounter with the criminal justice system will resolve itself into a memory. Escape is for people who can't face themselves, and when escapees get caught, as they always do, they're ridiculed for their stupidity.

With twenty minutes to go in the class today, I asked the students to wait a moment while I went off to fetch their new syllabi. In a desk by the Xerox machine, I had squirreled away a stack of paperback books which are to be used in the upcoming weeks—the books are gifts, this time—and a small pile of syllabi. It took me three or four minutes to collect them and to run off a few extra copies of the new syllabus on the machine. When I came back, Laird was tottering on a chair back beneath a window. He was pressing his fingertips gently against the pane and walking them into the corners around the window frame. He beamed impishly at me, a cute, pudgy kid caught with his hand in the cookie jar—cherubic face, floppy bangs, aw-shucks smile. The other kids were gesturing and hissing instructions.

"Dude. What are you doing?" I asked.

"I'm escaping," Laird confessed.

Everyone laughed. Laird smiled genially and climbed down from his chair.

"Theo," he said. He planted himself on the arm of a chair and then let himself slide into its depths. "I'm just kidding. I swear."

At first I was sure he was kidding, but it turns out that no, there is a plan, that he has outside help—automatically worrisome—and that the whole thing is set to go off in a matter of weeks.

I asked a half dozen questions. When exactly? Why? Where? The answers: Soon. Because. Here.

His plan is not much of a plan, and I'm not sure I believe him about his accomplice. "He's just gonna be a getaway driver," Laird assured me, "and he's getting paid for it."

"Okay, Laird, whatever," I said.

"Okay, Theo, whatever," he said.

I learned more about the plan. We spent the last ten minutes of class going over the details. In Laird's view, it's all about timing. For two hours every evening after dinner, he is admitted, alone, into the schoolrooms in order to clean them. It's an arrangement Jim has made on his behalf because Jim is nice and wants to be kind to Laird, to extend him a measure of teacher-to-inmate trust. In these two hours he must sweep four small rooms and one big one and empty two wastebaskets. Everyone knows that the classroom cleaner gets to watch two hours of TV every night in kingly privacy in the library. Laird has taken advantage to case the joint: he taps, he spies, he peers out the window to check on the frequency of sidewalk traffic (infrequent, always), and he turns up before the school camera every few minutes with a broom in his hand.

We're a medium-security jail. There are undoubtedly a few weak spots in the mediumness. People have escaped before. In the law library, the windows are a sandwich of Plexiglas (outer layer) and thick chicken-wire (stuffing). Running through the stuffing are two iron bars draped in cobwebs and covered in mold—the meat of the operation.

Even I can tell that the bars aren't likely to do much to prevent an inmate from squirming through. They're a foot apart—much too far apart to daunt Laird. He would have to do away with the Plexiglas and the wire somehow. If he could do that, and if that didn't trip an alarm, which it surely would, it's conceivable he could wiggle away into the fresh air. If he did, he'd be free, but he'd be standing in a pool of floodlit front lawn. Above him—I doubt he knows this—would be the office where the guards hang out at night. To his left, the booking room. And across the street, gaping gas station attendants dialing the police. Then he'd have to scurry across the lawn, break for the street, and vanish into the wind. As he says, it's all about timing.

Of all the foolish notions that occupy Laird's fantasies in jail—I
need a new lawyer! Better press! A new venue!—this is by far the
most foolish. It's a new falling off for him, or really an old one: once
again, he's nurturing a long-shot criminal scheme. Once again, he's
confident that it'll work. Once again, he hasn't given a thought to
what's *likely* to happen.

Laird is not without people who are well-disposed toward him.
His dad still talks to him and gives him books, though Laird did try
to kill him a few months ago. His lawyer wants to help him. So do I
and so does Jim for that matter and a half dozen other staff people
here in Woodstock: his case worker, a few guards, some of the brass.
He might relax into our company at this point; he might hang his
head and turn to us. Anyway, we're all he has. We mean well. Yet
apparently he has other plans. I've been trying in class to cool off
these romantic, against-all-odds fevers into which he occasionally
descends. I've presumed that circumstances have done most of the
cooling down on their own: an arrest, appearances in the newspaper,
sessions in court, grim-visaged lawyers, detectives, and journalists—
all of this must soothe his heated visions. No, it doesn't, apparently.

"I need a cell phone," he said as he was explaining about the
basement cleaning routine. "Do you have a cell phone?"

"No."

He needs a cell phone because the timing of the operation must
be coordinated among the conspirators. Just as he's prying off the
final Plexiglas sheet, he'll ring his friend. When he's ready to fly away,
a former inmate in Woodstock, someone Laird knew as a fellow
skiing teacher at Mount Ascutney by the name of B.J. Filieault, is
going to come swooping into the Woodstock Sunoco. He's going to
have a passport for Laird in his car and ten thousand dollars in cash.
Laird will wriggle through the window, scurry across the lawn, across
Route 4, and dive into the waiting car. It'll be a commando kind of
operation with BJ as the commando, and Laird as his war buddy, left
behind but not forgotten.

"Where's he gonna get all that cash?" I asked.

"Don't worry. He's gonna have it."

"You're an idiot," I said.

"Okay," he agreed flatly.

He talked some more about his plan and the more he talked, the less I said. It was a monologue of teen drama non-sequiturs: "Ten thousand dollars in cash!"—pause. "Dude, I *need* a cell phone!" Pause. "BJ owes me big-time, dude. I gave him three thousand dollars in cash. And more coming. So..." Laird spat out the details of the operation and watched me take it all in. Somehow, my opinion on the feasibility of the whole thing did apparently matter, just a little bit, to him. I was gratified to see that. But as he talked, he also lost himself in the details of the operation. After a few minutes, he was talking just to watch the thing approach. I began watching it too. He saw it in its shimmering simplicity, steeling him for the future. He was a little impatient with it and anxious about it, but he was also willing to wait. He was uncertain about his accomplice. That was a sticking point. Yet when he worked his mind around it—"BJ hates the system even more than I do! And he needs the money bad"—he was like a kid welcoming the end of a movie he's seen several times before. In his mind, everything was resolved. The only major part of the orchestration yet to fall into place was the actual physical doing of it.

"But you know something?" he said, sighing, as he countered one of my objections, "This isn't like the biggest supermax prison in the country or anything. This is Woodstock. I mean I know how to get out of a local jail."

"Okay," I said.

"Don't worry, bro," he answered. "I'm okay with it."

And where did he learn his escape skills? Did he have a teacher? Had he ever practiced? I didn't ask. I'm not sure he could have answered. My guess: the movies. In the eighties movies Laird grew up on—especially those about Vietnam—the hero shrivels for a while in his cage and then, in a dark hour, a rescuer comes along to whisk him away. It's the redeemed captive script: a nightmare turn among hostile peoples and then glorious rebirth in freedom. In the Vietnam movies, the hero had been betrayed by his nation; it was too ashamed of him, and too cowardly to take responsibility for him. He has to force himself on the conscience of the people he loves and even then they turn away. Eventually, of course, he is delivered and restored to a new life among his comrades.

"So, where are you going to go?" I asked.

"Away, dude."

"And you'll be a fugitive for the rest of your life?"

"Looks like it," he said. "I'd like to go home sometime, I guess."

"Great," I said.

The other kids watched our discussion in silence. They'd love to see Laird fly the coop. They'd love to fly the coop themselves. They attribute magic powers to the family money Laird claims to be in charge of: they seem to think he can—is—buying his escape. They assume—preposterously, I think—that this is the sort of third world jail where all the guards are for sale. Frenchie says he'd do it too, if he had the money. Perhaps he's just trying to egg Laird on.

When our discussion was over I wanted to be more angry than I was. After jail I climbed into my car, smoked a joint as per usual, and walked off into the woods from Cloudland Road. I walked farther than I've been in a long time. I'm not sure how far I ended up walking. Far. My head was filled with images of the kids clustering in the library, then snaking through the basement window, and walking up through the woods. I saw them huddling in lean-tos and beneath boulders along the trail. Every aspect of their plans had gone as expected—better than expected.

I saw them as I sometimes see them in my sleep, as a gathering of smirking, silent ghosts. Laird was their spiritual leader, their symbol, more doomed than the rest and more idiotically hopeful. He walked along next to me, chatting and turning his face every once in a while toward the sky.

"It's okay," I said. "You're not going to expire in Woodstock. You're going to come out of this okay in the long run. But don't do anything stupid. Don't get yourself deeper into trouble. Things are bad enough as they are. Please."

Laird listened politely.

The more I walked, the easier it was to descend into my fantasy. I invited it to develop and it smoothly unfolded itself, like a dream you deliberately prolong before waking.

Soon, the other kids were creeping along behind us in the darkness, listening and talking with each other. I stopped in a clearing on the side of a hill. I looked out over the patch of woods falling away at my feet. I could see dark hills silhouetted against the horizon and yellow lights off to the west in Bridgewater and Barnard. I looked at the stone wall tumbling gently from the field into the forest and then at the kids in front of me: "You kids think you're free because you don't have jobs, because you don't have futures. You think you're free to waltz away into the forest whenever you feel like it. You're fooling yourselves. And you're making the situation much worse because you won't stare at the facts. You run away from everything. Even in jail, you're running away."

"Really?" They didn't say anything for a long time after that. They looked at my little backpack and eyed my front pocket. I've pulled my wallet out of this pocket in the past and have shown my IDs and money and my rolling papers.

After my speech they didn't want any more counseling. They'd had enough of it. They knew my point of view and had affably dismissed it. Now they were staring jealously at my pockets. They wanted things: money, drugs, credit cards. They wanted me to shut up with my big-brotherly advice and fork over some goods: something, anything. They were like children in a famine-stricken nation. They were gathering closer around me, more menacing now than ever before, more needy and desperate and bitter. They held out their hands. More hands fluttered over my pockets. Fingers pried into my backpack. I stepped away.

"I've got lots of stuff to give you," I said. "Think of all that junk I give you in class! Come on."

"Not really," they said. "You give us nothing. Nothing we need."

"You all are amply provided for," I said. "Aren't you getting educated? Aren't you getting fed? Aren't you watching all the TV you could possibly want to watch? And you have lawyers. You have teachers and social workers and nurses. We're trying to help you. You kids know that, right?"

It was too dark to see more than the outlines of the trees now; they were black clumps against a flat, darkening sky.

Into the silence someone said, "Interesting," but I thought I could hear him drawling out the word in mockery. A chorus of soft chuckles followed—maybe it was my own breathing.

We stood in the clearing for a few minutes. I watched the moon come up. I put down my backpack and let myself think for a while. "Anyway, we're not taking your advice," someone muttered. The person got up, kicked at some rocks, and shambled off across the field, toward the ruined stone wall and the trees beyond. Then Laird turned around and walked off in a different direction toward different woods. And then Will was gone, and finally everyone was ambling away, each one at a different angle, across the patches of snow.

When I'm in their presence in school in the daytime, they're cheerful and thoughtful and literate kids, especially considering that they're screw-up teenagers, but at the end of the day, when I leave for home, they can get a little nasty. "Fuck you and yours, too," someone called out in the darkness.

This is the sad pathetic part about working with these teenagers. To begin with, I do it for the very personal, private thrill of rescuing the kids. Yet I'm not at all the rescuer they have in mind, apparently. First, I'm stuck in a Holden Caulfield scheme and they're thinking more along the lines of *First Blood Part II* or some other POW film— *Missing in Action,* maybe. Second, they really do want to beat it back into the deep woods. My students are seventeen and eighteen and the ones in their twenties are, emotionally, the same age. The point is that they have lifetimes of development to look forward to. Yet they take themselves for goners, for people who're destined for the shadows and have nowhere to turn now but darkness.

Gloom is not my idea of a future; being a lonely walker in the night on some dumb ridge above Woodstock isn't a life plan for me. Their lonesome traveler desperation is real to them. It does real stuff in the world, all by itself, sometimes with guns, and then retreats, denying everything, into the daylight.

The more the kids pretend that their lives are taking them further into the darkness, the easier it is for them to look on the dull, two-dimensional world where they go to school, where their futures will unfold, where they're locked up with contempt. In Laird's case, it's hard for him sometimes even to believe that the rest of us are alive. We have the flat, monochromatic lives of people stuck in a photograph. He lives in brilliant, exploding color, off on the frontier where life hovers in dangerous proximity to death. He drops in from his frontier to visit us every little once in a while. So when we see him, he's just traveling on through, just a nice, parentless kid in transit. The little epigrams Laird writes and passes to me as poems speak in the breathless, disembodied voice of someone floating through time: "From a time without love / Or beauty we came! Let's pray? / we are not going back! —Me." And: "When time stops / will love? —Me."

So he's headed off for the land where time stops. He just wonders if people will love him still when he gets there. All the kids are a little spacey in this way. They've already glimpsed the ending of things, the limits of their destinies, and now, owning all the certainty of someone who's seen the future, they're not bothered with the here and now. Leave your destinies alone for goodness' sakes! I want to say. That'll all unfold in its own good time. But I don't know how to say this, how to express myself so that they'll pay attention.

CHAPTER THIRTEEN

Time Travel

JAIL DIARY, MAY 1, 2000

In Ray Carver's story, "So Much Water, So Close to Home," four men hike into the mountains on a fishing trip. While they're setting up their camp, one of them wanders away to the nearby river. The body of a young woman is floating, naked and facedown, in an eddy. The men hem and haw for a while as they decide what to do. They consider hiking out to call the sheriff, think better of it, and return to the campsite to drink and play cards. Later in the night, in their drunkenness, they decide that they should keep the corpse from floating further downstream. They stumble down to the river's edge by the beams of their flashlights. One of them wades into the water, loops a nylon line around the woman's wrist, and anchors her to a tree.

Yesterday, as they read over this synopsis, the students were intrigued. When he was finished reading, Tobin dropped his sheet of study questions to the table and asked: "Well, who the fuck killed her then?"

"Read the story," I suggested.

It was the end of class and a guard, Frankie, was waiting for people to gather their things and leave.

"What did they do to her? Fuck her?" Frenchie wondered.

Other people asked: They just left her alone? Why? Is this a true story?

"Read it and find out," I told the inmates. I stood in the door frame and pressed Xeroxed copies of the story into their hands as they filed through. Suddenly, with Frankie the guard watching me and the kids talking about rape and screwing and naked corpses, I

felt like I was sending the inmates off to study evil, not Ray Carver. It
felt like I was throwing hunks of meat at creatures in a lair. It seemed
that the creatures were going to return the following day,
disappointed and angry with me because I'd given them only dirty
Ray Carver realism and not dirty porn.

"Thanks, Theo," Tobin said on the way out. "You're all right, you
know, man?" He gave me a smiling wink and slapped me on the back.

"What's your problem?" I asked.

I shouldn't have worried. When the students came back today,
they had given the story a thorough going-over. They knew the
characters' names, how they were associated with one another, and
how some of the characters, if not actually rapists, were guilty of, as
Will said, shitty morals.

I agreed with Will: "Well said, Will. I think you're exactly right.
I'm glad you're doing the reading carefully." He smiled back at me, a
little indignantly.

"Of course I am," he muttered.

Carver leaves out the smutty details of the crime—you never find
out who killed the girl or why or how she came to be eddying in a
fishing hole without her clothes. She exists strictly as a corpse, a
hazard of trout streams in Carver's America. The students—Slash
and even Rhino—understood the point well enough, it seemed, and
didn't miss the absent, foul details at all.

I asked them about how plausible the situation was, in their view.
"Very," said Slash. His eyes beamed. He's seen corpses in rivers
before—the Connecticut, the Battenkill, the Black River. "There's
not just rotting old tires in the Connecticut," he said. "Every week
something comes floating through Brattleboro," according to
Slash—old men, retarded people, suicides.

"What if you guys were fishing and a corpse came swimming into
your hole? Would you fish or hike out?" I asked.

"I'd have a cell phone," Laird said.

What if he didn't have one?

He *would* have one.

I was more interested in hearing the inmates compare the river in
"So Much Water, So Close to Home" to other rivers they've read

about over the past few months. Almost everyone remembers
something, at least, from *Huck Finn*. And several weeks ago, I
marched everyone through the Hemingway story "Big Two-Hearted
River." In class today, I recalled how the Mississippi was a sort of
river deity in that book—a provider, a taker-away, a vein of eternal
power—a spiritual presence at any rate, to which the heroes of the
book had to reconcile themselves as they grew up. I reminded people
of the scene in which Huck and Jim, planted up to their waists in
river water, greeted the dawn as it rose over the Illinois shore, pagans
communing with their muddy god.

"The Mississippi was like a spiritual body of water—is that what
you mean?" Laird said. "Whereas this river is just like dead bodies."

"Yes." I said. "Well put."

"Are you saying it's like you can go to the river in Mark Twain and
it gives life but here you go to the river to like die?" he asked.

I'd said it before when talking about Hemingway, but yes, that's
what I was saying.

"Or you go to the river to like throw a corpse in it?" Will added.

The discussion broadened out gradually into one of those dreamy
comparisons between the old America and the new America, the kind
that give bitter consolation to nostalgic, trapped people everywhere.
Everyone's screwed now, says this line of talk. *We've all missed out.*
I should have seen it coming and should have warded it off.

I didn't. I watched the inmates cast their minds back to the
halcyon days of outlaws and train robberies and vigilantes who shot
from the shoulder. Most of the younger people here are wise enough
to talk about this cowboy paradise ironically, as if they're not truly
nostalgic and not true believers in anybody's myth. Yet beneath their
skepticism I detect a genuine credulousness. No one doubts that if
society were arranged now as it was then, the inmates here would be
powerful, respected people, in possession of mules and forty acres
and a small arsenal.

Who knows? Perhaps it's true. Sheriffs would leave them alone;
they would live by their own laws. Rhino in particular feels that he
was born a stranger to the twenty-first century. He's constantly
dredging up primal memories and converting them into suggestions

for policy reform: "We should have more mercenaries and shit," he said as our river discussion dissolved. "We should have more motherfucking posses and hangings."

"Un-hunh," said Laird.

"There's no fun even in capital punishment anymore," complained Rhino.

Laird said that he'd be a skier if he lived back then—back in the 1900s and shit—he'd get in all the fresh powder runs because there'd be nobody else at the mountain.

"You'd be hanging from a tree. You'd have been lynched inside of a week," I said.

"We would've hanged you ourselves," Slash said. "Then we would have took down your body and doused it in gasoline. You're a goddamn lucky sonofabitch to be sitting here with us."

A surprised look appeared in Laird's eyes for an instant and then he smiled his aw-shucks-I-forgive-you grin. He mumbled "I know" into his shirt collar and shut up.

JAIL DIARY, MAY 8, 2000

I've been away from the jail for a solid week. Every once in a while Jim shuts down the school—I don't know why. Probably the guy needs a vacation from time to time. He's the first to come in the morning, the last to leave in the afternoon, and he gets no summer break as regular teachers do. He's in jail practically as much as the inmates are. Unlike everyone else, however, he's kept full time in the basement.

Last Monday I showed up at the front door and got the news: Jim's away. When Jim's away, the inmates are not permitted into the schoolrooms. So they've had a solid week of cell-block languishing and their brains are sapped now from all of the stifled, angry waiting they do when they can't move.

Tobin explained to me this morning in the current events class that they've been watching a lot of TV upstairs. "What else have you been doing?" I asked. They've been playing a lot of Hearts. And? He turned his head toward the windows; a look of perplexed wonderment, of brain scouring, came across his face.

"Anything else, Tobin?" I asked again.

"I guess not," he said at last. And then he turned back to the newspaper. A minute later, he startled into attention and gave me a pleased, fellow-conspirator look. He murmured: "Or...you know...you know what we do, right? That's what we've been doing, man. All of *that*." I do know what *that* is. In the cell blocks, suspended in their aspic, the inmates argue with one another, and carry on—with infinite slowness and deliberation—the work of the jail bazaar. Goods and services are bought and sold and stolen. Haggling ensues. Every once in a while there are fights and once every day for an hour they're permitted outside into the rec yard. Almost all the inmates wear watches. They check the clock a lot: time for breakfast, time for head-count, time for outdoor rec, time to return to the aspic. Lately, however, they haven't been going outdoors a lot because of the cold and the rain. So says Tobin.

Normally, on Mondays, I detect flickers of self-congratulation and relief in the inmates' faces: I've made it through, yet again, they're saying. Another weekend through. They're happy to be going through their routines at a normal weekday pace.

Today, they hadn't all made it. They sat down to their papers and wouldn't look up. Jim had questions for them. What had piqued their interest in last week's news? Anything? Silence. Anyone see the papers over the weekend? Silence. Someone had watched a basketball game—he didn't know who was playing. Someone else had seen Dan Rather on the news, but maybe that was last week. What was he saying? Jim asked. I don't know, Richard answered. "I guess it was about the news. You know. It could have been his news show, probably. " So much for current events.

In my class afterward, I began my violence in the American landscape syllabus. I meant to jolt the inmates into life with a very short introductory short story. But before that began, I wanted to find out how my students have been. I had new patience for their court sagas. I had new interest in their dumb escape plans—Laird's hadn't gone off yet, evidently—and new concern for their bouts with one another.

This is how May finds my class: "So, Tobin," I prompted. "you haven't been in the paper lately."

"I haven't?"

"Not that I've seen."

He smiled proudly.

"Any news from your lawyer or anything?"

"Probably. I don't really know."

"Do you have like any court dates coming up or anything?"

"Maybe," he smiled. "That would be okay, I guess."

I turned to Laird.

"Laird, dude. What's going on with your thing?"

He sighed: "I have no fucking idea."

"Have you like heard anything lately from your lawyer?"

Another sigh: "He doesn't call me back."

"Have you been in touch with your dad?"

"Not really. He sent me a Harry Potter book, but I don't know where he is. I heard he's in like California or something."

I turned to Joe, the school bus driver. "Emmons?"

"I talked to my caseworker last week." Sigh. "I'm supposed to be getting shipped, I guess. I don't know actually when. I'm waiting for it." He'll be going to the Northern State Regional Correctional Facility in Newport, Vermont, or possibly to Virginia, I assume.

"And Will? How about you?"

"I don't know." Silence. He shrugged his shoulders and rolled his head toward the window and then back to me. "I'm still trying to get some fucking like evidence thrown out I guess. I don't know."

Finally Slash dropped his folder of legal papers on the table. He slammed his two fists on top of them and leaned forward on his elbows. "We're all in the fucking dark here, Theo. We live in a fucking mine shaft. I don't have a cell phone like you do. I can't call random people when I feel like it. I don't go home every night to make love to my girlfriend like you do. Do you want to call my lawyer for me?" I didn't. Neither did I have a cell phone, but I took his point and didn't say anything.

Frenchie said he'd just learned in the paper that he's going to court pretty soon. Next week, maybe. His "I'm too retarded to stand trial" routine isn't working, apparently.

"Well," I said. "Court finally. That's good." He gave me a blank look.

"No it isn't," he said. "I'm fucked."

I didn't know what to say. Will was smirking from his corner. Tobin was stretching his arms.

"Teach your fucking class, why don't you?" Slash suggested. He stared at me for an annoyed second and added: "We don't come down here for this touchy-feely shit, you know. Come on."

I passed around copies of a short story—another Denis Johnson study of losers at large in the Midwest called "Car Crash While Hitch Hiking." I had stapled page two of Walt Whitman's poem "On Crossing Brooklyn Ferry" across the front of their packets. I asked the students to turn to that first. Both writers play a similar trick on their readers: they project themselves far into the future and address their audience as if they're recalling what life was like so many ages ago in the present. Whitman remembers the "scallop-edg'd waves" he used to see from the deck of the Brooklyn ferry and the sea gulls and the crowd of young men aboard, and Denis Johnson dilates on the ecstatic moments surrounding a car crash. In both cases the writer stands mesmerized before the dazzling contemporary world, walks himself out into its midst, and then disappears. Off he goes magically into the future from where he telegraphs good news: things are working themselves out, he says. I've survived, am still intact, am still coasting forward these many years hence, so take heart.

To give us a precedent for Denis Johnson and to reassure the students with Whitman's breezy, fellow-wayfarer confidence, I began by reading a section of "On Crossing Brooklyn Ferry" out loud. In the lines I read, Whitman is standing at his staging post off in the future somewhere and addressing the screw-ups in his audience. Way, way back in the past, he says, when I lived in hilly Brooklyn and took the ferry back and forth to Manhattan, I had some unhappy moments too. I didn't realize how common my condition was. But take heart, he says. Thus:

It is not upon you alone that dark patches fall,
The dark threw its patches down upon me also,
The best I had done seemed to me blank and suspicious
My great thoughts as I supposed them, were they not in reality meager?
Nor is it you alone who know what it is to be evil...

The students gaped at me. We don't know what it is to be evil, their looks said. Don't look at us. They've told me they don't like Whitman, and won't read him. In the past they haven't and, except for one or two lucky classes when things happened to work well, they've not showed much interest.

I stared back at them. "Imagine you guys talking to the punks who're checking into Woodstock fifty years from now. What will you say to them? You're codgers; you're twisting your gnarly beards around in your fingers." I kept reading:

I am he who knew what it was to be evil
I too knitted the old knot of contrariety
Blabb'd, blush'd, resented, lied, stole, grudg'd
Had guile, anger, lust, hot wishes I dared not speak...

I asked each student for a gloss on "knitting the knot of contrariety." "Fucking up on purpose?" asked Laird.

"That's called ODD. Oppositional defiant disorder," said Will.

"Right. That's the term of art, isn't it?" I asked. He nodded.

Will said that knitting a knot wasn't just fucking up. There was more involved. "You have to know how to knit; you have to work your talent to knit a knot of contrariety. Come on, man," he pleaded, smiling. "Give us some credit."

"Fine with me," I said.

I read a bit more of the poem and talked for a moment about how Whitman liked to tuck himself in among the busy, purposeful passengers aboard the ferry. From their midst, he'd gaze at the flags and the sun and the waves lapping up against the wharves of Manhattan. He'd eye the other passengers and the large and the small steamers in motion. He would salute the whole panorama in his mind, figure up all the things he had in common with it, and a moment of mystical unity would ensue.

I read a stanza of "I too" and "Just as you" clauses. Whitman makes eye contact with everything—Manhattan, birds, the sun— within visual range and many things outside of it. I looked up at the students when I was done: "You see?" I said. "The hustle and bustle of a port—the busy city, the busy passengers—and through it all the ever-flowing, ever-ebbing movement of the tides."

I was running out of monologue. I noticed some strained looks, not quite bored but getting there.

Finally, I read the lines of consolation Whitman offers his fellow grudgers and blabbers and knowers of evil. You're not so different from everybody else, he says, and you're quite the same as me. We're all of us merging in with the crowd, hemmed in maybe for the moment, but all the while advancing over the tides. I realized long ago, he says, that I was "one with the rest, the days and haps of the rest," and since then I've been keeping an eye on my fellows, you: "Closer yet I approach you," he says. "What thoughts you have of me now, I had as much of you—I laid in my stores in advance / I consider'd long and seriously of you before you were born."

"I mean . . . Amazing!" I exclaimed. "Clairvoyance! Time travel. He's looking into his crystal ball—well, it's the big cyclorama of the city, really—and he's kind of seeing . . . us. He's there on the ferry and gone in the same instant—way far forward into the future."

A thinking prisoner could conceivably hear in those lines of the poem a word of encouragement directed at him. On a good day, a prisoner might think: Can he really do that? *Is he really talking to me? Perhaps he is.*

That's sort of his advice for you guys, I suggested, I mean for all of us, really.

No, it wasn't apparently. Or if it was, it wasn't being openly received. The Whitman section of the class may well have gone over into a blankness. I hope it didn't because these trapped, languishing, hour-counting kids do need some encouragement. They're not getting out anytime soon, despite their escape plan, and on some level, I'm pretty sure they know this. On some level, I'm hoping they're paying attention to Whitman.

During their week away from school, the kids had mislaid their copies of "Car Crash While Hitch Hiking." When we were finished with Whitman, therefore, I had them settle into class by reading the whole story through, each person taking turns narrating out loud. It took about ten minutes; it's a short short story. Only Slash refused to

read, which was fine with me. He had some legal documents to
study—he's too anxious to leave off scrutinizing the motions and
countermotions he has in his folder. The rest of the kids were game.
Because of the cold and rain outside, everyone was huddled down
inside sweatshirts and baseball caps. The class shivered quietly to
itself as it read, but otherwise it did not fidget or complain or
argue—usually a promising sign.

When we were finished reading, I suggested we talk about the
present of the story first. It's a miserable situation, well worth
blabbing and grudging over. Our drug-addled narrator-hitchhiker
has been deposited by the side of the road. In the pouring rain, he
wraps his sleeping bag around his shoulders and gazes at the passing
traffic. His head is spinning from the drugs his last ride gave him.

"Any of you people ever been here?" I asked.

"Maybe," said Will.

"Do you guys know anyone in a similar situation now?"

A moment of teacher versus class staring followed and then there
was a round of murmurings and nods from Frenchie and Tobin and
Vandriel, who happened to be in class today. "Yup," he burped. He
stared at me suspiciously through matted bangs.

This is what happens in the story: a civilization of lushes washes
by the hitchhiker as he stands on the side of the highway. The drivers
who pick him up, it turns out, have each embarked on their own
private, seedy errands:

> A salesman who shared his liquor and steered while sleeping...
> A Cherokee filled with bourbon...A VW no more than a bubble
> of hashish fumes, captained by a college student...And a family
> from Marshalltown who headonned and killed forever a man
> driving west out of Bethany, Missouri.

It's a nation in transit, certainly, like Whitman's America—but there's
not much fellow feeling in the air, and not much purposeful
busyness in the travelers. The only creature within sight who's got an
ounce of feeling for his neighbor is the story's narrator, a druggie
spiritual descendent of Whitman. He manages a mystical vision
from time to time and lives on friendly, hallooing terms with natural

phenomena. Just before he gets in the fated car, he has an I-thou moment with the rain:

> My jaw ached: I knew every rain drop by its name. I sensed everything before it happened. I knew a certain Oldsmobile would stop for me even before it slowed, and by the sweet voices of the family inside it I knew we'd have an accident in the storm...

I wanted the students to feel the trapped helplessness of the hitchhiker: he climbs into the Olds, the rain cascades over the windshield, he can see the accident approaching, it's 3 AM and there's a baby sitting on the seat beside him. Locked into the backseat as he is, there's nothing he can do about the impending crash. There's nothing he wants to do.

"Do you guys have a sense of what's going on here?" I asked, feebly.

Silence, some nods.

I wanted the class to see that clairvoyance—or at least a special kind of self-confidence—resolves some of this claustrophobia. It lifts you out of your stalemate with time. So, to begin our discussion, I had them focus on the agonizing approach of the car crash. I asked Will to read that section aloud:

> I'd known all along exactly what was going to happen, but the man and the woman woke me up later, denying it viciously.
> "Oh—no!"
> "NO!"
> I was thrown against the backseat of their car so hard that it broke. I commenced bouncing back and forth. A liquid I knew right away to be human blood rained down on my head. When it was over I was in the backseat again, just as I had been. Our headlights had gone out. The radiator was hissing steadily. I was the only one conscious. As my eyes adjusted I saw that the baby was lying on its back beside me as if nothing had happened.

On the second time through, with Will narrating, the story finally got through to the students. "Dude!" Laird exclaimed. "Oh, my god!" He choked and laughed a little bit, but couldn't say anything

more than "Oh, my god! Wow." His eyes were bulging in their
sockets. "This is like, oh my god," he said and smiled again.

"That's what happens when you do speed and hash together. I've
done it like a million times," said Will.

Laird was lost in his private memory recovery moment. "Oh my
god!" he said again as everyone ignored him, "I totally had a dream
like that!"

I was curious about what was going on with Laird. He looked at
me and tried to explain. Apparently, he'd also seen something just
like what was described in the text: an accident in the night, a family
of three... he was just an observer, just someone passing through.

"It was, I dunno... one of the big reasons..." He'd had a dream
apparently, only—"it wasn't a nightmare—in fact it was a very
reassuring, good dream." He'd had it just a few weeks before he came
to jail. "Oh my god!" he exclaimed again. It seemed like he was
trying to persuade himself of something.

No one could figure out what he meant to say or confess. No one
seemed to care. Still, the students did want to talk about the agony of
a car crash and the premonitions that are occasioned by imminent
violence. We talked about dreams and inklings and the soothing
shock of death narrowly averted—for longer than I would have
liked. We also had to consider the simple beauty of Ketamine—how
it induces a kind of death that's similar to what happens in a coma or
an overdose or the final stages of cancer. Will and Slash have—at
least in their own minds—been at death's door many times,
apparently, and I listened to stories about their narrow escapes. Ever
since he was a child, people have been pointing guns at Will. And
ever since he was a child, he has been frying his brains with drugs.

"You can be fucking depressed as hell," Will said, "and Ketamine
almost makes your mind more depressed, but it also makes it burn.
You're like on fire—that's as close as you can come to true ecstasy
without dying—that's about a hundred times stronger than just
Ecstasy."

I didn't know what to say. At least the students were reflecting
quietly and listening to one another. The TV was on, playing
without sound, and had been for the whole class period. It's part of

my ill-advised liberalness that I sometimes let the kids watch MTV in silence if they can't stand the class. It flickered behind me as I chatted, but no one, I noticed, was watching it. Is this story true? Laird asked pointing at the text. How much of this shit is true? he wanted to know.

We couldn't get away from the car accident. The students wanted to talk about clairvoyance but not the good kind that sees forward to a wiser, older self. They were interested in run-of-the-mill car accident clairvoyance—the kind that sees disaster and the pleasure of a good wreck and nothing more. The more I tried to push the students onward, the more I annoyed them. Finally, I had to raise my voice and address the students by name. "Will, shut up," I said. "Laird, shut up." That didn't work. Eventually Slash saw what I meant to do and gave his fellow prisoners appropriate instructions.

"Shut the fuck up and listen to Theo," he said—there was quiet—and then he turned gallantly to me.

In the end of the story, the narrator is brought to the hospital. Though he's unharmed, the doctors on duty want to give him a cautionary X ray: "There's nothing wrong with me," he says.

> —I'm surprised I let those words out. But it's always been my tendency to lie to doctors, as if good health consisted only of the ability to fool them.
>
> Some years later, at the Detox at Seattle General Hospital, I took the same tack...

And with that the scene shifts forward in time to some other happier, more easeful event that transpired at a hospital in Seattle. The nightmare car crash and its victims are forgotten—the present falls away all together in fact, never to be revisited, and the accident remains a gory incandescent slide show. What little narrative it has ends, almost in mid-sentence. Its significance, if it has any, is that time has washed over it and carried it into the distant past.

I read the paragraphs in which the present dissolves and deliver my big point to the class: crises envelop and dazzle and terrify, yes, I said. But they resolve themselves too, like everything else. Will was paying attention.

"It's not time as much as drugs. It's drugs that help. I'm telling you. That's what does the trick," he said. He read us the final paragraphs of the story:

> A beautiful nurse was touching my skin. These are vitamins, she said and drove the needle in.
>
> It was raining. Gigantic ferns leaned over us. The forest drifted down a hill. I could hear a creek rushing down among the rocks.

When he read those lines, something in his voice faltered for a moment and it seemed obvious that he was trying hard to connect with them, to persuade us of what he saw there. We really did listen to him then: we gave him all the authority he's claimed over the past months as a drug dealer and pharmacist. It was a comforting, rain-foresty image and Will gave the reading everything he had. It worked, at least for me. He was proposing one very plausible way to read the story—great trauma resolved by a shot. We were all quiet for a few moments, thinking about the rain forest and the babbling brook in its depths. It was cold in the room but at that moment it felt humid and warm—the rain forest dripped and babbled in our imaginations—and the slow students, Emmons, Frenchie—ran their pencils carefully beneath certain words on the page.

We were together and listening to one another, respectfully, even urgently. It was an unusual moment in class history.

After Will's little speech, we didn't have much to say. I, for one, was almost a bit too tired of them to argue with the class. The point they were supposed to get—that broad, poetic vision will give them the most meaningful kind of escape there is—they didn't get. It was something they didn't want to hear, or couldn't hear, apparently.

CHAPTER FOURTEEN

Collapse

Whereas a lot of kids who're in their late teens and early twenties now still hold a warm place in their hearts for Stephen Spielberg's wise children, for the kids in the Woodstock jail, that warm place was owned by Stephen King. His kids wandered around inside their imaginations like little emperors, princes of the realm. He was the only writer they had read carefully, the only one whose classics every last kid had read, and the only writer whose books get stolen from the library every time they appear on the shelves.

Many of the King books are about unloved children, lost in the vastness of the American continent or lost in institutions that are meant to stand in for America. They stand on the brink of adulthood and don't like what they see. They are observant, morally courageous children who're often haunted by their *parents'* sins, and often killed by the indifference of adults. Sometimes, as in *Pet Sematary*, they slink back from the Great Beyond and reappear as gory emblems of society's guilt.

Characters like this, it seemed, spent a lot of time whispering in my students' ears. The kids were instantly alert when I talked about Stephen King; they corrected the errors I made in reciting the plots of the books and filled in the names of the characters when I couldn't remember them.

Perhaps the terrible psychic power that King's kids possessed had a way of making the jail seem less daunting. Danny Torrance in *The Shining*, Charlie McGee in *Firestarter*, Carrie in *Carrie:* these kids do get splashed in blood from time to time, but it doesn't really stain them and they use their powers like the Old Testament Yahweh, raining destruction on a sinful land. For the prosecuted, lonely, waiting, anguished kids in jail, that way of looking at children was enthralling. They could and did enthrall themselves with it all day.

I wanted to teach some Stephen King—I knew the students would do the reading, for one thing—but I also wanted to introduce them to things they didn't already know. The goal was to jerk them out of their routine, to help them see their lives with the clarity of an observer. So I looked around for things with the potential to sharpen their focus on themselves; and I started by looking for books that had had that effect on me when I was their age.

When I was a little younger than the youngest Woodstock kids, when I was about fifteen, I was obsessed for a time by a Larry Clark book of photographs called *Tulsa* that I located one day on a remote shelf in my dad's library. I pored over the pictures and wondered if they could somehow be used as a kind of pornography, but they were too spooky for that. I didn't have a clue what they were for. The photographer didn't clear up the mystery at all in his paragraph-length bio that introduced the photographs. It had all the warmth of a scrawl inside a tomb:

> i was born in Tulsa, Oklahoma in 1943. when i was sixteen i started
> shooting amphetamine. i shot with my friends everyday for three
> years and then left town but i've gone back through the years. once
> the needle goes in, it never comes out.

The book was an album of beautiful horrors: lanky, angelic drug addicts clutching their spikes; decrepit moms dozing in the sunlight like bears; an intruder into the drug den beaten and bloody. Everyone in that Tulsa world lived hard by the edge of savagery; it was an address they were perfectly fine with, as far as I could tell. I was jealous and wondered how you got to Tulsa, and how I could be that tough myself.

What I needed at the time was someone who could help me notice and value the gritty realism in my own life. It didn't look like anything in Tulsa—it looked more like *Green Acres* but with a feuding mom and dad—but it was my mystery and it did need some attending to. I didn't see the use. My own life had less reality for me than it should have and I would have been happy to pack everything about it into a sack and drop the whole trivial mess into a swiftly flowing river. I really did leap once from a bridge onto a shelf of black ice, not in order to kill myself, but in order to see what would happen. I didn't break through, but did manage to split the back of my head open. I lay on the surface of the ice for a moment hoping that the blood would pool around my head like a beautiful crimson halo while my friends stared at me. Of course I had no such luck. My hair matted and stuck to the ice; there was hardly any blood at all.

To the kids in jail I was trying to offer the perspective my friends must have seen when they looked down on me from the bridge. I was trying to make their lives real to them, and trying to help them confront the adult world not in the self-absorbed way I did, or the spoiled way I did, or the reality-denying way I did, but as certain heroes in books do, that is, with dignity, and moral force, and honesty.

I put Danny Torrance, the hero of *The Shining*, at the end of the unit on kids and violence and America for that reason. He turns out to be a good role model for kids: in the end, he sloughs off the visions of doom with which he's beset throughout the novel. He takes matters into his own hands, and, perhaps a little improbably, destroys the sinister Overlook Hotel in which his family is imprisoned.

Earlier in this unit on violence, we spent time with some of Danny Torrance's spiritual kin: those seeing children—Tarwater in O'Connor's *The Violent Bear It Away,* John Grady Cole in McCarthy's *All the Pretty Horses,* and Nick Adams in Hemingway's story "The Killers."

I thought the students might take an interest in the fate of Francis Marion Tarwater, Flannery O'Connor's boy prophet in *The Violent Bear It Away.* A smooth-talking devil whispers over his shoulder in the opening pages; his uncle-guardian-tormentor keels over at the breakfast table and Tarwater makes directly for the whiskey still. Afterward, when he awakens from his drunkenness, he promptly sets his childhood homestead on fire and sets out for the city, home of sin.

All the themes for a good class with the inmates were present: family history, revenge, the hero who seeks his destiny in the great wide world. I wish I could say the students filled themselves up on the material like Tarwater at the still, but they didn't. On the first day we had a fine discussion about the fire that consumes the uncle's shack: There's a pink moon above the conflagration that descends into it as the shack burns; there are huge silver eyes that stare at Tarwater from its center; there is rutted, ugly field nearby and of course a black, black night. All of this reminded Will of a concert and a bonfire he'd been at a few months back: every detail was precisely the same, including the pink moon and the field. But the next day,

Will and his friend Tim, the sculptor, tossed their books on the table; won't be here for a little while, sorry, said Tim and left.

"I can't get into this," said Will. Maybe there was too much religion in the book; maybe the print was too small. I concluded *The Violent Bear It Away* a day earlier than scheduled and then went hunting for my departed students in the hallways. Come back, all is forgiven, I said—no more religion. I depended strictly on their goodwill and couldn't afford to lose two of the regular attendees.

During the two weeks when I scheduled *All the Pretty Horses* and "The Killers," my class was visited by a band of ex-parolees who were all arrested together a few days earlier, apparently, for violating the conditions of their release. They had spent the last five years together at Vermont's warehouse for long-term prisoners which happens to be in Virginia. There at the Greenville Correctional Center, amid the gun towers and the three-thousand-plus inmate population, they had learned how to measure their hatred. They paid it out carefully, in doses calculated to avoid getting themselves in trouble.

Unfortunately for me, they seemed to search out the jail library like homing pigeons, day in and day out, probably because they wanted to be out of the way of the guards and Jim and the cameras. My class didn't get a lot of work done in those weeks. The old convicts weren't interested in Cormac McCarthy and downright refused to read the Hemingway.

On some days—when the reading had bored the inmates, or when there were too many brand-new people, or when my regulars were in court—it was just me talking to the Virginians, reading passages out loud, gesturing at the cover of the book, and spinning paperback copies of *All the Pretty Horses* toward them, those hairy weight lifters, those gigantic illustrated men. From behind their matted beards they watched the books turning on the table. They left off mumbling to one another for a few moments and then resumed their private discussions. I was pretty sure they wouldn't be doing the homework.

The arrival of the Virginians was the beginning of the end for me. For Laird and Will, both of whom were destined for Virginia, it was more like the end of the beginning. It was a foretaste of life in the years to come.

These older, seasoned convicts used to settle into their chairs in the current events room—six or eight of them at a time—all at once, foul smelling and pissed off, and begin a campaign of sotto-voce harassment. They did it invisibly at first, and then gradually with more and more flair. In a typical current events class, one of them, a hairy giant named Tom, would sit down next to me, and peck at my right arm. Move, he would demand. Asshole? Move. His nostrils would flare, and I would move. Tom had a shaggy mustache and shaggy bangs hanging into his eyes; he was in his late thirties and claimed to have robbed every bank in the Northeast Kingdom.

"Got any food, Thea?" his friend, Mark, would ask.

"Hey faggot?" another one would whisper.

Laird would turn his head and everyone around the table with the exception of Jim and me would snicker and guffaw. The noise was loud enough to make the tables chatter against the floor.

I liked to inspect the tattoos of the old-timers: purple barbed wire on their necks; dragons on their forearms, a Medusa-woman on Mark's bicep. She was a snake-haired harpie whose eyes were black coals: they glowed and shot off sparks. Her viper's tongue flashed out of her mouth like a whip. For hours at a time, Mark would rub his hand over her—back and forth, up and down, around and around, as if he she was still causing him pain—and then he would peer down into her eyes to have a closer look.

There's a jail rule about other people's tattoos: staring suggests too much involvement in the other guy's person. You're supposed to take the tattoos in through peripheral vision, I guess. I ignored the rule and stared like a visitor to a gallery. Mark glared. I apologized. Mark threatened:

"Man can get shanked for that, man. Don't be looking over here."

"I was only looking for a second," I confessed. "Not really at all. Sorry about that."

"Don't do it again," he warned. "I don't like that shit, okay? Do you want me staring at your pansy ass?" I didn't and told him so.

The new arrivals were still beaming and puffed up from having had their parole taken away—a cop had busted all the residents of their halfway house in one fell swoop. Apparently some other convict who didn't get arrested had left a roach lying on a tray and the probation officer had happened on it one morning. And then he'd happened on the house residents, who were drunk and stoned and couldn't account for the roach. They were all immediately packed off to jail.

When Chris, a bank robber and veteran from Virginia, filled in the story for Laird, Laird shook his head slowly in gallant sympathy.

"Fucking DOC," Laird mumbled, his eyes narrowing in indignation. "Who busted you?"

"Fucking cop," Chris said.

"Fucking Damone?"

"Fucking Damone, yeah."

"Fucking DOC," Laird agreed. "What the fuck's the point, you know? A fucking roach?"

Chris had nothing else to say to Laird; he turned away and Laird took the cue. But whenever one of the old-timers expressed a need or a complaint, Laird was on hand to address the matter.

"You don't know HTML?" he would say. "If you don't know HTML, I can teach you like in a day." Tom gave him a nasty look. None of the ex-parolees had much use for web-designing software code. They wanted cigarettes and letters from home and secondhand porno mags.

When they hit Laird up for their nicotine fixes, Laird assured them he had plenty of cigs on hand in his cell. And when they wanted food, Laird agreed to share some of his canteen. They were his new friends, and he wanted to be welcomed into the group.

With the new prisoners, there were nearly twenty people in the current events class. Jim had to bring in extra chairs from the music practice room. He had to ask the inmates to settle down three or four times before introducing his topics. "Gentlemen," he would say when he'd finally coaxed everyone into a state of relative quiet. "Gentlemen. What's in the news?" Mark—the owner of the Medusa tattoo, he was supposed to hold the Vermont record for DWIs, thirteen, he said—refused to make eye contact with Jim at all.

The new people wouldn't stand for a regular discussion of current events such as we had been having in the past. They drank a darker, bloodier drink than Jim could serve up from the *Rutland Herald,* and every time he proposed his bland cocktail, the inmates—soon it was everyone, new and old alike—countered with a concoction of their own. It was a brew cooked up from stray items in the paper and stories they'd picked up during their time in Virginia.

Rhino knew it well. He liked to savor it, to gurgle with it and slosh it around in his mouth and pat his tummy as it slurped down his throat. I could see him warming up to it as soon as the Virginians began talking; he laced his fingers across his belly and leaned back in his chair, his eyes chuckling like a customer at a bar.

One day, an item appeared in the newspaper concerning two small-time felons who had been locked up in Woodstock in the early nineties. They'd been in for burglaries of various kinds, but had escaped one day from a work-release crew, and had gone on to commit much graver crimes, thereby ending the work-release program. It seems that one of these two hoodlums-turned-killers wanted a new trial.

We talked then for a half an hour about the murder of Robin Colson in Newfane, Vermont, in the spring of '91. The discussion that ensued was a sort of good-versus-evil contest in which there really was no contest at all but rather a wave and then the subsiding of the wave. Jim had been positioned somewhere along the beach; he did his best to hold his piece of ground, but he was vastly overmatched and was left inundated and defeated. The whole thing was a turning point for me, as it may also have been for Laird, Vandriel, and Will, though they, being destined for Virginia, had to turn in a different direction.

Most of us were roughly familiar with the story of Chris Bacon and his partner in crime, Charlie Gundlah. The story was part of the inmate lore around the Woodstock jail, and still part of the community memory in southern Vermont. It was another home invasion tale: wandering hoodlums who'd never done more than rob a convenience store and sell drugs had embarked on a wild crime spree that ended in an act of chilling violence.

We heard again how Bacon had been just a kid at the time, nineteen, and not nearly as ill-tempered as Gundlah, who was ten years older. We heard how one spring morning the two of them walked away from a brush-cutting crew that had been mobilized from the Woodstock jail. We heard how they had taken themselves on a bender that culminated in the stabbing death, on April 19, 1991, of a music teacher, Robin Colson, in Newfane, Vermont. Yet in this telling, the story had details that must have come from Bacon himself, who many people on hand, including Slash, knew personally.

After Bacon and Gundlah ditched their crew, said Slash, they started wandering into people's houses. They found stashes of pot and smoked it down. They stole somebody's scuba knife.

They stole a stake from a horseshoe pit. For four days, they walked around southern Vermont, breaking into empty houses during the daytime, borrowing the drugs and the whiskey and whatever weapons Gundlah thought might have been useful.

When they were armed to the teeth and totally stoned, they appeared at Colson's doorstep. It happened that she had been a teacher in Bacon's elementary school though apparently the two did not know each other. Slash knew her slightly. About thirty, pretty. Single. Everybody knows everybody in those small towns down there. Gundlah wanted her car, a Subaru station wagon. "Can we use the phone?" he asked.

Jim had had enough at this point. There was no current events value in the discussion and nothing to be gained from rehashing the story. "Gentlemen," he urged, "let's move on."

As Slash talked he allowed himself to get angry about the scandal all over again. Or was he really angry about the depravity of the inmates? Maybe. It was hard to tell.

The real culprit, he said, was the fucking DOC that let those two assholes out. The fucking DOC that gave Gundlah a "don't incarcerate" recommendation the first two or three times he was arrested. The fucking DOC that wanted to keep him, Slash, in jail for obstruction of justice and could see its way to letting Gundlah roam the state with a goddamn Weed Whacker and a rake. He was also pissed that a kid like Bacon should be subjected to whatever mind games Gundlah had played on him. His eyes burned at Jim as if Jim were responsible.

"Stephen," Jim said.

Robin, it seems, was by herself. She knew what was going to happen. She tried to shut the door, but Gundlah kicked it. He asked for her car keys. She went into her bedroom. Gundlah was trying to be nice about the whole thing. He was going to kill her from the beginning, but he wanted to do it professionally, mercifully, by strangling her. But she started screaming. Bacon said he had no idea what was going to happen. He thought Gundlah was just going to tie her up or something. She died fighting, clawing from the ground. Gundlah kept kicking her. He had his stake from the horseshoe set. He used it to crush her larynx. Then, to make sure she was dead, he stabbed her in the heart with the scuba knife.

After she was dead, Bacon and Gundlah dug a grave in the woods near her house. They buried her beneath a mound of leaves and flat stones.

The more Slash talked, the more outraged he became, but over what I couldn't tell.

"They were sick motherfuckers," someone said.

"And Bacon had like two weeks to max out his sentence," someone else said. He'd been in jail for holding up a gas station convenience store in Thetford.

"Now Bacon's living with all the lifers too," Mark said. Now Mark had a story. "Down in Virginia—" he began.

"Mark," Jim interrupted

"Down in Virginia. Check this out, Jim. Please," he pleaded. Jim shook his head.

"Gentlemen," he said and rolled his eyes. Mark kept talking. One of the lifers, one of Bacon's neighbors, stabbed a guy in the neck down there. Guy comes running out of the cell—blood squirting all over the place. Bacon tried to put a compress on it.

"Mark," Jim said

"Wait, Jim," Mark said. "This is funny. The lifer guy jammed his shank into the base of his roommate's skull and twisted it. The motherfuckers in Vermont, they had this guy classified as a nonviolent offender, right? What the fuck?"

"Okay, Mark," Jim warned.

Rhino was gibbering happily, running his hand over his mustache. The other prisoners shuffled their newspapers; they watched Jim and waited for him to lose his patience.

Slash turned on Jim: "Why was Gundlah let go on a work detail? You work for the Department of Corrections, Jim. What the fuck's the deal?"

Finally, Tom interrupted. It wasn't just Bacon who was nuts, he said. "Another guy I knew down in Virginia, this guy killed someone in New-fane too." Larry Plante, it seemed, was on probation when he killed a friend of his by stabbing him in the head with a ski pole. "Another sup-posedly nonviolent DOC beauty—planted a ski pole into Larry Manks's head—and stole his fucking cowboy boots, too," said Tom. "He was arrested wearing the guy's fucking boots and his leather fucking jacket. Ski pole was planted right in his goddamn scalp. Now he's down in fucking Virginia carving letters into his arm," Tom told us.

Jim had to end the class early. Another ten minutes went by and finally Jim called into his radio to summon a guard. The inmates were told they could come back for the next period but if they did come back, they had to be signed up for a specific class and had to be ready to do the work in that class.

A half hour later, when they trooped into the library, they seemed a giddy and flushed group of athletes—as if they'd just arrived from the locker room and were ready for another round. I braced myself and stared at my lecture notes.

Laird sailed through the door today, circled the table, and dropped a letter from Hofstra University into my lap. I had ten seconds to glance at it—the admissions committee welcomed his interest...his record of achievement at Gould gave them great confidence in him. They wished him the best of luck in his search for a good college match and urged him to contact them at any point in the future with questions. "If I'm a so-called cold-blooded killer, why did they write this?" he demanded. He pulled the letter out of my hands. "Why?"

"Maybe you didn't tell them?"

"They know I've had a problem with the DOC," he said.

As soon as the hour ticked two, I started babbling madly. Let the content of the class take over, just keep talking, I was telling myself. I rely heavily on my notes in situations like this. I had a brief program drawn up designed to introduce the students to the giant symbolic apparatus that Stephen King deploys in *The Shining*. My sense is that the students know the plot well, but they're not reading the book as the impassioned polemic it is, and they don't see the backdrop of the novel—the deserted hotel, its population of spirits, the father's alcoholism—as anything more than a collection of horror-shop tricks.

My notes had me beginning the class on page 63, when Wendy and Jack Torrance, parents of the psychic Danny, stop at a pull-off on the high mountain road that leads to the terrible Overlook Hotel. My notes said: "Panorama of endless firs, plunging mountainsides, and in distance THE MIGHTY OVERLOOK: Sublimity of American landscape, its DANGERS, its terrible beauty. Swallows you up. Erotic tremors for Wendy, Jack." After making a little speech based on these notes, I read a passage from page 64 that shows King illustrating the soul-touching, perpetual allure of the westward voyage. We see the action through the eyes of Danny, the visionary child, who's gifted and afflicted by his ability to shine: "And in the bug, which moved upward more surely on the gentler grade, he kept looking out between them [Wendy and Jack] as the road unwound, affording occasional glimpses of the Overlook Hotel, its massive bank of westward looking windows reflecting back the sun." My notes said: "Emphasize: the shining beacon/city on the hill, the lateness of the day, the beauty of the day, the strength of Danny T's vision."

I organized my class today around an overlook of the Overlook past. The view takes in a magnificent sweep of American history—I meant to stress the grandeur and nobility of its early decades. It happens that the history of the nation's best and brightest can be glimpsed by scanning the names in the hotel's desk registers: Roosevelts and Rockefellers visited often; "Henry Ford and Fam." dropped by in 1927, according to the hotel records. In 1956, "Darryl F. Zanuck and Party" had reserved the entire top floor for a week.

But King is at pains in the book to stress that a great falling off occurred somewhere shortly after World War II. There's a long narrative of decay and greed and malevolence to be followed by observing the history of the hotel, and I wanted to give the students a crack at commenting on this second act in American culture as well. So my plan in class was to A) establish that the Overlook Hotel is King's metaphor for America and B) to examine the relations between the hotel and the Torrance family.

"They're the caretakers of the hotel now," I announced as I was beginning this part of the discussion. "That tells you something, right?" The inmates shifted uncertainly in their chairs. They were thinking, reflecting. Good

King's trick, and the part I like most, is that the family of the hero child is itself a crystallization of America's postwar decline; it has the same problems on a personal, familial level that haunt the hotel and entire continent. Thus Danny Torrance need only look into his parents' minds (with his special "shining" power) to see what America has in store for him—and for all other children, by the way. Insane violence, self-destruction, alcoholism, and, of course, barbarous behavior toward kids. So, before I examined the doomed history of America through the hotel desk registers, I wanted to have a brief look at the dangers gathering over Danny's family.

In the opening chapters, the boy undergoes his first seizure of many. As he waits for his father on a curb outside a rented apartment in Boulder, his imaginary friend, Tony, beckons to him from a spot far off at the bottom of the street. Like a sleepwalker, Danny rises from his curb to see what Tony would have him see. He's a modern pioneer-child climbing up a western ridge to peer into the American past. The haunted Overlook appears before him, and many horrible things besides: It's where he's headed, where his father is coming from even now after an appointment with the manager. It's his destiny made manifest:

> Sometimes thinking very hard made something happen to him. It made things—real things—go away and then he saw things that weren't there. Once, not long after they put the cast on his arm, this had happened at the supper table. They [his parents] weren't talking much to each other then. But they were thinking. Oh yes. The thoughts of DIVORCE hung over the kitchen table like a cloud full of black rain, pregnant, ready to burst. The thought of eating with all that black DIVORCE around made him want to throw up. And because it had seemed desperately important, he had thrown himself fully into concentration and something had happened. When he came back to real things, he was lying on the floor with beans and mashed potatoes in his lap and his mommy was holding him and crying and Daddy had been on the phone. He had been frightened and had tried to explain to them that there was nothing wrong, that this sometimes happened...

Obviously, there's a division in the familial house, isn't there? I asked.

And this division is supposed to be reflected elsewhere, of course, in other houses. Right?

"I didn't read the book," said Mark.

"I didn't know it was a book," said someone else.

I didn't get very far with my discussion plan. To people who've seen the movie and haven't read the book, the story is about Jack Nicholson terrorizing Shelly Duvall. Jack Nicholson roams the halls of his hotel with an ax; he slams it through the bathroom door. No amount of lecturing can coax people into the belief that the boy in the story has an emotional life and that we're meant to be attached to its development. We ended up skipping over my whole program because the guys from Virginia and Rhino and Slash wanted to talk about scenes they remember from the movie: the blood pouring out of the elevator; Jack at his typewriter, "Honey, I'm home!" "Redrum! Redrum!" and all of that.

The new guys segued from the Overlook to Other Jails, that topic of endless fascination to the inmates. At Other Jails, people amputate their own testicles and roll them down the hall like olives; they help each other commit suicide in preset operations that run with the efficiency of a marine drill. If you want to go, you've just got to say the word and they'll string you up like a slab of beef. At other prisons, you buy with a pack of cigarettes the privilege of buggering other people's "wives"; people wake up from afternoon naps with shanks sticking out of their kidneys. The Aryan Brotherhood and gangs of lifers execute people every day. The inmates, especially Laird and Will, talked about these stories like hearty old cons—knowing the terrain, laughing, embracing their destiny, and being a little rueful about it besides. I tried to drag the class back to Stephen King and succeeded for a while, but instead of reading the book or talking about it in an intelligent way, we visited each horror scene independently, as if there had been no plot or design or writerly scheme to set them off. We just strolled by the gore as if we were looking into rows of museum dioramas—each event disconnected from every other event and each one producing its little jolt of satisfaction. The inmates know the text well, and Laird and Will were our guides.

I sank back into my chair after some useless efforts to quell the inmates—it only makes them madder. At one point, Slash apologized.

"Don't apologize if you don't mean it," I said. "What are you apologizing about?" I asked

"Okay, nothing," he responded. Then: "Well, what the fuck do you expect, Theo? You didn't come down to the country club, you know."

JAIL DIARY, JUNE 1, 2000

I think things might be getting a little dicey with Jim. I think he's ready to move in a new adjunct teacher. He seems to poke his head into the library two or three times every class these days, as if he's angling to catch me filling the inmates' baseball caps with contraband. It's not merely this checking-up though, that has me on edge. He's asked me twice in the past two weeks what my long-term plans are. We both know that I can't be a part-time jail teacher forever; for one thing, the Corrections Department won't allow it. Either they hire you full time or you move on.

We've both pretended that I'm busy pursuing other things in my off time, and we've pretended that together we will bide the time until a good offer comes through. Now this agreement is faltering, it seems. Or anyway, he's withdrawing from it. Jim has taken to wondering when, specifically, the better job I've been hinting about is likely to materialize. He's not subtle. He heaves a big sigh and hitches up his trousers like a farmer about to spec'late 'bout cows with another farmer. So, he sighs. So. In terms of your other employment. How's that going?

He did this once last week in front of a guard upstairs. The guard's face was as blank as it always is, but when I turned my back, I felt him send a wink over to Jim. It seems like everybody's up to date on my situation. Erratic inmate attendance, course materials that verge on provocation, too friendly with the inmates.

We are already deep into the Woodstock summer. In the schoolrooms, and especially upstairs in the corridors, I smell a new odor on top of the floor cleaner and the cafeteria grease: cut grass.

A mile from the cell blocks, in every direction—up on the hillsides, down in the river flats—rolls of hay stand like giant dinner buns in the fields. Late in the evening, long past dinnertime, they're still casting their shadows across the stubble. When the inmates go to sleep in their cells at eleven, they can still hear the tractors bringing in the hay. They can see a dusky gray light lingering in the west: so says Laird. I'm guessing that they can't physically see it, that they just know it's there. From what I can see, it's really only visible from bluffs and ridges outside of town. The inmates complain about it anyway—they hate going to bed when the night is still young. And they hate the long summer evenings—anything that drags itself out reminds them of the larger expanse of time they have to endure, and is permanently disagreeable to them.

So bedtime itself has lately become an issue that I hear about in mutterings and sighing complaints. The teenagers are the worst affected. They feel that an essential human right, namely staying up late, a right even more fundamental than freedom itself, has been pried from their grasp. Impassive, overgrown baby-sitters in green uniforms have done the dirty work—and they themselves, the prisoners, haven't so much as put up a word of resistance.

Inside the jail of course, no one smells the farmy, fresh hay smell of the June mowing. What we get there is suburban lawn-trimming odor. It comes drifting in from the rec yard mower and from the clothing of the inmates who push the mower around. It's a sweeter, homier smell than the odors outside of Woodstock—it's lawn mixed with essence of dandelion.

The smell reminds you of the last few days of high school, those late June days when all the kids around you are about to flood out into the world. Nothing is easier than to look at the prisoners and see them, in your mind's eye, loosed from the jail and traipsing along forest paths, plunging into streams like kids on vacation, and emerging with their white flesh shining in the sun. Today in class, three of the inmates had been to court in the morning—Laird, Frenchie, and Joe—different court houses, apparently, but dressed in their legal finery as they were, they seemed as though they'd been out on the town together. They seemed like sober, Christian young men, returned to the mission after an early, desultory round of proselytizing.

Laird in particular looked bright and beautiful. If you saw just the image of him this morning—in a photograph, perhaps—and didn't know anything about him, you'd see his sunny smile, the tint of orange that hasn't yet washed out of his hair, his wire-rim glasses. He would stand out as the decent kid, the self-respecting one, the slightly nerdy, chubby, overly friendly one who gets picked on for no good reason by the others. You'd notice his world-accepting smile and his studious glasses.

As I watched them file into the library, I was overwhelmed with an unwonted feeling of gratitude. The inmates are on trial for their lives, basically, and yet they're still anxious to come to class every day, still busy with the homework, still trying to keep in my good graces. They have bigger things to worry about than whether or not they're keeping up with the homework assignments I'm giving them, and yet they are earnestly keeping up.

I've got to get *The Shining* finished. It's not exactly what I want to be reading right now but I've gotten this far into it and I've got to finish it. As soon as the inmates sat down today, I started talking about what happens at the end of the book. Danny faces down his father—he faces down the whole of the Overlook—the sprawling history of corruption and violence his dad was trying to hand on to him. He looks at this coldly and resolves to blow it all up.

As soon as I opened my mouth to talk, I noticed that Rhino was stuffing pencils into his nostrils. He had three of them up there and was putting his hand out toward the other prisoners for more pencils.

I ignored him for a moment and kept talking. The great boiler in the basement of the Overlook, the giant cylindrical metal tank that whistles and groans when the PSI rises over 100. Everybody remembers this, right?

Rhino had five pencils dangling from his nostrils by then and had removed his hands from his face. He spread his palms wide and then opened up his whole wingspan like a giant bat in a cave. How about that? he laughed. How the fuck about that?

A round of stifled applause spread through the room. The inmates thumped their feet on the ground.

I had more students than I knew what to do with today, perhaps because there's a new kid here now, a teenager who says he's been charged with attempted murder. It seems he barged into a house somewhere in southern Vermont armed with a gun and a pair of knives. The teenage girls in the house, possibly friends of his, said he'd tried to stab them. He shot at someone else. He seems like a nice enough kid—frightened and anxious to fit in like the new kids always are. His name is Rich. His eyes bulge when he's addressed by the older inmates. They call him Crazy Rich because no one can figure out why he's done what he's done, and he's not talking.

Altogether in class, there were fifteen inmates. I knew the names of four of them.

It seems that the one thing that can keep Mark from getting released is a bad word from his parole officer. When Rhino had finished his performance, Mark took the opportunity to deliver a lecture about what will happen to his PO if he takes back the parole Mark has already been given once. If he does it, he will put two bullets in his heart, he said. "I will walk up to him, put the silencer on his chest, pull the trigger twice, swab off the burn marks and walk away. Easiest fucking crime to get away with in the world," he said. "Just one thing you have to keep in mind: No witnesses."

I was looking at Rich during this speech. He showed no reaction.

"That's the way it's done," said Rhino, staring at Rich. "Isn't that what you did?"

It seems that Laird has some people he'd like to get back at as well. He's angry with a certain newspaper up in Bethel, Maine, where he used to go to school. Before he could launch himself into a lecture about that, I grabbed at my *Shining* notes and started reading them: In the Presidential Suite, men in suits and narrow ties are piled in a bloody heap. They are beginning to stir before Danny's eyes, I said. But now the kid finally has some control. So he stares at them, and faces them down. Do you guys remember this? I asked. FALSE FACES! he says to himself. NOT REAL! Do you guys remember this?

Laird was hardly listening to me at all. He was wrapped up in a discussion of how best to exact revenge on the newspaper in Bethel that had been printing lies about him. I'm gonna burn down the whole fucking town, he shrugged. That place is so full of liars, man.

"You should burn down the fucking jail, while you're at it," Rhino suggested.

"I hope you do burn down the jail," said Slash, "but just wait until I've left. Then I'll come down here to piss on your embers."

"I'll come down to pour gasoline on you guys—that ought to help," said Rhino.

I started scribbling a bit in my notebook, not knowing what else to do, and seeing this, one of the Virginians suggested that I write a poem.

"Okay," I mumbled.

"I'll write you the poem right now," said Tom.

He chanted: "It's a dirty fucking hole. The government can suck and ride my pole. It's a dirty fucking hole."

Laird sat up in his chair, smiling. "I like that one," he said. "We could make that into a rap or something."

Frenchie picked up his cue: "It's a dirty fucking hole.... The government can suck and ride..." Soon, five inmates were tapping on the table and singing in unison: "It's a dirty fucking hole. It's a dirty fucking hole," over and over again. Then more inmates joined in. They were looking at me and at the new kid, Rich, as they sang. It was a sort of song of initiation for Rich, and for me, a song of victory. The victory was theirs of course, and I wanted at that moment to concede it to them.

"I'd like to finish with *The Shining*," I said. "I've prepared a goddamn lecture. Some people here have done some homework, some preparation for this class. Okay?"

"Let's watch the fucking movie," someone said.

Another chant began, possibly from Frenchie's corner of the room: "Fuck those books, we want the movie, fuck your books."

Someone decided that that would be a good time to toss his copy of Stephen King into my lap. First one copy came skidding across the table, and then another rolled end over end, and then a small flock of paperbacks was fluttering through the air.

Fortunately, today was the last day for *The Shining* and the students were supposed to turn their books in anyway. I packed them into my backpack and sat for a while with the inmates as they talked about the movies they wanted to see, and the crimes they felt they might like to commit someday. For the first time in my experience as a jail teacher, I got up before the class was officially over, and slipped out the door. I made an excuse to Jim—I had to meet a friend a bit early today—and climbed up the basement stairs, feeling distinctly like a fugitive. Just let me the hell out of here, I was thinking at the front door. The guard on duty must have read my mind, because he saw me coming, fished my keys out of their secure cubbyhole, tossed them into the tray beneath his window, and gave me a big congratulatory smile. Another guard, in a weird gesture of chivalrousness that I've never seen in a guard before, pushed the door wide open in front of me, remarked on the beauty of the weather, and told me to have myself an excellent day.

In June I discovered that it was highly unlikely that my University Within Walls scheme was going to pan out. There would be no for-credit class, no Introduction to Western Literature offered, at least not in the near term. The reason was threefold. The education people within the DOC were not enthusiastic about a venture that would distract from its primary mission: providing high school equivalency diplomas to inmates. The Community College of Vermont was not enthusiastic about giving away credits to inmates when the rest of the citizenry had to pay for them. They wanted $5,000 per class, and an additional sum per student. I didn't have the money. When I inquired, a foundation in Woodstock noted that most of the jail's residents were not generally from Woodstock. The Woodstock Foundation's funds, I learned, were earmarked for projects that would contribute to the well-being of the town and its citizens. The jail was a state operation with almost no connection to the town.

I didn't break the news to the inmates, but I stopped talking to them about my University Within Walls scheme, and its accompanying Teach for Incarcerated America subplot.

The demise of the project didn't matter much to Laird. He was planning daring legal moves for his trial, a trial that would in time be preempted by his guilty plea. He would eventually accept a sentence of twenty-five years to life and a concurrent sentence of twenty to life for the attempted murder of his father. But in June 2000, he was eyeing his impending rise into the world of media celebrities. He felt he hadn't yet risen as high as he might. There was much more limelight to come, at least as he saw the future. He spoke often of the book he and his father were writing together about "my case." But the truth was that the estrangement between father and son was deepening. Originally, back in January and February, Bill had made an effort to visit his son in jail every week, or at least every other week, but something about Laird's attitude—his requests for money and clothing and CDs—began to grate on Bill. I didn't know this then, but the father was coming to jail because he expected something of Laird. He expected that Laird might talk to him about why he'd tried to kill him and why he'd killed his mother. He'd hoped that the two of them could explore their tragedy together. Bill wanted to write about it and suggested to Laird that he do the same: thus, "the book." Laird liked the idea and talked about it to his friends in jail as if it were really happening but he had no interest in actually collaborating with his father or in actually exploring the fateful family history. He certainly had no interest in writing. So there was never any book. For that matter, there was not much inquiry into the past, at least not from Laird.

Laird preferred to pass the time chatting about the guards and the other prisoners. He talked about CDs and movies. He never mentioned his mom. "She was like the invisible, unmentionable subject," Bill told me later, "we never talked about Paula at all." So by the summer of 2000, Bill was visiting the jail less and less. He was trying to figure out what kind of relationship he wanted to have with his son. He knew he didn't want one in which the parent provisioned the kid and the kid went off into his separate world without talking, without understanding, without regret.

In June 2000, Laird announced casually that he was in negotiations with TV producers. They were, he claimed, interested in the rights to his story. I never heard anything further about the TV producers, but various versions of TV celebrity reemerged in his planning. He wanted to call a news conference. There would be a big revelation at that hour, he promised. It would make people rethink everything they thought they knew. It would blow their minds. And the whole thing would happen out there in the public eye, he vowed, in front of the lights and the cameras, with his dad and everyone else looking on. Will said he was heartily looking forward to such an event. He would help Laird prepare himself for the cameras.

With Laird contemplating his rise back on to the media stage, and the inmates from Virginia imposing themselves on every class, I had some difficult teaching work to do. But the classes weren't all horrible. I diverged a bit from my planned syllabi and did make some progress, particularly when the Virginians began to drain away.

PART THREE

CHAPTER FIFTEEN

Alone

In the late summer of 2000, the core of my literature class disintegrated. Mike Tobin disappeared, as did Tim and Joe Emmons. They were given their twenty minutes' notice at an hour when I was not in the jail and shipped away. I had to find out from the remaining inmates that they had been "shipped." Slash, in his turn, was sent to the "farm," a minimum-security facility in Windsor, Vermont, where he waited out the final year on the five-year sentence he'd gotten for obstructing justice. Frenchie was shipped away to the St. Albans jail after an altercation he'd had with a shy eighteen-year-old inmate. Rumor had it that Frenchie had propositioned the kid and when that didn't succeed, he'd threatened to kill him and had beaten him. Frenchie picked up another charge—assault—for that crime and was sentenced to an additional year in jail.

After Rhino, Slash, Laird, and Frenchie dispersed from Woodstock, Will was given his sentence: three to seven years for armed robbery. He was transferred to the state prison in Newport, Vermont.

At his sentencing hearing, he apologized to the court: "If I could go back, I'd definitely change things. It was a weird time in my life. I don't know what made me do it. I've had nine months to think about it. I hope that when I get out, I'll be a changed person." The statement was included in the newspaper account of his sentencing that appeared the following day.

In class, I read the statement out to Will and to the eight other inmates who came to my class on that day. I read as solemnly and slowly as I could to take away whatever irony Will might have wished to recover for himself in the presence of the other inmates. I was relieved to see that he didn't try at all. He sat perfectly still, with his arms folded on his chest and his eyes cast downward at the table.

"I think you really meant that, Will," I said when I had finished reading. It seemed to me that he had likely thought carefully about the statement beforehand and had wanted to make an unvarnished, personal statement to the court.

I paused after my reading of the article and tried to catch his glance. He didn't want to look up. I stammered: "So congratulations for standing up there in front of everyone. Okay? You said your piece. Good for you."

He kept staring at the table, but finally he took his eyes off of it and looked up at the other people in the room: There were two motorcycle men who'd dropped in for the day; Tim from Brattleboro was there as were Crazy Rich and Joe Emmons. "I was definitely sincere, definitely," he said loudly, and to all of us. He didn't think being sincere had helped him any with the judge—he didn't think the judge liked him or hoped for anything from him—but it was his only shot to say something in public, and he wanted the moment to come off well.

Since I knew that after a sentencing hearing an inmate is due to be shipped from Woodstock within hours, I had brought to class a sweatshirt embroidered with Phish logos. It had the name of an Indian reservation in Florida and the date of a concert stitched in next to the cursive "Phish."

I tossed it across the table to him. "Good luck and stay out of trouble, will you?" I said.

He unfolded the sweatshirt on the table. He was embarrassed by the gift. For the first time in the six months I'd known him, he smiled and sank into his chair and blushed. He pulled himself together quickly, though. He said the name of the Indian reservation on the sweatshirt out loud several times and mentioned that he'd been planning to go there, to a Phish concert, when he was arrested. He seemed still vaguely annoyed that the police had intervened.

Rhino was released in the early fall of 2000. He was in the news again several months later when a woman named Carrie Lavallee, who turned out to be the mother of eight children and a recovering heroin addict, was found floating in the Connecticut River.

Rhino had been the last person to be seen with her. He denied any involvement in the killing, and was left alone for several weeks, but a search of his car eventually turned up bloodstains and a substance that the police identified as "human tissue" on the rear window. No one ever found out for sure what had happened since there was a plea agreement rather than a trial, but Rhino was eventually sentenced, in 2002, to a term of twenty-five to fifty years.

Laird's escape plan was foiled on a sunny afternoon in November. Laird said afterward that the guards had "rolled in" on him. He talked as though there had been a battery of armed vehicles and cops in riot gear, but it came out in later conversations that the guards had just tapped him on the shoulder. He was downstairs in the current events room at the time, typing a letter to a friend. The guards invited him to follow them up a staircase and into the booking room. There he was presented with the contents of his cell. The guards had packed his luggage for him, using the standard jail suitcase, which is not a suitcase but a translucent blue trash bag. Violent offenders get shackled at the waist and feet when they're transported. There in the booking room, he was locked into his chains, trundled off to a waiting van and driven north to the Northeast State Correctional Facility in St. Johnsbury, Vermont. The NSCF wasn't any stricter or more maximum or more vicious than Woodstock, and Laird's removal there was, it turned out, more a matter of DOC prudence than punishment. The guards had of course been listening to Laird connive over the jail phone with his accomplice. They'd noted the details of his plan: the longed-for cell phone, the window grate removal project, the $10,000 in cash. And when they felt they had sufficient evidence to accuse him of plotting an escape, he was promptly transferred to the St. Johnsbury facility.

In St. Johnsbury, Laird was charged by the DOC with an escape attempt. A Major A-1 Disciplinary Report is the most serious kind of jail rule infraction that an inmate can make, and it results in a permanent blot on an inmate's record. The blot might prejudice a judge at sentencing or make it harder for the inmate to get parole when the time comes. But there were no "street" charges, and no criminal investigation, and therefore no threats of an additional jail sentence. There was just his speedy removal from Woodstock and a lessening of the likelihood of parole.

In the year 2000, one in every six male teenagers in Vermont was under the supervision of the Department of Corrections. In the previous three years, there had been a 77 percent rise in the state's population of youthful inmates (defined as offenders under twenty-one). There was a growing gang problem in cities like Rutland and Burlington and Brattleboro; the gangs brought heroin, and that caused further problems. There was a 79 percent rise in youthful property crimes in 2000 over the previous year and a 60 percent rise in teenage drug crimes.

I didn't know these statistics at the time—I had a vague sense that things were perhaps deteriorating in the world of certain teenagers in rural and suburban America and it seemed logical that the detritus should pass a spell in the local jail.

Yet I never felt that the Woodstock jail was buried under a wave of disaffected youth; I never felt we were living through an epidemic. There was probably never more than one teenager for every eight inmates in Woodstock when I was there, but the teenagers did make their presence felt. They strutted more, and conspired more, and tried, at least, to live life in jail in the larger, daring, laughing way they had led it on the streets. They were the jail's singers, the would-be escapees, the importers of contraband, and the inmates most likely, therefore, to get into further trouble.

Of all the cliques in the Woodstock jail—heroin addicts, sex criminals, motorcycle men—the teenagers were, however, kindest to their own. They served up jail tours and tutorials for the new kids, and within hours, the new ones were traveling the hallways in the company of their brethren, moving from one place to the next in herds, like college freshmen. They traded clothing with one another and CDs and candy and true-crime books. Whereas the older inmates made no pretense of lending an ear to one another's troubles, the younger kids did. They passed their poems and their correspondence around to one another, and kept up-to-date about one another's girlfriends. The trusting ones submitted their legal documents to Frenchie for advice on the law. At twenty-four he was a graybeard among the teenagers. When dilemmas were put to him in the right way, he uttered pronouncements under his breath. He didn't make a lot of legal judgments, but those he did make, he made with solemn authority, motioning imperceptibly with his hand. "Call your lawyer," he would breathe, or "You gotta contact prisoner's rights," or "Grieve it," meaning the kid should file an official grievance with the jail administration. The questioners would nod in silence and the conversation would end. I think few doubted that Frenchie would succeed in persuading the Windham County District Court that he was incapable on grounds of mental deficiency to stand trial. It was presumed he would be released from Woodstock into a comfortable mental institution and, from there, back to his old haunts. When, in June 2000, a headline appeared in the *Valley News*, "Experts: Suspect Is Mildly Retarded," no one raised an eyebrow. The text listed Frenchie's charges: one count of sexual assault, one of kidnapping, one of domestic abuse. It said that the psychiatrists were inclined to recommend leniency since his IQ of 86 made it difficult for him to assist in his own defense.

The more I watched the inmates come and go, the easier it was to detach myself from them. I took some time off at the end of the summer and came back in September.

During the fall, I made overtures to all the teenagers who seemed willing to talk: I invited them into the library, offered them copies of the books I wanted to teach, and arranged for movies to be shown on the library VCR.

I churned out new, alluring syllabi every two weeks and taped sheets of paper to prominent spots on the cinder-block walls in the current events room. There they were duly ignored along with all the other school announcements. To the passing inmates I proposed: "The Literature and Films of the Wild West," "The Belly of the Beast: Writing from Inside" (we began with Edward Bunker's *The Education of a Felon*), and "True Crime, the Novel" (Truman Capote, Norman Mailer, and James Ellroy.)

With every passing week, I trained my eye on a new kid, or on a new clutch of kids, whose outward demeanor, I guessed, might possibly overlay an impulse to study. Some of these students would drift into the library during classes attended principally by the older drunks or the unpopular sex criminals.

I made greater efforts to attract Jim Vandriel to the class. Laird had told me that he pretended, even to himself, that he was fine about having accepted his twenty-year plea, but at night in his cell he sometimes babbled in his sleep and sometimes emerged from his bunk with tears running down his face. He had zero interest in literature—some interest in music, some in computers—and when he came to class, he sat in stony silence and refused to read anything that was given to him.

Most of the kids in jail knew that they were undergoing a divorce. They were divorcing themselves from the great apparatus of kid rescue: diversion programs, guidance counselors, friendly English teachers, juvenile courts, sports, and all the other measures that society employs to lead young people out of the dangerous places in adolescence. Many of the kids had never been truly married to this system in the first place, though they did trust it to be there. Anyway, now the relationship was through. Some of the young people had misgivings about this new event, the separation; some were delighted by it, and some were frightened of it, but almost all the kids looked on it, eventually, as a good reason to stop paying attention to their teachers. In September and October of that year, I tried to persuade the teenagers I met that, despite the divorce, now was no time to be giving up on school. They seemed to think that now was an excellent time. All the other reciprocal relationships in their lives were faltering. The demise of school was the least of their worries.

"But school still has a lot to offer you guys," I insisted. "Look around you!" They turned to cast jaundiced looks at the adults in the newspaper reading class: a troupe of rapists and murderers and kidnappers. I could see what words were on the teenagers' lips. They did, it seemed to me, have a point. School, in the old sense, was finished. Now they were into something new. In the wake of the University Within Walls demise, it became more difficult for me to promise that the new thing in their lives might be college. I wanted to make promises to the kids, but, usually sooner rather than later, they figured out that I was in no position to make them. They turned their attention elsewhere.

I was turning my attention elsewhere as well. As a teacher of undergraduates at a public university, I was never so drawn to my students that I felt the need to pack myself off to the library in search of books about their lives. But that fall in Woodstock, a curiosity took hold of me. I found myself entering key words into library search engines: TEENS TROUBLE AMERICA VIOLENCE, I typed and scanned the results. I turned up William Finnegan's frightening, warmhearted, heartbreaking book *Cold New World* in this way and read it in two evening sittings. I also holed up with the Russell Banks books, *The Sweet Hereafter* and *The Rule of the Bone*, which was set in an upstate New York enclave that was a near twin to Woodstock. Its star was a Huck-like first-person narrator, who, in slipping free from his family, finds himself at odds with "sivilization." To make matters worse, he is beset by a conscience.

Some of the best books about adolescents in contemporary America are books of photographs: Mary Ellen Mark's *Streetwise*; Lauren Greenfield's *Fast Forward: Growing Up in the Shadow of Hollywood*. Many of the young men in those pictures seemed to me to have just recently passed through the current events class.

I also read obsessively about a handful of suburbs in America that had recently been in the news: Littleton, Colorado; Pearl, Mississippi; West Paducah, Kentucky; and Evergreen, Washington, home of Kip Kinkel and family. I was interested less in the analysis and more interested in what the perpetrators themselves had said: what their diaries revealed, what they liked to read, what they told their friends, and what they told the police. I was directed in this way to *Rage*, a Stephen King novel, which he eventually pulled from bookstores because he thought that it might have helped Michael Carneal kill three of his classmates in Kentucky. As in *Apt Pupil* and *Carrie*, an unhappy young person goes on a spree. The book was written at the end of King's own adolescence and ought to have been laughably out of date, but it read to me like a diary that might plausibly have been kept by any of several of the Woodstock students.

That fall, I also started listening more carefully to a commentator on the local radio whom I had met when I was a student at Middlebury. Ron Powers had written a book about Mark Twain's youth that I'd read. Lately, in his radio essays, he'd begun to discuss errant kids in the suburbs and the small towns of Vermont. I listened carefully, wondering if he was going to shed some light on people I knew. He seemed to have looked into the problem a lot more carefully than I had, though he had not, as far as I knew, set foot in a jail.

I looked up an essay he'd published in a literary magazine about teaching writing at Middlebury College. He was rooting as hard as he could for the kids he taught, it seemed to me, some of whom had apparently come through a lot. But there was also a lament in his writing for the baffled families of teenagers, for baffled small towns, and for a public culture that was turning its back on its own difficult kids. That essay affected me a lot. I read it over again more than once and wondered what I might say to its author if I were to write him a letter.

By late 2000, I was beginning to sense that I'd overstayed my welcome in jail. If I had been honest with myself, I would have put my finger on a number somewhere in the vicinity of six months. The sense came not only from Jim, but also from me. I was having difficulty keeping any one student in class for longer than a week. This difficulty didn't so much worry me as make me angry over the heedlessness—the ingratitude, the philistinism (so shocking!)—of today's youth.

Meanwhile, I was becoming pleasantly heedless myself. I watched myself submitting to the rhythms of jail—the radio calls, the flow of the class periods, the fire drills, the bull sessions with the criminals—and decided that this wasn't such a bad way of passing the time after all. Hey, I'm getting paid for this, I said to myself. I waited for the next check to come in the mail.

I was still interested in the comings and goings of the inmates but I followed their movements like a retiree on a bench by the ocean: the vessels came in, the vessels left. Each one bore slightly different markings and each one hailed from a different port of call. Some of the vessels looked like they'd been submerged for decades. Others looked as though they'd breezed in on a morning gust. Yet nothing in their physical appearance, or inner qualities, for that matter, caused me to stir very far from my bench. I suspected the new ships of being exactly like the previous ones. Their logs would be filled with a familiar slate of charges: drug running, assaulting women, arms proliferating. I told myself that I could find out what I needed to know from reading the newspaper.

CHAPTER SIXTEEN

Travelers

At the end of January 2001, I watched the front pages of the local papers blackening with headlines. The *Valley News* proclaimed: "2 Bodies Found in Hanover, Police Investigate Deaths of Dartmouth Professors." The *Boston Globe* had tall capital letters: "FACULTY COUPLE AT DARTMOUTH SLAIN." It printed color snapshots of the victims below the headlines. The pictures had been taken at a happier time and showed Half and Susanne Zantop relaxed and smiling. The *Globe* story for Sunday, January 28, 2001, said:

> Dartmouth Teachers Killed
> HANOVER, N.H.—The bodies of two longtime professors at Dartmouth College were found in their home here on Saturday. The police said late today that the deaths of the couple, Susanne and Half Zantop, were homicides.
>
> A guest arriving at the home found the bodies and called the police, a neighbor, Audrey McCollum, said.

On Monday, January 29, the *Globe* wrote:

> HANOVER, N.H.—The midwinter calm of this academic town was shattered yesterday as members of the Dartmouth College community grappled with the mysterious slaying of two popular professors.

About twenty miles away from Hanover, at the Woodstock jail, the current events class was inundated that Monday with inmates who normally spent the hour after lunch outside in the rec yard. The weather had recently turned fiercely cold, so those without hats or coats or proper footwear retreated indoors to the school. It stayed cold outside for the next several weeks, and so every day, I nudged myself in with the crowd and scanned the day's headlines. On January 30, 2001, the *Globe* read:

> Slayings Cast Pall over Dartmouth
> HANOVER, N.H.—As 30 state and local investigators combed this college town yesterday and vowed to take their search statewide if necessary, authorities would not offer the smallest explanation for why, or even how, two popular Dartmouth professors were slain in their home.
>
> The lack of information in the baffling double homicide of Susanne and Half Zantop in turn fed simmering anxiety in town and on the Dartmouth College campus.

On Wednesday, January 31 in the *Globe:*

> Officials Say No Arrest Near in N.H. Killings
> HANOVER, N.H.—In a case shrouded in mystery, the state's top law enforcement official said yesterday that investigators are not close to making an arrest in the slayings of Dartmouth College professors Half and Susanne Zantop, whose bodies were found in their off-campus home Saturday night.
>
> New Hampshire Attorney General Philip T. McLaughlin dismissed the blood found in a Dartmouth dormitory Monday afternoon as being unrelated to the slayings, but offered few other details.

On February 2 in the *Globe:*

> Dartmouth Couple May Have Known Attacker, Police Say
> HANOVER, N.H.—Breaking the official silence about how two Dartmouth College professors were murdered, New Hampshire Attorney General Philip T. McLaughlin said yesterday that Susanne and Half Zantop were stabbed to death, possibly by someone they knew well enough to let into their home.
>
> Investigators said the Zantops usually kept the doors of their secluded home a few miles from campus locked, and evidence suggests they let their killer or killers into the house.

Five days after this disclosure, the New Hampshire authorities, apparently at an impasse, announced that they were bringing in the FBI.

In the current events class, as I turned the pages of the papers, I eyed the faces of the inmates, particularly the new inmates, for telltale signs of inside knowledge. I kept my eyes peeled for displays of nervousness or knowingness or excessive nonchalance or an evil combination of these. I found the nonchalance around the table to be at an altogether normal level, as was the nervousness (absent, as usual) and the knowingness (the same). The inmates flipped past the front page within a few minutes to the smaller-time crime columns—the DWIs and the drug cases—and from there on to the sports pages. When they were done, they rested their hands on their bellies as they normally did, and belched loudly, as they normally did, in order to show that it was vain to try to correct them in even the smallest of their habits.

I glanced at their pallid faces and then glanced at photographs of Half and Susanne Zantop—there were pictures of their house, their campus, their students—and felt sick. The whole thing made me ill in a way I hadn't yet been ill in jail. I felt the stink of the library toilet leaking into the current events room, where it mingled with the odor of the inmates' breathing. I smelled the odor rising from the inmates' clothing (cigarettes, sweat) and watched them cough into their hands and scratch their T-shirts. They mumbled indifferent words about the headlines and checked their watches. They smuggled newspaper sections into their legal folders so that they could lie down upstairs in their bunks and peruse the sports section at leisure.

The self-satisfaction of the well-fed inmate—he's had his lunch, he's had his post-lunch cigarette break, he's now fingering his pile of newspapers—sometimes seemed to envelop the entire institution. It radiated from the crisp uniforms of the guards, and the fresh paint on the window trim. You could hear it in the laughing voices of the inmates as they taunted one another in the rec yard and see it in the shiny, jacked pickup trucks that filled the employee parking lot. It was everywhere that February—a thick patina of self-regard and comfort. It seemed as immovable and as deep as the snow. We were a colony of allrightniks, with no responsibilities or ideals beyond taking physical care of ourselves. That's surely the way things ought to be in a jail, yet just then, the imperviousness of our colony—its aloof smugness—seemed pitiless. There was no effective way for the general population of inmates to reckon with what criminals were doing in the world. Murders, local murders committed by people much like us, had as little relevance to us as happenings on another planet. We weren't directly implicated and therefore we weren't interested. The institution's genius was for absorbing everything under the sun into its eat-smoke-sleep-eat program. Everything else tended to get in the way.

I wanted to provoke the current events class into some human response to the murders of the Zantops. Jim wanted to avoid the topic. The inmates seemed glumly indifferent to the teachers' differences.

We flipped through the newspaper articles——the Zantops' throats had been slit, their heads stabbed, it had happened on a sunny Saturday during the day, in Half's study, beneath a shelf of books—and we flipped on to the next thing. As long as the lunch schedule wasn't messed with, we could not, as a class, be bothered.

But I was bothered. I was starting to feel angry at the inmates and jealous of the judges who got to punish them. From what I could gather in the newspapers, it seemed that the Zantops had led their lives so modestly and adventurously and creatively that even their high-achieving colleagues felt themselves to be underachievers by comparison. Everyone who knew them agreed: Half and Susanne had truly lived out the meaning of what they taught, namely humanism. In the *Rutland Herald*, Professor Marianne Hirsch, a colleague of Susanne's in Dartmouth's Comparative Literature Department, recalled: "They had several elderly couples, who they had kind of adopted as surrogate parents, they took care of, going to fix things at their houses, inviting them to dinner, doing all the things children should for their parents. They did that not to be altruistic, but because they saw an interesting side to people, and wanted to be part of their lives." Professor Bruce Duncan in the German Department said: "What people say about them is true. You want to speak well of the dead but you don't have to put any effort into it with them. You couldn't help but like them. They had strong convictions, but they were tolerant. They really were remarkable people who just meant an awful lot to everybody in one way or another. This is really unimaginable. There is really no explanation I can think of except a crazy random act." I wished that I'd had such beneficent professor-parents when I was in school. I wished that I'd had such professor-parents period.

After the first week of headlines, attention to the case seemed to die down for a while—there was no new news, only new rumors—but then, in mid-February, the front pages blackened again. On the eighteenth, the *Rutland Herald* announced:

Police: Pair Planned Slaying of Zantops
HANOVER, N.H.—The murder of two Dartmouth College professors was apparently planned by two Vermont teenagers who are now the focus of a nationwide manhunt, authorities said Saturday.

A New Hampshire prosecutor said police have evidence linking the two Chelsea youths to the secluded home where professors Half and Susanne Zantop were slain three weeks ago.

Arrest warrants were issued for Robert W. Tulloch, 17, and James Parker, 16, officials said at a news conference. The pair are believed to be on the run but were last seen only two days ago, officials said.

Also on the eighteenth in the *Rutland Herald:*

Chelsea Neighbors Express Disbelief, Support for Families
CHELSEA—Nine months ago, the whole town was watching as best friends Rob Tulloch and Jimmy Parker cruised to victory in a raft race on the First Branch of the White River.

That was nine months ago.

Now Tulloch, 17, and Parker, 16, are nowhere to be found. They are the subjects of a nationwide manhunt that has shaken the quiet hillside hamlet where they ruled the river during last May's festival.

The two friends emerged from the cold water after the spring race, all smiles after they capsized at the finish line. The spill was intentional and friends and neighbors gave a cheer.

Now neighbors are dumbfounded.

On that day, February 18, the boys were found at a truckstop off of I-80 in New Castle, Indiana. The *Rutland Herald* reported the next day:

Vermont Teen Murder Suspects Arrested in Indiana
NEW CASTLE, IND.—Two teenagers wanted in the slaying of two Dartmouth College professors were taken into custody at a truckstop Monday after a sheriff's deputy learned of their whereabouts while monitoring CB traffic.

Henry County Sheriff's Department Sgt. William Ward heard a

trucker say he was carrying two teenagers who were looking for transport to California. Ward, who had heard the suspects in the Dartmouth murders were headed West, pretended to be a truck driver and said he would pick the boys up at a truckstop along Interstate 80, just south of New Castle.

Also on February 19 in the *Boston Globe:*

TWO WORLDS COLLIDE IN DARTMOUTH DEATHS
The suspects and the victims inhabited different worlds, and the authorities are offering few clues about how they might have collided.

The victims, Half and Susanne Zantop, who were found stabbed to death in their Hanover, N.H., home on Jan. 27, were urbane German expatriates and longtime professors at Dartmouth College.

The authorities said the two youths wanted in the killings— Robert Tulloch, 17, and James Parker, 16, of Chelsea, Vt.—were arrested in Indiana yesterday on a lawman's hunch. What they did not explain was why two good students from a tiny logging town would have wanted to kill a married couple 45 miles away.

Suddenly, everywhere I looked there were images of Main Street in tiny Chelsea, Vermont: across the Internet, on TV, on the front page of every paper. There was Will's General Store and here was the snow-covered South Common; there, for an instant, was the carved wood sign at the town line.

Perhaps because my connections with the students at the Woodstock jail were dwindling, I started to get interested, maybe too zealously interested, in the lives of the two suspects. I considered applying for a teaching job over at the Grafton County Correctional Center where Tulloch was being held. I sketched out a syllabus: Dickens's *Great Expectations,* Kafka's *Amerika,* Kerouac's *On the Road.* Travel and the Discovery of Self, or Journeys of The Spirit...or something. My problem was...my problem was that I didn't know what my problem was. I did know that my urge to get involved had little to do with my teacherly, benevolent, adolescent-aiding spirit. If I had one, it couldn't be blamed for this. There was something else at work. Whatever it was, it was becoming a little unhealthy, a little repetitive. After a few days of listening to me talk about Parker and Tulloch, my friends started to say: Move on, for Christ's sake. Get over your-self. Drop it. Go forward.

Out of stubbornness or resentment or a combination of these, I ignored the advice. I took notes as I read the newspaper, and cut out the articles about Parker and Tulloch as they appeared. I took a renewed interest in scribbling on legal pads during my time in jail school, and rushed home afterward to look over my scribbles. I half hoped that the truth about the kids in Woodstock and Chelsea would emerge from my doodles and ran-dom notes, and when nothing at all emerged, I was sincerely disappointed.

Still, I kept trying to stitch the stories together somehow. Outwardly, there were curious similarities: restless, dreamy, middle-class kids wander-ing in their cars down the backroads had perhaps slipped through the looking glass sometime during the night. While they were gone, horrible things had happened. Then they were back in the daylight world, trying to fit in again, trying once again to be high school students.

In addition, there was the apparent suddenness of their violence, a strange interruption in otherwise placid lives. Yet, the more one looked, the easier it was to find evidence of careful, even loving premeditation. Parker and Tulloch, for instance, had purchased two enormous military knives from an Internet arms dealer about a month before the Zantop murders. They had purchased ankle holsters for these knives so that the weapons could be withdrawn, Navy SEAL–style, in the midst of a struggle or, casually, perhaps, as if reaching for an undone shoelace. A surveillance notebook was found in Tulloch's room: the notes appeared to consist of a handrawn map of an unknown house and scribbles describing the move-ments of the inhabitants. Parker and Tulloch were already known to the sheriff in Chelsea as snoops: they were casual housebreakers who some-times lounged and sometimes cooked food inside the houses they were burglarizing. So perhaps the murders were the result of an evolution of behaviors, or of a bizarre refinement of them and not, as it seemed at first glance, an inexplicable departure.

Of course, none of the snippets of evidence reported in the newspaper proved that Parker and Tulloch and my students had much in common. Perhaps the salient facts about the Vermont kids were those that distin-guished each kid from the next. I didn't know and didn't know how to find out. The inability to proceed pestered me and disturbed my sleep. I

didn't want to sleep; I wanted to know more about the kids in the newspapers and the jails. I was becoming a bit obsessed with the topic. I didn't
admit it, even to myself, and stopped talking about it in public. Yet my
preoccupation with Parker and Tulloch seems to me now the first unraveling of my own experience in jail. It was my own private cul-de-sac at the
back of which there turned out to be a little pathway that lead further on.

Like everyone else who followed the case, I wondered about the families of the suspects. The Parkers, I discovered, lived about two miles from
Chelsea village, on a hillside. Mr. Parker owned a construction business
and ran an adult basketball league in Central Vermont. He had, more or
less by himself, been responsible for building the town's much admired
baseball field. In the Parker family, there was also a mom (an aide in the
school) and an older sister was now away at an arts school in Chicago. The
Parker kids had been well-liked, if occasionally eccentric, students at the
Chelsea School. Jimmy was a class clown who drove his car too fast
around the South Common. The sister came home from school now and
then with a shock of pink in her hair, a fashion statement that had apparently raised an eyebrow or two in Chelsea's General Store.

Jimmy Parker's best friend, Robert Tulloch, lived in a big yellow
house on Main Street with his mom and dad and three siblings. A Tulloch
neighbor, Steve Gallagher, called the Tullochs "good hardworking folks"
in the *Rutland Herald* and described their son as "a healthy, normal boy."

"My heart goes out to them. I hope, for their sake, that everything
they're saying is not true," he said. Mr. Tulloch was a furniture builder and
a carpenter. The family had moved around a bit; they'd been in Chelsea
for ten years. Before that, Florida.

Michael Tulloch's eldest son, Robert, was the president of the student
council. He was a member of the debate team, had finished his high
school credits almost a year early, had no plans for college, and loved rock
climbing. Both boys were said by the other kids in school to be comical,
funny kids who made their classmates laugh. "There was no sign of any
trouble," said a neighbor.

Soon enough though, signs of trouble appeared in the news. *ABC
Prime Time Thursday* aired a segment a week after the boys' arrests that
claimed that investigators were focusing on neo-Nazi propaganda found

in Tulloch's bedroom. No sooner had the reports aired than they were denied by the official in charge of the investigation, Philip McLaughlin, the New Hampshire attorney general. Those rumors died, but a note of unpleasantness was seeping into the newspapers. A town official in charge of the voting list announced that he'd been keeping a suspicious eye on the Parker family: "Jimmy Parker wasn't quite wild but his parents were permissive [and he's]...shunned by a major population of the school. This does not surprise me in the least," he said, meanly, I thought.

Of Jimmy, a classmate said: "Nobody liked him at all. He was always doing stupid stuff to irritate people."

Yet he was evidently the junior partner, the follower, in the projects he undertook with Tulloch, whatever they'd consisted of. The *Rutland Herald* quoted a Chelsea classmate, Emily Dumont: "I guess you could call [the two teenagers] inseparable," she said. "Wherever you saw Rob, you could bet Jimmy wasn't far behind."

Now both families lived in the eye of a media storm. The State Police Mobile Crime Lab parked itself on Main Street in front of the Tulloch house, along with a fleet of cruisers, and the networks, the satellite trucks, the bustling reporters and their boom mikes. The Tullochs erected a sign on their front lawn that was photographed and appeared in the papers: "Private Property, No Media Allowed!"

From Woodstock, thirty miles to the south, it seemed as though a temporary sort of insanity was enveloping Chelsea. On February 22, citizens held a special meeting in which 250 people packed into the Unitarian Church; it was advertised as a "town meeting–style discussion," but the media were pointedly excluded. When the residents of Chelsea left the building, they were approached by reporters. A panic descended over the group and dozens of the citizens sprinted off into the night, too saddened or alarmed or high-minded to talk. Those who did talk made comments that seemed strangely out of synch with the occasion. The *Rutland Herald* interviewed one meeting participant:

> "It was an awesome evening," said Robert Sherman, a Montpelier
> lobbyist who lives just outside Chelsea village. He has been helping
> the people in the community deal with the media attention that has
> brought satellite trucks and scores of reporters to town.

I didn't get it. What did Sherman mean by "awesome"? He didn't say or wasn't asked. And had people in Chelsea brought in the local lobbyist to help them in dealing with the media spotlight? Did they really need help in dealing? It seemed likely that they didn't. But excluding reporters from a town meeting was an odd thing to do, the reaction of a people under siege. Maybe they did need advice after all.

Toward the end of February, reports began to emerge about the boys' movements in the days after the killings. On Monday, January 29, they were in their current affairs class at the Chelsea School, where the Zantop murder was discussed. Tulloch seemed to have a gash in his leg and told a classmate, Kip Battey, that he'd cut it against a sap spigot while hiking through the woods. Parker was said to have sold a snowboard to a friend sometime between Sunday, the twenty-eighth, and Tuesday, the thirtieth; he mentioned that he planned to leave Chelsea soon to go rock climbing in Colorado. On Wednesday, January 31, the boys purchased two bus tickets to Amarillo, Texas, and left White River Junction, Vermont, on the 1:50 PM bus to New York City. On February 2, Parker made an apologetic call home from St. Louis: he and Tulloch were now running out of money, and Tulloch's leg needed medical attention. On the fourth, a Sunday, the two kids flew home to Vermont.

Two weeks later, on the evening of February 15, investigators knocked at 10 Bradshaw Crossroad in Chelsea, home of the Parker family. An Internet weapons merchant in Massachusetts had recently shipped two SOG Seal 2000 knives, special delivery, to a James Parker at that address. Two plastic knife sheaths, of the kind that are sold with such knives, had been found at the scene of the Zantop murders. Would James Parker be willing to come to the sheriff's office in Chelsea to have himself fingerprinted?

Both Parker and Tulloch gave written statements to the police on the evening of the fifteenth; they admitted having bought the knives but said they'd sold them to a stranger, two or maybe three weeks earlier, at an Army Navy store in Burlington, Vermont. At three o'clock on the morning of the sixteenth, Parker drove his silver Audi to pick up Robert Tulloch in Chelsea village. From there the two drove to a truck stop in Sturbridge, Massachusetts, where they waited for truckers willing to help them light out for California.

None of this description cleared up the mystery of the kids' motivations, or explained the more immediate, confounding mystery of what on earth had brought Parker, Tulloch, and the Zantops together.

Back in Woodstock, I found that some of the inmates were following the case perhaps more closely than I had thought and had worked up some theories of motivation. When I pressed them, the older prisoners guessed that Half Zantop had been sexually involved with one or both of the boys. The motive for the killing, they presumed, was therefore revenge for sexual abuse. The teenagers, meanwhile, guessed that Parker and Tulloch had been searching for drugs, or money, or both in the Zantop home and had been surprised in the act. Not wanting to get caught for burglary, they did what they had to do to silence the witnesses.

In Chelsea, things continued to deteriorate. A dispute had erupted over whether or not it was right for citizens to contribute to a legal defense fund—wait, it was not for legal defense, but rather to help the Parkers and Tullochs get by. It was a "family support fund." It was being organized by the sixth-grade teacher at the Chelsea School. "I won't pay to help murderers get off," said one townsperson in the newspaper. Further disputes simmered: "There's a climate of permissiveness among certain parents," said certain townspeople to reporters. No, the whole thing had been blown wildly out of proportion by the media, said others. No, it was the kids' own damn fault, said another chorus. "People are feeling shocked and somewhat alone... They're not looking for answers," said the school principal. Shocked and alone I could believe; not looking for answers, as the rest of the world was—that seemed to me either unlikely or unwise.

The families of the perpetrators kept utterly silent throughout. What could they say? They said nothing, at least not publicly. Audrey McCollum, the Zantop neighbor who had been one of the first at the scene of the crime had sympathetic words for those close to Robert and Jimmy: "I ache for their family and friends," she said. "They must be asking themselves, 'Where did we go wrong?'"

In Woodstock, it turned out that the inmates did know, after all, what weapons had been used, who'd been stabbed where, and whose blood had been found in a green Subaru belonging to Jimmy's mom (it was Susanne's). Yet the rapists and drunks and wife-beaters were too high minded to dwell on murder. "I don't read about any of that stuff. It just

makes me sick," one felon told me. He'd been arrested for fondling incapacitated and drugged patients in a hospital.

I began to root silently for the inmates to be assigned puritanical
judges who would visit draconian punishments on them. I wasn't making
much progress with them in any case. Maybe the judge could make some
progress on his own. I cut my hours down at the jail to just a handful a
week, and went off to visit Laird at his new jail in St. Johnsbury.

There had always been a part of Laird that envisioned himself ascend-
ing a great plume of media celebrity. Laird's own position in the heavens
seemed to me to have vanished long ago, but now, with the death of the
Zantops, his star was emerging again. He claimed to have known not just
Parker and Tulloch (plausible because his cousins lived in Chelsea), but
the Zantops as well (implausible). They had tutored him in German, he
said (ludicrous). He talked to me about the media interviews he was refusing and those he was giving. In his accounting, the reporters viewed him
as a sort of Rosetta stone, a wise child who could crack the code of teenage
violence. This Rosetta stone was a fascinating and widely coveted object;
everyone wanted a piece of it, apparently. And now his negotiations with
the movie companies were picking up speed.

The picture would be based on his experiences in life thus far. He was
talking to all the big studios, he said: Paramount and Fox and Universal.
He was driving a hard bargain when it came to the writers. He had told
them that he didn't want any of the hacks or B-movie specialists, but only
the best, the best of the best. When he finally met with the writers, he was
going to tell them everything he knew about the Zantops and Jimmy and
Robert. He wasn't going to waste that information on the local flacks from
the *Rutland Herald*.

So Laird had learned to like life in the public arena. He'd become a
well-known intelligent bad boy, at least in his own mind—and now he
was missing the limelight, it seemed. He wanted to be back before his
audience.

How was his dad doing? I asked.

"Haven't heard from him," he said.

"And your court case?"

He was supposed to be taking a plea: twenty years to life, but his
lawyer was forcing it on him and he wanted out of it. He wanted to go to

trial. "Let it all hang out there for the public to see," he said. "Every bit of it. Bring it on." He had a steely, combative look in his eye, as if he was already facing his enemies, and already defying them to think ill of him.

I left the compound in St. Johnsbury, wondering about his urge to be in the headlines, and thinking also about the media army in Chelsea that was just then, after nearly a month of occupation, beginning to break camp. The snow was melting on the baseball field in Chelsea that John Parker had built. Jimmy Parker was in his cell at a juvenile facility in Concord, though his seventeenth birthday was approaching, and he was soon to be shipped on to an adult facility.

And Tulloch, how was he faring? It was hard to know because he was locked away in his jail cell in North Haverhill, New Hampshire, and talking to no one, of course. His trial, if there would be a trial, was at least a year away. His parents, for their part, were surely trying to mend their lives. The father, Michael Tulloch, was perhaps back constructing the Windsor chairs—those functional sculptures—that he built in a woodshop behind his house. The Chelsea School debate team and the student council were getting on with their business. Everyone wanted to be normal again. Surely, however, something had changed.

I had seen a lot of this before—the mystery that would never be solved, the astonished parents who wouldn't ever be quite the same, the kids sealed away in their jail cells—but somehow this time the whole scenario seemed more permanently sad, more hopeless. There were more ruined lives this time, and I felt more acutely the aura of futility, of absolute senselessness as it glowed from the newspapers.

Driving home from St. Johnsbury after my talk with Laird, I thought a lot about Bill Stanard. I saw him sitting in his handknit sweater beneath the bookshelves in his house in West Windsor. He'd given Laird a copy of Jean Anouilh's *Antigone* during Laird's first week in jail, and some echo of that play began to surface in my head. What had Bill wished to convey? What was Laird supposed to have understood? The pith of the message must have had to do with the isolation and impotence of someone who finds himself trapped in a tragedy. I remembered that much about the play from high school. A day later, I looked up *Antigone* in the library and found a fitting speech given by the Chorus.

Headstrong and childish and exultant in her righteousness, Antigone has forced her uncle Creon into turning her over to the machinery of the state. He will have to have her hanged, though he's still hoping, somehow, that through a sleight of hand or back door deal, he can get her out of harm's way. Reflecting on all of this, he leaves the stage. The lights come up and the Chorus, a single actor in this incarnation of *Antigone*, strolls downstage to announce:

> The rest is automatic. You don't need to lift a finger. The machine is in perfect working order. It has been oiled ever since time began, and it runs without friction. Death, treason, and sorrow are on the march; and they move in the wake of storm, of tears, and stillness....
> The silence inside you when the roaring crowd acclaims a winner—
> so that you think of a film without a sound track, mouths agape and no sound coming out of them, a clamor that is no more than a picture; and you, the victor, already vanquished, alone in the desert of your silence. That is tragedy.

At home I threw myself into writing about my experiences in jail. It was the only thing I could think to do and all I wanted to do. I had let my writing project languish in the previous months, but as February gave way to March I was back at it, poring over the old jail diary entries, guessing at their meaning, hoping that they might coalesce into a pattern and that the pattern would somehow amount to more than the sum of its parts. I caught glimmers of a theme now and recorded what I could see of it. When I had nothing to say, I wrote a lot anyway, and filled computer files and legal pads with notes. I worked myself into a state in this way, especially after dinner when there was nothing else to do in dull Woodstock but write. Then, when I was done, I lay awake in bed and thought about the prisoners crawling into their beds, a few miles and a few hundred worlds away. In the morning there would be one unbroken, impenetrable paragraph filling the computer screen and, at the end of it, a note from my girlfriend: "You are nuts —me."

Parker's and Tulloch's lives, I decided, and the lives of my own students, for that matter, could be decoded only with the aid of a map. It would have to be a curious, inventive map since the kids lived in their own curious, inventive geography. A Parker-Tulloch map would render the landscape near Chelsea in intricate relief, with special attention paid to climbable rock faces. Those could be found in the woods near Vershire, Tunbridge, and Thetford. There would be approach trails and shortcuts and cool lookouts on the map that no one, not even the local hunters and snowmobilers and landowners, knew about. You could, if you wished, sketch in a sap spigot somewhere alongside one of the trails. It would be protruding dangerously from the bark of a giant maple. Tulloch, at least in his own accounting of events, would have passed by there shortly after the murders.

The map would have to have panels that unfolded into a much more exotic, far-flung, hazier kingdom. That realm was a reachable, even a convenient, jaunt from Chelsea, though no one in town would have known much about it. It was well within reach, in fact, and shrouded in haze only because most people didn't know how to search for it. Kids would, however. That was what the Internet was for. You could begin with Google and go on from there.

To pencil in the physical geography of that region would inspire, it seemed to me, a major cartographic headache. But there were some vague coordinates with which to begin. The place had a major city, for instance: Syracuse, California. This was the destination for which Robert and Jimmy had tried to buy bus tickets at the Vermont Transit window in White River Junction on Wednesday, January 31, 2001. It had been four days since the killings. The investigators working the crime scene up in Hanover had no leads. They were planning no arrests. It was a good time to leave the area without the slightest aura of suspicion following along.

Later, the newspapers interviewed the clerk. She'd rightly denied the existence of a Syracuse, California, had suggested Santa Cruz, and San Diego, and had then laid out an atlas in front of the boys. They didn't have the $159 per ticket it would have required to go all the way to California, so they settled on $139 tickets to Amarillo, Texas.

Thus, out in the distant quadrants of the map, one would have to sketch in a mythical, imaginary city. It would be called Syracuse, California. Nearby this fanciful destination, there would surely be plenty of rock climbing. And there would be a patch of treacherous forest for which a SOG Seal 2000, the foot-long military knife, would be necessary equipment. The ads on the Internet for the SOG 2000 showed compasses propped against a background of wet rocks and knives. The copy hinted at what life might be like in such a wilderness:

Evaluation [of the SOG Seal knife 2000] included the following tests:
Tip-breaking strengths, blade-breaking toughness, sharpness and
edge retention, handle twist off limits, two-week saltwater emersion
test, gasoline and acetylene torch resistance, chopping, hammering,
prying, penetration, cutting of 6 different types of rope and nylon
line, low noise and reflectivity evaluation plus an intense hands-on
competition in the field.

Customers who purchased such knives would know that in the future, in
their hour of need, the knives could stand up to circumstances. When
local conditions forced you into twisting the handle beyond all normal
twist off limits, or made you submit to burning by acetylene torch, the
blades would resist. When necessity required a two-week salt water emersion, or low noise and reflectivity in the field, or prying and hammering
and penetrating, the SOG 2000 would stand the test.

The landscape where all of that was possible—its necessities, its threats,
its opportunities—would have to be sketched in on the map as well. Maybe
it could be done with symbols and icons, as on those early modern maps
made by Renaissance cartographers.

Whatever curious atlas eventually emerged, I thought it might be
interesting to begin drawing lines of movement on it. I wanted a narrative
of time to plot across the coordinates in space. I wondered if Parker and
Tulloch had tried to get to Syracuse, California, before, or whether they'd
tried slipping away to similar destinations in Vermont. If so, where had
they gone? What had they found? What had they brought home?

In Laird Stanard's imaginary universe, all the roads had seemed to
lead toward home. He had been bargaining with his parents for a sort of
permanent home leave from boarding school (he would have a car and
drive himself down Blood Hill every day to school) for a year before his
crime. "Not until you're eighteen," his father had said. In December 1999,
he had left Gould at the Christmas break determined to come home once
and for all. He'd packed his whole dorm room into the car, saying he
wanted to sort through his things at home, but knowing he'd never be
back. On the night of the shootings in West Windsor, he'd waited until
his parents were asleep, taken the family car and a family shotgun, and
had gone out to a nightclub called Destiny's. He'd gone on to another

party, but eventually he'd brought the car, the gun, the alcohol he had in his system (two shots and a beer), and all the dangerous volatility of an unhappy seventeen-year-old home with him. With the shotgun concealed behind his cargo pants, he'd pushed open the front door. There was his mother, annoyed that he'd stolen the car. She was prepared to give him a good dressing down.

After making some sketches on a sheet laid over a DeLorme atlas of Vermont, I wondered if a similar pattern in Parker and Tulloch's movements might have been at work. They had left home on Saturday morning, January 27, 2001. The police evidence—a footprint, fingerprints, and the knife sheath—said they'd been at 115 Trescott Road in Etna, just outside of Hanover, New Hampshire. The boys came home for a little while after that, surely drenched in blood—what a nightmare that must have been—and left again a few days later. If they had really had the Kerouac urge to be on the road, they could have kept going beyond St. Louis, off beneath the arch somewhere. But they came home, perhaps knowing in the backs of their minds that they were bringing something fateful into the houses of their parents. They repeated the cycle one final time. This last time, they left in the dead of night and returned on a government plane, with the nation's media assembled out on the tarmac, snapping pictures and yelling questions. Up in the hills to the north across the Connecticut was the bland, sheltering, sheltered community; there were the speechless parents, watching on TV. Here were the sinister children, eyes cast toward the pavement, shuffling in their chains. They were coming home, their secrets revealed, their identity proclaimed for all the world to see. If the kids wanted to make a statement to Mom and Dad, this was surely one the parents would not miss. But why couldn't they have had their showdown with their parents in some normal, teenage way? They could have marched into the living room in their muddy boots, for instance, told their parents to go screw off and stolen the family car. That ought to have been a sufficiently satisfying way to disrupt the family harmony or proclaim a new, uncontrollable identity; it was certainly the time-honored way.

I've never tried to make contact with people in the news before, but that spring I wanted to get in touch with Robert Tulloch, the older half of the pair. From tidbits in the newspaper—and from his picture—I guessed

that he might also be the more worldly, more self-aware, possibly more desperate half. He was the one who was said to have a girlfriend; the one I
imagined to be the leader of the two. It was clear that he didn't have the
family advantages Parker had. He was also the one whose parents hadn't
bought him a car, the one whose family house was showing its age, the one
without the private lawyers. And because he was seventeen, he was also the
one who was automatically relegated to the adult courts and the adult jails.

I didn't know exactly what I would do with him once I did get in touch,
but various notions presented themselves to my imagination: I'd lend him
some books. I'd write to him once a week. I'd help him cope however I
could during that first year in jail, the first year being the deepest point in
the well, as everybody who's spent some time in jail knows. I would be the
sort of correspondent and visitor who sticks around, as I had with Laird and
the other Woodstock kids, when the media storm died down. So I wrote
Tulloch various letters of which this is a (slightly abridged) typical example:

Dear Robert,
Lots of newspapers have written about how bored and tired of
Vermont you were. I somehow doubt a kid's relationship to his town
and state can be as simple as all that. Obviously, some stuff in
Vermont is good, some bad. Would you be willing to talk to me
about leaving Chelsea and coming back? About playing and working
in Vermont?
   I rode my bike through Chelsea last week. I noticed girls with
their baby strollers walking down Route 110 for exercise, I guess, and
little kids playing softball on the rec field. It was evening. I passed a
senior couple ambling down the highway after their dinner. In the
store on Main Street, there was a group of teenage girls talking
loudly. An old man was yelling at his dog; the dog was penned up
inside the truck cab and going crazy over the passersby.
   The whole time I was in Chelsea I was thinking about what it
would have been like to grow up in a town like that. Woodstock is
not the same. To be honest, I'd be happy having a talk just about this
kind of thing. I'm also interested in how a smart kid—this is the way
the papers describe you and okay, I believe them—ends up in jail. I
work in the Woodstock jail as a teacher and have some students who

sort of remind me of you. Anyway, if growing up in Chelsea is a painful topic, I understand. I'll ignore it.

So please write and say ok and I'll try to arrange a visit through the authorities. If for whatever reason, you feel that the visit isn't working out, I'll understand. I'll drive back home with no hard feelings. I hope the jail is treating you okay.

Theo

I never heard from him.

CHAPTER SEVENTEEN

Robert and Jimmy

An important piece of evidence for me was a photograph of Robert Tulloch and Jimmy Parker taken by a newspaper photographer from Montpelier. A number of local reporters had been present in May 2000—ten months before the Zantop murders—at a make-your-own raft-and-see-if-it-floats contest in Chelsea. There was a scattering of stories in the press and a few pictures here and there, one of which resurfaced later.

In the photograph that caught my eye, it's a sunny spring day and the town's kids and hippies and ski bums have come out to float their productions down the First Branch of the White River. There are mountain bikes liberally distributed among the little kids, and, in the background, a few parents, among them one worried-looking John Parker, Jimmy's dad. Normally, the First Branch is a creek, but in early May it gushes over rocks and crashes into bridge abutments. In the photograph, Tulloch is the captain of his raft and has paused for an instant in his task of tugging it toward the water's edge. His face is turned upward and back toward the assembled townspeople, as if he's letting the scene imprint itself once before setting off. Parker, like his dad, looks a little concerned and crouches at the stern of the raft. His brows are knit in a perplexed, anxious expression that makes Tulloch's easy self-possession seem exceptional and plucky. Naturally, there's no hint of malice or crime in the eyes of the kids, though it has since turned out that even when the picture was taken, in May 2000, the boys had begun to consider violent crime as a way to raise money. The picture shows a simple sunny day in Chelsea at the height of spring. The river is up. Two local boys have been out scampering in the woods. You can tell because Parker and Tulloch's raft has a bit of the forest in it: it's a comical, slapdash creation made from two fresh saplings and

262

twine. In the instant that the picture was taken, Robert and Jimmy stood above their raft, poised and resting for a moment, before they were to float away on the little creek that runs through town.

I know from my own experience as a kid at raft races that this is an accurate—maybe sentimental but accurate—depiction of one kind of boyhood in Vermont. Your parents are standing a few feet away—they may be a bit worried, but they've stepped back and are keeping quiet. There are admiring little kids underfoot and older, jawboning local types in the background. For a few moments, as you prepare to slip away, your mind wanders. You know that soon the cameras will be put away, and the parents will return to their lives. May will erupt into June. The river will subside; the corn in the fields will sprout tassels and silk. The teenagers who surround you will climb aboard whatever rafts they've managed to cobble together: college, jobs, marriage. Soon, in the blink of an eye, the whole scene by the river's edge will disappear. But for a moment or two, the adolescents at the center of that image—there they are poised in their instant of reflection—are miraculously holding everyone together. People are proud of them. The older folks may be a little worried for them, but they're proud. So everyone's come down to the river's edge to be pulled together by a handful of teenagers, and the kids are doing just what people want from them. Well done, teenagers, you want to reply to the picture. What a delicate trick it is. Congratulations.

After the Zantop murders, this photograph inevitably means something else. With the Zantop murders in mind, I gazed at the picture and saw the kids urging themselves into catastrophe. I could see the pleasure of anticipation in their eyes, and the excitement of an imminent shock in their relaxed, healthy limbs. The townspeople were gazing cluelessly at their kids. The rest of the story could easily be filled in: The kids would be overwhelmed. And then the entire town would be engulfed. The whole thing would happen in excruciating slowed-down time, so that everyone near and far—even around the country—could watch it from moment to moment and make comments.

Robert and Jimmy would of course be swept under by the force of the current. For months, the town would continue standing by the river's edge, mutely, perhaps more suspiciously, but with deepened helplessness and deepened bewilderment.

Later on, when more facts about the case became known, it would turn out that Parker and Tulloch really had been lingering, at least in their minds, at the borderline, just this side of overwhelming, for quite some time. This borderline, it turned out, was indeed part of the local geography. There was nothing particularly sinister about it—it was no freighted, symbolic stopping point such as Jack and Wendy Torrance are offered in *The Shining*—but it did have some effect on Jimmy and Robert, apparently.

In a 350-page document called "In Re: Zantop Homicides," dated December 18, 2001, Parker talked about the origins of the murders to Kelly Ayotte, a New Hampshire prosecutor. In the interviews, Parker says that during the summer and fall of 2000, a few months after the raft picture was taken, he and Tulloch considered kidnappings, burials, bank robberies, and, on one occasion, thought about using rocks to bludgeon two people who happened to be standing on the side of the road next to their camping car. Why? Ostensibly, they were trying to raise money for a trip to Australia.

In trying to trace these plots back to a particular frame of mind or circumstance, Ayotte asked Parker about the development of his friendship with Tulloch. Was there a conscious beginning, she wanted to know, a point in their history together when the plans the two were making turned criminal? The question had evidently occurred to Parker already. He responded immediately with a tale that hardly seemed to address the question. For him, his criminal projects had begun eighteen months before the murders, not in frustration or contempt or vengefulness, but at a quarry up on the East Randolph Road outside of Chelsea. It was a place he had passed by every day of his life, on the road between his house and school, but he hadn't really explored it, he said, until sometime shortly before his sixteenth birthday when he and Robert went out together for a hike.

The East Randolph Road winds up from the valley floor for about three miles until it tops out on the ridge just to the west of Chelsea. Down on the valley floor, where the stores and the school and the town offices are, the prevailing quality of the countryside is mildness: the pastures roll mildly, the cows, the brook, the traffic—everything is quiet and mild. But to the west of town, there's a narrow gap in the hillside—the East Randolph Road—that is girded with a denser forest and steep walls. Halfway up, on one side of the road, the walls give way to friable cliff. Walk up a pathway and through a patch of woods and you can stand on a tiny ledge

200 feet above the road, you can hurl stones into the void. You are stand-ing at the rim of a disused quarry. Its edges are made of an uncertain mix-ture of clay and grass and loose rock. The trees crowd up to it and their roots stick out into the air like vines. Somehow, at least in Parker's mind, this quarry is where the two boys' plan to murder people was born. In the plea-bargain interview, Ayotte asked, "Is there another set of goals that you [and Robert] talked about?"

> Parker: Well the major thing, that this whole thing was about, meaning murders, is that in the spring of '99, I remember we got dropped off at the bottom of my dirt road, Hook Road. My mom was driving so I don't think I had my permit yet, so it might have been before May 24 of '99. I'm not sure though. Um, there were some quarries up there that I never checked out. These are the ones in Chelsea, not in Barre. Then, we went up there and we were kind of walking around, checking things out, just playing around on the big boulders and climbing stuff and then we were walking back up. It's like two miles from the bottom of the road, so we were walking back up and he suggested, I don't know how it came up, but he suggested, you know, maybe we could steal cars and joyride cars and um...

So they were on the way home from the quarry, and that's when the idea came to them. The next pages of Parker's testimony are kind of harrowing. It turns out that the boys went to several different quarries in the succeed-ing months, stole a truck at one of them, nearly dumped it off a ledge, but decided to keep it around for another day. They thought about stealing cars from the valleys, joyriding them in the hills, and then dropping them like rocks into the quarry water. The thought of joyriding led them to think about fleeing not just to a quarry, but across the countryside, hun-dreds of miles away, with no particular destination in mind, and for that, they realized, they'd need money. In order to get money, they decided they'd have to steal it. In order to avoid being caught stealing, they decided that they'd have to overwhelm their victims. In order to cover up that crime, they decided they'd have to kill their victims and bury the bod-ies. The planning took on a momentum of its own. They furnished them-selves with black plastic bags for the corpses and plastic zip ties for use as handcuffs. They dug a grave near a house whose residents they intended to kill. They bought knives. Later, they clothed themselves in special black Ninja outfits and hovered in the woods outside prosperous looking houses. Tulloch took notes. They considered leaping on the homeowners as they arrived from work; Tulloch and Parker would seize them and drag them inside and force them to give over their money and their credit cards. Then a new idea came along: they would pose as students from a nearby prep school, The Mountain School; they would say that they were interested in the environment; they would have a phony list of questions, a survey, and a secret cue (Parker would ask: "Can I get a glass of water?") The interview would be over then. The boys would reach for their knives. The killing would begin. When Jimmy Parker gave his interviews to Kelly Ayotte, he described what had happened inside the Zantops' house:

> *Jimmy Parker:* Robert was interviewing and I was writing down, I might have asked a few questions. And um, so I thought we were just going through the interview and I was thinking, you know, this guy is all right, you know, we don't need to kill this guy, um and I thought we were going to leave and he said, "You know," I mean he said something about like we need to be more prepared or something because we weren't prepared at all. I mean, we weren't supposed to go through the whole interview anyway. Um.
>
> *Ayotte:* Half said that?
>
> *JP:* Yeah.
>
> *Ayotte:* And when he said that, what happens?
>
> *JP:* . . . . And this was like his closing thing, we were just kind of talking about how to interview and um he was like, he said, "Let me give you somebody's number near your area that you can talk to." I'm not sure if he checked his computer, but I know he looked through the phonebook and couldn't find it. He might have looked more places. I don't remember. But I do remember him getting his wallet out to, ah, probably get a name out of there or something and um he opened his wallet to look through it and it looked like there was a lot of money in there so at the time, or during when he was looking for his stuff, Robert took the bag [a backpack] from me, and I was like oh, okay, here we go, you know, so he took out one of the knives while he wasn't looking and you know pulled it out of the sheath, he still wasn't looking,

he was looking through his wallet and he jumped him. I don't think Half noticed until he was actually stabbing him and he was on him and they were um, he was on top of him pushing him back towards, there was like a bookcase to the left of the computer and um so he um so he was over him and um kind of like sort of on top of him and he was stabbing him in the chest and he was screaming really, really terribly and um.

Ayotte: Half was?

JP: Yeah. And Robert didn't say anything. He jumped on him and knocked him back on the floor. There were papers kind of, something fell over, he fell onto something, and he was kind of leaning against the bookcase like with his shoulders or something, I'm not sure. And Robert was stabbing him, you know, after he had screamed, his wife ran into the room and opened the door. At some point I had got the other knife, I'm not sure when, it was probably after he screamed, and I got the knife and she came in and um she was like grappling on the floor with her husband. I'm not, like it wasn't a lot of struggling, really, you know, she was just kind of holding on to her husband's leg or Robert's leg and screaming something in German and I grabbed her and kind of lifted her up by the shoulder with my left hand and told her to shut up and I think Robert was still stabbing. This is all going really fast and um so Robert stopped and we were looking at each other and he said, um, "Slit her throat!" and um I paused for a very small amount of time and slit her throat and let her fall to the floor.

Ayotte: What happened after that?

JP: And then I think at this time Robert um cut Half's throat. He was already dead. That's what he told me later. And um so it gets weird at this point.

Ayotte: What did you do after that?

JP: I don't remember.

I didn't know these details in April 2001. I was still trying to understand the meaning of my own experience in jail and didn't know what, if anything, Parker had told the New Hampshire authorities. I did, however, know something about adventurous local teenagers, and knew something about how they liked to hang out in the places to which their schemes had led them.

The kids I had taught in Woodstock had done everything they could to find their way into a moral vacuum. If the portal for Parker and Tulloch had been a quarry, for many of the kids in Woodstock, the doorway had been the jail itself. Some had been tossed inside when they were seventeen and let out a few weeks or a few months later. After that, they had gotten more sincerely interested in crime. For other kids, the way in had been somebody else's crime scene; they had seen a body, or a broken store window, or had ambled through an unoccupied, art-filled house. Some of the kids had been present when burglaries unfolded in perfect, undetectable order and after that, all vacation houses everywhere had seemed like refuges, like friendly B and Bs.

I had heard a lot about what might be done in places like this when I taught my classes. They welcomed sex and drugs and rock and roll, of course, but they also invited radical, possibly violent departure. You could be set upon by dangerous forces, or, if chance willed it, you might just set upon somebody else. Anyway, you were totally disconnected from the normal world. Since there would be no responsible adults nearby to witness what was going on, you could act with impunity. Everything was permitted. Nothing would make it back to the real world and if it did, it would come back weeks later, dazed and unsure of itself and without sense-making context of any kind.

CHAPTER EIGHTEEN

Book

By April 2001, I was down to one class a week in jail. At home, I looked over my jail journal entries and newspaper clippings and typed up a book proposal. In it, I wrote:

> My younger students tend to be frustrated travelers. Will robbed a convenience store; Russell stood on a table in his high school cafeteria waving his handgun, then he hit the road in front of school, meaning to hitchhike to who knows where. Frenchie kidnapped a homeless girl, and started off on a trek to visit Wal-Marts around Vermont. No matter the particulars of their crimes, my students all aimed to break with the past, and to set off on the open road, in audacious imitation of movie heroes. Somehow, they were arrested. Each half believed that his destination was the roadside shanty town depicted in *Mad Max, Terminator II,* and *The Stand*—a community of equals arising after terrible calamity—and they half believed that such a society could most reliably be found in prison. Many of my students are suicidal, and, like the characters in those dramas, they're preparing themselves for what happens after everything ends.
>
> In my prison classroom, the students, especially but not only the teenagers, style themselves as belonging to a tribe of Americans that is fated to travel the countryside. Its members mete out justice to anyone who impinges on their native liberties, and its spiritual kin are the people on TV who come forth to attack oppressive regimes (police, banks, schools) on principle. There's also a strong current of apocalyptic feeling in my classroom: my students find the landscapes

described by Flannery O'Connor and Denis Johnson to be more or less accurate depictions of the nearby forests. They have seen, or would like to have seen, sunsets that recall celestial massacres, and birds dripping with blood. I see my students sometimes as a community of believers united, at least, by these apocalyptic suspicions. They act as if, at this extremely late hour in the day, nothing much matters anymore. Their murders and careless, purposeless, hopeless robberies are an effort to hasten the end, which, they assume, probably isn't all that far off anyway. Their crimes are also acts of faith: they're inspired, almost ecstatic attempts to vault over the shabby facts of everyday life in Vermont. They'd like to touch down in places they read about or see on TV. The texts that really unite my students are movies. A salient moment for the young and the old in my class is the speech in *Taxi Driver* in which Travis Bickle prophesies a great rain, and promises that it will wash the streets of scum. Other movies that promise an imminent ending are popular in jail: The *Mad Max* movies, the *Terminator* movies, *Blade Runner.*

Our classroom discussions often reflect my students' faith that they are indeed arriving at the end. They're more bored now than they've ever been before, and they're badly impatient for a calamity of any kind to sweep through the prison. They see the signs…the millennium, sicknesses, terrorism…and draw their hopeful conclusions.

My students are fascinated by the newspaper coverage of their crimes. Their murders, and those of peers like Parker and Tulloch, are described as "senseless," "meaningless," and "unmotivated," and the teenagers themselves seem "cold" and "distant" to the reporters, but camera and prose always bear in on the details of the crimes with the tightest possible focus, as if some sort of meaning might be found there. Invariably, the result is a splashy, mesmerizing crime scene, a mysterious protagonist, and no context whatsoever. As it happens, that's an effect that's highly valued among clever adolescent criminals. They watch plenty of TV and know the signature of the evil society-defying genius when they see it. From their point of view, reporters who turn over the clues in the columns and stories are delightfully adrift. Nevertheless, they're useful, for they help to propagate the right images.

When I had just about finished the book proposal, Jim from the jail called to say that he wasn't going to be requiring my services anymore. He suggested that I check back with him in a few months, or call some other jail in a different part of the state if I was still interested then.

CHAPTER NINETEEN

My Escape

One day in April 2001, just as the snow was retreating from the fields, I sent a letter to Ron Powers, the radio commentator and author of essays I admired. I mentioned that I had met him once at Middlebury, that I had been working in the Woodstock jail, and had discussed his radio commentaries with an inmate and former Gould Academy schoolmate of his son's, Laird Stanard. In the letter, I reminded Powers of the conversation he and I had had in Middlebury: I had told him that I wanted to be a writer, but didn't know what I should write about. Powers had responded, approximately, thus: "The subject will come to you if you look for it." Or something to that effect. I remember him being sage and gracious and restrained. I remember hoping that he would impart a draft of his writerly genius to me, immediately and without demur. He seemed an obliging enough person. It seemed vaguely possible that, at the end of the evening, he would pour what I wanted into a thimble or a tumbler or a magic hat, maybe, and pass his gift off to me as his eyes twinkled.

In the letter I wrote to Powers that spring, I asked: Would he be willing to look over some of the writing I had been doing lately? I had some jail diary entries and part of a book proposal to send him if he was interested.

To my astonishment, I had a book agent a few days later and not too much longer after that, a slate of meetings with publishers in New York City. I trembled in the elevator on the way up to my first meeting, light-headed with nervousness and coffee, and filled with dread. Inside the elevator, I eyed my fellow passengers. Along the back wall was a semicircle of sunflower-like creatures; they were, I assumed, actress-models. Or maybe they were actress-models who did some writing and book editing on the side. (The elevator belonged to a glossy magazine that was also part of a movie company and a publishing company. Who else would be in the elevators?) The sunflowers were far handsomer than my normal companions in the stairwell in Woodstock, but they made me shrink in a way the prisoners had not. Suddenly, I missed the lummoxes in Woodstock.

The book agent had told me at my first meeting that I'd have to talk to Tina Brown, who wasn't at all like what people said of her but much nicer, as a matter of fact, far nicer, and in any case, at the other meetings later on, things were bound to turn around for me. Waiting in the lobby upstairs, I considered sabotaging the occasion somehow.

A fine opportunity was at hand; conditions were fair to excellent. I was standing on the edge of an encounter with something foreign and distinctly equivocal. Something good could result or something bad. I was suspicious of the whole idea and intimidated by it and attracted to it. But the doubts I was having were rapidly pulling rank. The best thing for it, I thought, would be to walk into the meeting, make some jokes, and fumble with my papers, perhaps spilling them across the floor. It wouldn't matter anyway because no one at home would ever know where I'd been. If I told them, they'd hardly believe me. And if I did make a mess, the joke would really be at the other people's expense—the adults in the room—although they might not see it that way. But, I thought to myself, who the hell cares about that?

I considered the whole scenario backward and forward. The stress and the coffee I'd imbibed for the occasion would have made it easy for me to do almost anything, to really surpass myself. Whatever I came up with—a paper throwing incident, maybe a cup of coffee sloshed across the table—would have been a true, spontaneous, but also an artfully premeditated expression of myself. It would have been me through and through. I was sorely tempted.

I decided against it. I'd punted plenty of times in the past and knew the whole sorry-dumb comical routine from beginning to end: the glow of pride that turns into a glow of self-loathing; the sensation of life piddling away and the depression that follows swiftly thence. I'd have to go out and ride my bike around a bit to work it all off and, of course, it would come back. I'd have to go find another jail in which to while away more hours. So, no punting.

In the meeting, I explained what I wanted to write to a group of editors,

at least one of whom, to my astonishment, was taking notes. I lied confi-
dently about how confident I was that I could get the job done. I pulled a
silly number from the air when they asked me how long it would take.

Afterward, I wandered around the streets of lower Manhattan and
wondered if my life wasn't soon going to be changing, maybe dramatically
changing. I felt like a fugitive from justice. I felt that I might have done
something, a possibly harmful something, and that I should try to take it
back. There was a tinge of excitement in my throat, because the whole
thing had been deliberate after all, and I wanted my life to change. Yet,
until then, I hadn't thought much about how specifically it should
change, or how I should go about making the changes on my own. Now,
it seemed, I had wandered into territory that didn't belong to me and
there, through a process I didn't understand, had contracted a debt. So my
life would change. But these sensations—guilt, fear—were not at all the
ones I had had in mind.

I avoided returning to the apartment where I'd been staying, the
apartment of a cousin, because I worried that there'd be a message from
Jim, the literary agent. I ambled into a bike shop and looked at the New
York City bikes. I purposely took the wrong subway. When I finally got
back to my cousin Connie's, her husband, Bernie, met me at the door
with wide eyes, in a panic.

"Call your agent. Now," said Bernie.

"Okay," I said, and retreated down a hallway, far from the phone.

Bernie followed me. "Call your agent," he said again.

When I got on the phone, Jim Hornfischer told me that whatever I'd
done today, I should keep on doing tomorrow at the other meetings.

Oh, shit, I thought. Shit.

But it turned out that the other meetings were full of warm, welcoming people. We talked together as if we were old friends from college and
we'd happened on a sad topic that was nevertheless filled with unexplored
meaning. They were actually nicer than my friends from college and I
wished for more meetings with similar people, or more meetings with the
same people. In my early twenties, when I worked as a bike messenger in
Boston, I would to ride the elevators in the company of smartly dressed
professional types on their way to meetings. During those rides, I used to
allow my thoughts to linger on what stores of friendliness, what breath-

taking views, and what salons of mutual understanding awaited those elevator riders. They would offer one another coffee. They would say professional things to each other. They would look out the window. As it turned out, my imaginings were more or less on target: they corresponded to the actual world with all the accuracy and specificity of a railroad timetable. I was astonished and thrilled. Naturally, I wanted to go back for more meetings with the same people, or with different people, the next day.

On the evening of the first meeting, after talking things over with Bernie, I had dinner at my sister's house in Brooklyn. Hornfischer called again from Texas to say that I'd done well, and that if things continued to go well, I would probably be able to write the book. Would I be paid? Yes, he promised. But I didn't actually have to ask because I knew I would be.

Back at Connie's, after everyone had gone to bed, after I couldn't sleep, I pulled out a battered but still somehow entirely blank writer's journal. I made an entry:

9:15 PM
Cucumbers and chicken with Soph and hubby. Wine. Then pedaling Bernie's bike up to E. 78 Street. Beneath the Brooklyn Bridge I asked a guy in a Monte Carlo how I could get myself onto the surface of the bridge. "Where do you want to go?" he asked. "The surface of it," I said, "the road on it." There was no following his directions. Twenty times too complicated and good only for the Monte Carlo. I carried the bike over cement barriers and pushed it across lanes of traffic.

Urban biking. Pedal-carry-pedal-push. Climb up something, drag the bike behind, stand on top of a cement wall, and wonder how to get down again.

Finally, I found the right on-ramp. Way, way down on the surface of the blacktop, ten feet below my feet, the cars were barreling up out of the darkness. This is how you get to the bridge? I yelled. *Whoosh.* This was how you got to the bridge. I waited for a hole in the traffic and leapt. I heard the cars coming up behind me. Thank you for not running me over, cars, I muttered. But I knew they wouldn't run me over. I knew they'd see me at that last minute and swerve into the fast-food containers beneath the curb on the left. There was much excitement: the excitement of nearly dying, of nearly being smooshed against the curbstone and the concrete. Perhaps I should be moving past this stage in life; perhaps I am not.

Up on the bridge itself. The pavement whirred along beneath the pedals. I hopped another fence, onto the pedestrian part of things. Fully on the Brooklyn Bridge now, recognizable wood and cables from a million photographs. Lights of New York City, millions of office windows, skyscrapers, reflected in the water beneath me. Head full of thoughts of Laird and the others who propelled me down here to New York City. How foreign a place it is to me, and how much more foreign it would be to them. What tourists, what wide-eyed bumpkin rubes we would be if we were here together. We'd be thrilled, though, and pleased to be together.

And thinking also what I've thought a lot about lately: how, by doing evil, those kids have done something for me. I don't know how I feel about this.

Also in my head: Soph's wine, and the vodka Bernie gave me this afternoon. What was that about? Never had vodka with Bernie before. And in the afternoon. Totally novel, weird experience.

On the bridge, up in the air, the lights are everywhere—above, below, across. Swimming, then pulsing. Then jerking out of focus. "Cross from shore to shore, countless crowds of passengers! Stand up tall, masts of Mannahatta! stand up, beautiful hills of Brooklyn!" That's all I can remember from "On Crossing Brooklyn Ferry." I saw no hills or masts or anything like that, but I know what he meant, basically, and the lines are good ones, with excellent rhythm, and once they popped into my head, they didn't leave.

Over bridge apex, downhill. Then picking up speed. Then flying. The other bike riders coming along in the opposite direction. "It's okay!" I telegraphed. "I can jump you!"

Thinking about the book people at their book-movie-magazine complex, and about the agent, and the book I'm now supposed to write. Such opportunities are lying in front of me. I have, astonishingly, a future and something to look forward to.

Back into traffic in lower Manhattan, looking for a way north. I chose a one-way road. It was fine, beautiful. The taxicabs and buses bore down on me, but honestly it didn't matter. I was having my private bike tunnel several inches out from the parked cars, a foot or so off from the oncoming ones. Anyway, the traffic wanted nothing to do with me. It might as well have been imaginary traffic, though sometimes it did honk, sometimes it did swerve suddenly out of my path. Each time I skirted disaster, I was aware of a tiny bit of disappointment. That wasn't close enough, I thought. Come as close as you dare, okay? Okay? Make it closer. You'll be just fine.

I kept thinking of Laird and definitely of Parker and Tulloch, too. Of how pleasant it is once you've decided you exercise direct control over life and death. Cross from shore to shore, countless crowds of passengers! Flow on, river. Flood tide below me! I see you face to face!

And all of that. An awareness like that exalts. You could, if you wanted to, make the really big decision. You could do what other people don't do, what no one else has the courage for. Opt for the wild unknown, for the wide-open road. It would solve some problems that have lately emerged concerning the future. Namely, it would take care of the how-will-I-ever-write-the-book-that's-in-my-head problem. I'm seriously worried about that one and don't know if I'm up to facing it down. So I would be okay with an ending. It would be okay if it came... about, well, about now. It might seem a reward, a fitting thing to happen to someone like me. A crowning achievement.

I survived, obviously. When I got back to Vermont, I went immediately to the Northern State Correctional Facility, in Newport, Vermont, Laird's newest home.

"I just barely drove in from New York City," I told him. "I'm going to write the book."

His head had been barbered into the standard inmate fuzz-over-skull cut. He smiled his bald man's smile. Back in St. Johnsbury, some of the guards had smoothed out the unfamiliarities in his name by reading a few extra consonants into it. To some of the less skilled readers of inmate rosters, he'd become Larry Standard. Here, with his crew cut, and his face fleshed out from eighteen months of growing up in jail, he was Larry Standard in the flesh. The person who'd appeared on the front pages around Vermont at the end of 1999—never a substantial creature to begin with, in my view—had all but faded away. In his place was one of the affable, empty-eyed lunch eaters who had spent his days in Woodstock feeding and smoking cigarettes.

Larry seemed to recognize me from our last visit. That was good. He'd taken on some weight. He wasn't chubby like a kid anymore; he was bulbous like an old person. It was fine and normal to see that in the veteran felons, but in someone his age, it had a jarring effect, like white hair on a college kid.

"Remember that book?" I asked. "The one I wanted to write. Sort of about you and all?" I told him I had most of it written already.

"Great," he said. "That's awesome."

"I mean I've got a book contract now. It's all official."

"Oh. Yeah? Who's it with?"

"Miramax in New York City. It's a book company, but it's also got a movie division."

"That's so awesome," he said. He didn't look like a person in awe. His head was nodding. His fingers were playing with his inmate ID. He offered me some polite congratulations and we wandered into other topics, but as he talked, I could see that his face was slowly falling. After twenty minutes, it became obvious that he didn't feel like putting in the effort to conceal it. I knew that look from previous visits. It said: "Thanks, Theo, for coming. This is a big change in the routine for me, though and I kinda want to go back to my cell now."

"I'm still working on my own movie deals, too," he said to the visiting room table. "I'm still talking to Universal and stuff."

"That's cool," I said.

I changed the subject pretty quickly because I hadn't driven all the way up there to make him any sadder than he already was. I didn't want him comparing his life to mine or dreaming up any further schemes for success at all, for that matter. He didn't have a lot to show for himself at the moment, while I had always had plenty, and now had more. We sat in silence for a little while, him tapping a pencil on the visiting room table and playing with his ID, me touching a visitor's locker key in my pocket. The guard who presides over the visiting room—he stands on a risen platform at the front of the room—pays special attention to concentrating, meditative visitors. Silence can indicate mischief. A pocket of marijuana gets passed beneath the table, a packet of pills, held by a toe, gets dropped beneath the footpad of a waiting shoe. The miscreants sit like zen Buddhists, tapping their fingers to an inner rhythm. We might have resembled such a couple. I felt the guard's eyes alighting on us. They left. They returned.

"Dude," I said to Laird at last. "Did you ever listen to Liz Phair or anything?" On the way up in the car I'd been playing a tape of one of her albums. She seemed to be unusually preoccupied by guns. The album seemed to have been written by someone who'd been mistreated by her friends. She wanted to emerge from her basement and show them all just how wild she could be. It was indie, college radio music. Maybe it had been popular at Gould.

"Who?" Laird wondered. "Never heard of her. Elizabeth totally loved that chick...whatshername? Ani DiFranco."

"Oh," I said. We talked for a few minutes more about people we'd known in Woodstock. Some of them had migrated up to Newport as well; others had already been shipped on to Virginia. Laird was saying less and less and his silences were growing louder. I didn't want to keep him from doing whatever it was he wanted to do and so when the next silence came along, I pushed back my chair, gave him a hug, told him to hang in there. Then I left.

You can leave any time you want when you're just visiting. You make eye contact with a guard, stand in front of the door, push it when it buzzes, and off you go.

Will and Tim and Joe had similar, nonplussed reactions. They were happy for me, but it wasn't news of their success I was bringing them, and beneath their smiles, I sensed indifference and the shame of the lieabout. They had nothing to show for themselves; no way to match my excitement. They were embarrassed, and soon, so was I. I didn't blame them for wanting me to take off.

When I went to visit Will, I said: "Remember when I said that I was writing a book? And you told me to put in lots of stuff about the education you were getting? I'm putting that in, okay?" I said that I was also going to write about how intelligent a kid he was, despite his cockamamie theories.

"Good fucking luck with that," he deadpanned. "I'm not a kid anymore, by the way."

At no time during our discussion did he turn on the charm, or urge information on me, or try to go over the book plot with me so that I could get the tragic details of his incarceration down right. He wanted to talk about his plan to get himself transferred to a jail in South Carolina, where it was much, way much easier to get parole. That way, he wouldn't have to go through the hated Vermont antiviolence program that really, in fact, only made people more violent. I believed him on that score.

We talked about those things until the hour and a half had run out, and the guard announced that visiting was over.

In the months that followed, I made arrangements to have a conversation with Bill Stanard, Laird's dad. I wanted to find out how he had gotten on since the shootings. I also wanted to know how his feelings toward Laird had evolved. During the two and a half years Laird had been in jail, I'd noticed Bill wanting less and less to do with Laird. Bill was no longer visiting. He wasn't taking collect calls anymore and he was scarcely writing. I wondered about this widening gulf. Laird seemed to think that his father was anxious to wash his hands of him once and for all. I guessed that Bill's search through the books on his shelves was leading him away from reconciling with Laird. Why? What had he found?

I'd met Bill for the first time at Laird's sentencing hearing. I learned then that he was selling his house in West Windsor and moving away, perhaps back to Rhode Island, perhaps further afield. At the courthouse, he greeted me with the chipper smile and the gay, apologizing, twinkling eyes I knew from a certain criminal defendant who happened to be, that day, accepting his sentence of twenty-five years to life. "You're Theo. *Great* to meet you," Bill had said to me as he pumped my hand during a break in the proceedings. He thanked me for being a help to Laird in Woodstock. He said he admired what I was doing with my students.

By then, word had gotten back to Bill about my book writing project; he seemed curious but guarded. When I finally interviewed him officially and on the record, he wasn't guarded at all. We spoke over the phone, he in Newport, Rhode Island, me in Vermont. We had a free ranging, lively conversation in which we tried, sometimes awkwardly, sometimes in hurried bursts, to share our conclusions about Laird.

He started by telling me that he was certain Laird had meant to kill him and Paula as they slept in their bed. Paula had surprised Laird at the front door. She was angry and dressed him down right away: "And here you take the car *again*. You've ruined our trust in you," he recalled her saying. She was also furious because Laird had promised to be in bed an hour and a half earlier: "I told you to be in bed by midnight," she'd scolded. Bill heard the harangue from the upstairs bedroom. Then he heard the gun shot. He heard nothing from Laird himself: his expression was the pressing of the trigger.

But Paula, it seemed, by waylaying Laird at the front door, had saved Bill's life. She had stepped out of the darkness and had ambushed the ambusher. Laird did creep up the stairs, apparently in pursuit of his dad, but he retreated and by the time Bill walked downstairs, Laird had lost his composure. Either that or he just couldn't see. Anyway, the blast was fired from such close range that his shoulder, Bill's shoulder, had been burned.

I asked Bill what life had been like for him in the weeks following this episode. I assumed it had been a dreary, and probably spooky, winter. I said that I assumed he must have felt deeply estranged from his normal life. He was suddenly alone, suddenly in the news, and suddenly the star witness in the state's first-degree murder case against his son.

He got through those months, he said, by crafting a wooden boat. He needed to do something with his hands and he wanted to employ himself in an occupation he loved. Rick Fallon, the downhill neighbor whose teenage daughter had been a friend of Laird's, had done what a good neighbor does. "Rick would just come up every day and just check in," Bill said. "'Hey, how's it going?' and just check in." That had been reassuring in a low key, low stakes sort of way. Bill quickly realized, also, that there were other parents around who'd watched helplessly as their kids lost control. He found good company in a book by the parents of Reagan's would-be assassin called *Breaking Points*. In it, Jack and Jo Ann Hinckley describe their son's disintegration and recall how dozens of parents of similarly disturbed children had reached out to them when their son first appeared in the news. Bill had had similar contacts.

In those first few weeks, Bill also made a point of visiting Laird every week during the A-Block visiting hours in Woodstock.

"As soon as Laird was in jail," Bill said, "one of my duties, I thought, was to go visit him. I mean here my kid is in jail, I have to go visit him. I knew he was going to be in for a long time because whatever the heck happened, I knew he wasn't going to get off on a technicality. He was going to spend some hard time in there and I started thinking, I should get him ready for this, so I suggested that he have a kind of approach. And I said,

'Whether it comes from the Buddha, whether it's a philosophy, whatever it is, you're going to need something—whether it's a psychological or philosophical thing, you're going to need something.'"

But Laird, apparently, had been in no mood to receive advice; certainly he was not in the mood for philosophical advice. He was too absorbed by the details of his new life to take his eyes off them, even for a few moments, during a visit with his father. He wanted baseball hats. He wanted work boots, the better to clomp around the cell block. He was alarmed at how the guards were treating him. They made rude comments. They gave him a giant, oafish cellmate. He was also worried by the equivocal, uninter-pretable behavior of his lawyer. I was familiar with all of this and said so.

Those visits left Bill astonished and vaguely angry. A coarsening and a hardening of Laird's nature seemed underway. He babbled and lectured about his "case" but skirted all mention of his mother. Nor was there men-tion of Laird's second shot, the one that had been aimed at Bill's head. During the visiting sessions, said Bill, Laird acted as though the shootings had occurred strictly in the newspapers, but not at all in real life. And the newspapers, in Laird's view, had gotten everything wrong, a circumstance for which he could not be blamed. In this way, Laird skipped eerily, weirdly, over everything important in his discussions with his dad. Paula, it seemed to Bill, might never have existed at all.

"You bring somebody up in an atmosphere where there is good and evil," Bill told me, "where there is right and wrong, the right thing to do, the wrong thing to do—all the shades of gray. You sort of assume from his outward demeanor that he has absorbed this. I won't say that he's learned it but he's absorbed it. He's lived around it long enough so that it's sort of part of his fabric. And then all of a sudden, he ends up in this really tough situation and it's as if he's really just turned it off? I don't think you can turn off your morality."

I wondered what tough situation Bill was referring to. Living in jail? Being unhappy at Gould? Being seventeen? But of course it didn't matter. Sometime in his seventeenth year, Laird had checked out. Jail had wors-ened the situation but it was by no means the cause of it. I knew from my discussions with Laird that he had decided, sometime in the past, that he was capable of getting away with murder. I knew he assumed the police would greet him with the news of his parent's demise as they greet widows and orphans. He'd expected a consoling pat on the back.

I told Bill that I thought Laird did imagine himself to be a victim, an unfortunate whose way in life had been bitter and lonely. I said that in my opinion, a lot of people in jail, not just Laird, had that problem. "They look around and see the guards and the chains and the miserable conditions in which they live. They think of people who've slighted them in the past. That's all the evidence they need. They see what people have now who come to visit them. They see that and say, 'Well, I'm the unlucky one. I've had a hard row.'"

Bill interrupted. His voice was astonished, nearly appalled. He addressed himself to Laird: "You tried to blow away your parents. You were partially successful. *That's* why you're here."

"Right," I agreed. "I know. I know."

We changed the subject. We were both curious about the influence of Elizabeth Burton, the wiccan teenage not-quite girlfriend, on whom Laird had doted at Gould.

It seemed to me that Laird had been mesmerized by her, and that he had allowed his fixation to overwhelm his judgment. He had been desperate to impress her, desperate to woo her, and desperate to shore up the unstable relationship they had had. Judging by Laird's poetry, I said, it seemed to me that the death of her father had been a big issue between them. It was a topic he was forbidden to broach, knowing nothing about death as he did, but one she introduced when she felt the need. I mentioned a poem Laird had written in the fall before the shootings. It was addressed to Elizabeth and was called "Your Pain." It began:

Is the pain much? I bet it would be.
There is not much I can do to diminish your pain.
I wish that I could take the pain from you and put it to myself.

"I can imitate your pain," he'd written further down the page, "but I cannot share yours." Those, I thought, were the words of a kid who was jealous of suffering, who was anxious for real-world hardships to match those of his peers. His unhappiness, such as it was, was too subtle a thing, too uncaused and invisible to win anyone's sympathy. He needed to make his unhappiness real. I asked Bill if he thought that Laird, in doing away with his parents, was possibly trying to offer up a visible and outward sign of his plight to Elizabeth. He would present himself as her spiritual twin. Then, to top things off, he would imply that he had a lot of money coming his way.

"That was the first thing I thought of," Bill said instantly. "That Laird had just said to himself, 'I want all the marbles. And I'm going to take them. Now.'" But Bill also thought there was more than money-lust, and more than teenage-lust operating in Laird's mind. He was still haunted by the last long conversation he'd had with Laird before the shootings.

"The part that I wonder about is when Laird said, over Thanksgiving vacation: 'I wanna come home. I don't want to go to Gould anymore.' That's seems to be when everything changed. We said, 'Stick it out till the end of June.' That seemed to be when he decided to do us in, because that's when he stole the credit card, that's when he stole the car for the first time, went back to school, started running up the bills, had this sort of on-the-lam buddy movie going in his head with Elizabeth and ended up coming back and doing the shot-gun thing. We weren't going to be moved so therefore he would move us.

"And *that* leads into the next question which is, What is my relationship to him now? And my relationship to him now is that I don't want to be friends with, or I don't want to be a guardian to, or I don't want to be a mentor to, I don't want to be a *friend* to somebody who can make a decision like that and do what he did.

"And it really scares me," Bill continued, "because I didn't see it coming before and I'm not going to see it coming, if it happens, again." He paused and I could hear him thinking on the other end of the line. "I did something about six months into this. I told Laird that I thought it would be a good idea if he didn't have any children. I said, you know, the line of the Stanards I think has come to an end. He shouldn't have any children. I shouldn't have any more. And I said, 'You shouldn't.' I didn't blame it on him. I said there's very possibly a problem in our family. It's something we should watch out for."

A picture of Laird at the end of the line, isolated and alone and fingering the buttons on a prison phone, floated up before me. It wasn't the first time, nor was it the last, that I'd thought of Laird like this—standing by himself in the ruins of his life, busily pursuing a connection. He called them "hook-ups" and "deals." Now, it seemed, there was no one left to call except me. I wasn't even sure how much he liked talking to me; he often sounded bored and anxious to get off the phone.

To Bill I said that I hoped that somehow, in the years to come, a kind of piecemeal reconciliation could unfold, a rapprochement paid out in increments over years. But I wasn't counting on it. Laird was becoming a new, institutionalized creature in his Virginia cell block. He was becoming a sweeper of the prison wood shop and a cleaner of toilets. That person, I suspected, didn't really want his father back. He wanted a few dollars in his prison canteen account so he could buy sweets and shampoo and the occasional tin of sardines. Laird did not need a dad for that; that was the sort of thing his friend the teacher/author could do for him.

Nowadays, when I think about the inmate students I had in Woodstock, I try not to let those dull, desultory phone conversations impinge on my good memories. In general, I prefer not to think about the gloomy hours I've passed in gloomy visiting rooms. Each time I go, the inmates have aged. Each time a deeper voice comes out of them. It's the voice of the crochety, unflinching inmate for whom nothing has ever or will ever come as a surprise. It has a woodsy, north country accent, and talks mostly about the unreasoning ways of the DOC. And every time I go, a new, uglier tattoo has begun to move on the inmates' forearms. This one by the elbow was a scorpion, but the guy couldn't draw right and it had to be made over into a joint. That one is a bleeding heart. That one illustrates a piece of barbed wire, the international symbol of incarceration.

Instead of picturing the inmates in their visiting rooms, I like to picture them in their finest hour, or, at any rate, during the hour in which they appeared finest to me. Counting by the clock, it was actually a stretch of time somewhere in the twenty-minute/half-hour range in the early spring of 2001, in Woodstock. Thankfully, for once, nobody was counting by the clock.

During a brief interval of time, then, when the sunlight was splashing down on the red floor tiles and the guitars were banging in the music practice room, my regular students and a few old drunks who happened to be passing through, read passages from Whitman's "Song of Myself" out loud.

The students hated the assignment I'd given them: "Choose a part of the poem," I wrote, "that you understand, that honestly means something to you, and prepare to read it out loud to the class. Read it so that we can

feel your understanding, so that you express with your voice and your gestures and your silences, all the knowledge of the poem that you have.
Make sure to express this knowledge to us, your classmates, and not to the
floor. Please make eye contact, and speak slowly."

As an assignment, it required too much sincerity from the inmates
and probably too much preparation. Anyway, no one could admit to having done it when the time came. Laird said that he'd been bogged down
with legal duties. The DA had come through with his offer of forty years
to life. Laird had to consider it, he said, and get back to him. I wasn't sure
if the sum of forty years meant very much to Laird, but I knew that he and
his roommate, Jim Vandriel, were both too frightened and too tongue-
tied to talk about what it might mean. Sadly, there was no other possibility for that kind of exploration. For an inmate to be seen dwelling in
anything but pride on the length of his sentence was unthinkable. Talking
about it in public at all was not really done. You're supposed to tell the
other inmates that you had led a bold life out in the world, and were now
facing up to the consequences. Even at that early date, Laird knew that.
He was figuring out at the time just how to do it: how to walk around
with a permanent poker face. He often looked to me like a kid who
wanted to let the face fall away, was on the verge of it, but knew better
than to give in, and possessed anyway a quiet certainty about his ability to
triumph over human impulses. He's good that way; that's his specialty.

Outside, the first truly spring-like spring day was underway. It had
been an excruciating winter—a dark, seeling night, as in *Macbeth*, that
had scarfed up a lot of the pitiful light of day we'd had. There had been
murders and kidnappings and the specter of children turning against their
families. Some people in the area hadn't survived the winter at all, and
some of those who had—the people sitting around the table—had come
through permanently diminished, crippled. There wasn't all that much
life left to them. A lot of them sat dully, almost dead themselves, day in
and day out, as the rest of their lives dribbled away. In the spiritual as well
as the physical sense, they were inert. It had occurred to me from time to
time that that inertia might somehow be worse than death. Maybe now, if
death came for those youngest kids—those who'd truly doomed themselves—it would come as a tender mercy.

But on that spring day, these thoughts had obligingly left the room.

They had gone and disappeared, probably to haunt the people in the next room for a few minutes. We'd closed the door to the library. That always helped. And, as per usual, one of the teenagers—I think it was Steve, the folksinger—had stood on a chair beneath the window and pushed lightly on the pane, to see if it was any more inclined to give way today than on any other day. The sunlight filled his crazy blond dreadlocks: they were the very picture of the mixed tousled hay of head that Whitman was celebrating in our reading. As Steve stood beneath the window, he closed his eyes and bathed himself in his column of light. Squinting, and closing *my* eyes, I could almost see him as a child standing still somewhere on the edge of a field, or as a statue in a courtyard. He was frozen on the edge of something, not quite inside, not yet outside. The sunlight in which he stood gave him a natural radiance; he seemed a symbol of nature's benign intentions. The world would forgive him eventually and he would be set free.

We were in a funny mood that day and it was hard for me to settle the kids down. One of the old drunks had got up to go sit inside the library bathroom. The other kids seized the opportunity to prop a chair in front of the door, locking him in. We waited for him to push at the doorknob. Ten minutes of teenage breeze-shooting and homework-shirking rolled by. We paused every few moments to eavesdrop on the drunk's thumpings and angry calls for rescue. No calls emerged. It seemed he might have fallen asleep in there, poisoned by the aroma. Maybe he'd died. More minutes passed. The longer he stayed inside, the funnier the situation became. Will decided to slip him some newspaper sections under the door so that he would have something to read in case he was merely bored. He crept up to the door and lay with his tummy on the ground. Two teenagers followed, lurking over his back. Will whispered into the crack between the floor tiles and the wood laminate door: "Would you like the sports, dude? Business? Dude! I can hook you with the fucking business section if you want! Just gimme the word! Say it, bro! Use your words!"

Not a sound came from the toilet and the kids had to reassemble themselves at the table, laughing and giggling, but trying not to laugh too loud, for fear of waking the drunk.

When it came time for Laird to read his section of the poem, he didn't want to do it, but I pressed him, and finally he agreed. His reluctance made him self-conscious and that made him concentrate. He hadn't bothered to do the assignment—nothing depended on it after all—and I had to remind him which passage it was that we'd talked about the day before.

"Oh, that one. *That* one," he said as if he'd labored over many and wasn't sure which I was referring to. I had suggested that he might read from a section halfway through the poem, in which Whitman, "afoot with my vision" identifies himself with everything his eye happens to meet. In the passage I proposed to Laird, Whitman—or some idealized version of a poet-hero—is suddenly struck by a bright idea: "I think I could turn and live awhile among the animals," he says, "...they are so placid, and self-contained."

Immediately, he envisions a pacific animal kingdom. It is a meditative community of fellows, where all are equal, everyone is playfully irreligious, and no one ever complains.

Laird agreed to read the lines that follow:

> No one is dissatisfied...no one is demented with the mania of
>   owning things.
> No one kneels to another nor to his kind that lived thousands of
>   years ago.
> No one is respectable or industrious over the whole earth.

Laird was straining on even that much. He looked up and coughed. "You take it from here, Theo," he said. "You the man." Though I knew he was shirking, I didn't mind. I was really happy actually because this is one of my favorite parts of the poem. I had it close to memorized and so I scarcely had to look at the book in order to read the lines. I didn't want to look at the kids, however, because I knew I'd embarrass them. So I pretended to read, but really just said the lines out loud, more or less to myself:

> they show their relations to me and I accept them;
> They bring me tokens of myself...they evince them plainly
>   in their possession.
>
> I do not know where they got these tokens,
> I must have passed that way untold times ago and negligently dropt
>   them,
> Moving myself forward then and now and forever,
> Gathering and showing more always and with velocity,
> Infinite and omnigenous and the like the others among them;

I understand this passage as a brash, even a zany, assurance of the power of identification. The tokens he refers to are bit parts of the souls he inhabited before, in other lifetimes, other stages of evolution. To lay eyes on them inspires a recovered memory, and the memory is necessarily a personal one, bringing news of oneself.

In the lines surrounding that passage, the idealized poet-persona zooms back through history. He strolls over the hills of Judea; he visits the Alamo, and observes a ghastly war crime in which 412 young men were massacred. "The living and the dead lay together," he reports, "the half-killed attempted to crawl away. The bodies were burned during the night. And that was a jetblack sunrise."

Next, he skips forward in time. He feels himself one with the drowned sailor, one with the cholera patient, one with the handcuffed muntineers. There are floods of people to identify with, it turns out, oceans of them. *I am, I am, I am*, he says as he moves through history. *I am, I am, I am*, he says as he moves across the face of the earth.

Though there's every reason in the world to doubt it, particularly through the examples he gives, he insists that life is not the static, one-shot deal we presume it to be. He insists that there are hundreds of lives out there to be led, and that they can all be crammed into the span of a single lifetime. We are permitted not just three strikes, but an infinite quantity of strikes. The fundamental principle in the world therefore is mutability, renewal, self-transformation. Just because things don't look good now, one shouldn't infer that there are not another thousand lifetimes out there inviting you to live them. It just takes some imagination to make the magic work.

I explained the idea to the inmates as best I could. They sat patiently while I talked and made consistent eye contact with me. They seemed to understand. They seemed to know that I was talking about them. They seemed to like the poem itself, and seemed to appreciate that I was there, down in the basement, trying to bring a poem to life.

The theory of innumerable new lives for everyone, for now and all time, is an appealing one. It does, however, elude me. I can't believe in it, at least not all the time. But when you're sitting in a basement library on the first day of spring, and the sunlight is dancing on the floor tiles—perhaps there are clouds passing before the light from time to time—the kids around you may appear like promising high school students. They were

that way a little while ago, after all, so it doesn't take much force of imagination to see them that way now. They might seem like the sort of kids
who'll go on to do important, wonderful things in the world. And even if
you know they won't do that, but are doomed instead to grow bitter
behind bars, all you have to do is to put an old drunkard in the toilet, cast
a spell so that he falls happily asleep, and then will the kids into being
mild attentive students. Just for a few moments, please, you'll say (only to
yourself). They can do it. They *will* do it. Of course, in your mind's eye,
you can cast those kids in any light you choose: they can seem like future
engineers, or poets, or teachers, or computer hotshots–to–be. It's not that
much of a stretch, really, especially if the flickering sunlight cooperates.

Then you will naturally feel the power of the poetry taking hold.
Whitman's verses will read with all the force of vivid documentary. His
promises will seem utterly plausible and true. They seemed true to me
that day for half an hour or so during class. And then afterward, for a long
time afterward, the feeling lingered.

ACKNOWLEDGEMENTS:

I'm up to my ears in gratitude to certain people. Jim Hornfischer has pushed me onward from the very beginning. Elder sibling, steady hand, coach—he's done much more for me than any agent ought to have and I owe him a ton of thanks. I'm also grateful to Ron Powers who helped me see what was happening in my jail classroom. Without him, I would have slogged forward gamely enough, as many people do who're caught up in the life of an institution, but there would have been no book. I've incurred a deep karmic debt to JillEllyn Riley, nominally an editor, for me a shrink. I suspect some editing occurred as she helped me through the writing of this book, though if it did I hardly noticed what was going on. I noticed instead her sympathy, patience, good humor, and a current of calm life wisdom on which I drew more and more as time went on. Of course, I should have started earlier. I'm also in debt to Bill Stanard who reflected on the life of his family with me honestly and carefully. During the writing of this book, I was a great pain in the ass to my own family, especially to my mom. I owe them lots of gratitude for putting up with me. And Kate: Kate put up with more of me than anyone else, and endured gracefully when life with me was neither gracious nor really endurable. I don't know how I'll make it good but I'll try. Finally I owe gratitude to the inmates of the Woodstock jail. For no reason other than friendship, they welcomed me into their lives. I owe special thanks to Slash, Tobin, Will, Emmons, Laird, and Duane Bedell. This book is dedicated to all of those who're still in jail. I hope it will help bring them the clarity it brought me.